TV

THE BIG PICTURE

By STAN OPOTOWSKY

THE LONGS OF LOUISIANA

TV: THE BIG PICTURE

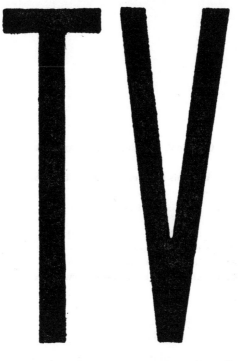

TV

THE BIG PICTURE

By STAN OPOTOWSKY

NEW YORK • E. P. DUTTON & CO., INC. 1961

1144818

TO MY MOTHER

WHO

ALWAYS

HELPS

CONTENTS

INTRODUCTION

This book was not written by an insider, nor was it written for insiders. This book was written for those who sit on the living-room side of the television screen. Furthermore, it was written by a recruit from their ranks.

There was a purpose to this. Television has become the primary medium of entertainment for a great majority of Americans. It is also a vital factor in what they buy, when they sleep, and even whom they elect to administer their government. Yet few of these addicts have an inkling of who operates TV or why.

The assignment was for an outsider, a man trained as a reporter but otherwise as naïve as any other casual TV viewer, to invade the industry and find out the whos, hows, and whys. A person already connected with TV would have begun, of course, with much more background knowledge of the industry. But background knowledge inevitably produces a by-product of prejudices and preconceived theories. The outsider, on the other hand, goes in with completely open mind—and this is very important in a survey of something as beleaguered as today's television industry.

I looked upon myself as the TV viewers' ambassador in the foreign land of networks, advertising agencies, and rating services. I asked the viewers' questions, not the insider's questions. This book is, in effect, a report back to my constituents in the living room.

As I threaded my way through the industry's maze, I was often surprised, occasionally shocked, but mostly informed about a medium which quite frankly is engaged in the practice of harnessing art to serve the purposes of commerce.

For twelve months I asked questions, I read, I watched. I interviewed a network board chairman in his sumptuous office one day and I interviewed an unemployed actor in a cut-rate beanery the next day. I interviewed a tough-talking realist in a New York advertising agency and I interviewed an idealistic actor on a Hollywood sound stage. I found myself studying dozens of trade publications, for this is a complicated industry whose technical literature runs from the slick, color-splashed advertising journals to the militant mimeographed union bulletins.

The job had its difficulties. Much of the research was done under a cloud of scandal, at a time when critics, professional and amateur, were harping incessantly on the medium's deficiencies and deceits. The result was occasional encounters with men who were afraid to be interviewed. In some cases they appeared ashamed of their industry. In others, they seemed to have a paranoic fear that the outside world will always misinterpret TV's motives, so why discuss them? It is interesting to note that almost every one of these men who dared not face an interviewer worked for an advertising agency. The network people and the artists seemed to be more confident of their position.

But for each frightened rabbit there were two bulldogs who

barked back at any criticism, and also a few owls who were quite willing to discuss the dilemmas of TV with candor about the past and hope for the future.

I found that most of the people in television are quick to concede the industry's shortcomings, and just as quick to explain why these shortcomings are inescapable. They often feel trapped by a system, and their despair occurs because they cannot conceive an alternative to that system.

I think that what impressed me most about these TV people is their anxiety to point out their detachment from the business as soon as they leave the office. They are downright eager to say that *their* wives would never watch "Queen for a Day" and that *their* children are permitted only a rationed and highly supervised diet of TV. It would be easy to brand these men as hypocrites, and to say that they foist upon the American public mediocrities they would not suffer upon their own families. But they are not hypocrites. They are convinced that it is "the system" that produces the mediocrities, and they consider themselves as much the victims as anyone else with a set in the living room.

Are these men right? In this book you will find the evidence they present to support their stand, and you will find the arguments to the contrary. You are the judge.

There may be some who will read this book while trying to decide whether to seek a career in the glamorous world of television. For them, there must be a warning. TV does have glamour and it does pay high salaries. But it takes a frightful toll. The man in TV, be he network executive or advertising-agency man or star comedian, works long hours under constant terror. Yesterday's hero is too often tomorrow's bum. The stakes are high, and an error in judgment can cost someone hundreds of thousands of dollars. It is an accepted part of the business that this someone will have his vengeance upon the culprit who lightened his pocketbook.

I leave television's backstage with compassion for those who feel that commercial necessity is an escape-proof prison, with

admiration for those who forever try to aim the treadmill uphill, and with contempt for those hardened few who consider
the great American audience a blob of dullards who deserve
all the shoddy deceits they can absorb.

In a job like this, the author is indebted to every person who
answered a question or a letter and to every secretary who
confirmed an appointment. But special thanks are due those
much abused publicity men who so often opened doors and
led the way through dark alleys. Thanks are due, too, to Arthur Berman, who served as a sort of special Hollywood op-
erative between my two visits to that land of bilk and honeys,
to Bob Williams of the *New York Post* for frequent guidance,
and to George S. Trow, Jr., who performed the manual labor
inevitable with these projects.

To my constituents in the living room I say that I have tried
very hard to present a fair and objective report for you. I thank
you for the opportunity to inspect the fascinating land of TV.
It was indeed a nice place to visit, but I wouldn't want to live
there.

                                                        S. O.

New York City
October 13, 1960

TV

THE BIG PICTURE

EVERYBODY'S DOING IT

You can tell the story with statistics: 88 per cent of the households in the United States have television sets. These sets are in use on an average of five hours per day.

You can tell the story with an anecdote: Michael Flanders reports visiting a British beach. Everyone within sight was clustered around a hut. Behind them was the sea. In front of them was a television set. They were watching a BBC telecast of the sea.

Or you can tell the story with a dire forecast: Because of television, predicted Fred Allen, "the next generation will be born with four eyes and no tongue."

You can tell the story in countless different ways, but the conclusion is always the same: An electronic box that has been in popular use scarcely twelve years has become a mighty social force dipping into all aspects of American life. Its impact has been felt on everything from law and education to

romance and the design of cigarette packages. Leonard Goldenson, the chairman of the American Broadcasting Company,
told Congress: "In television in this country, we have in twelve
short years, created and put into operation a communications
medium that furnishes sight and sound and is capable of simultaneously reaching virtually our entire nation. It is a medium with an impact and a communication opportunity
unparalleled in the history of mankind." Researcher A. C.
Nielsen put it more succinctly: Americans, he said, spend
more time watching TV than doing anything else except
sleeping. And that, he added, includes working.

The eagerness with which the American public grabbed at
the opportunity to become hollow-eyed zombies is graphically
demonstrated by television's growth. It took 62 years for electric wiring to reach 34,000,000 homes. It took 80 years for the
telephone to reach the same number of homes. It took the automobile 49 years and the electric washer 47 years. But it took
television only 10 years.

In 1950 there were 104 TV stations in operation. By 1960
there were 531. Between 1948 and 1950 alone the amount of
money spent by advertisers in TV leaped 229.2 per cent, from
$8,700,000 to $90,629,000. By 1959 the expenditure was $1,-
151,560,000. The public, meanwhile, had spent $23,000,000,000
buying TV sets.

Survey after survey has shown what a slave the set owner
is to his set. Sindlinger & Company says its research indicates
that on a typical day 72 per cent of the adolescent and adult
population of the United States watches TV and that the average person spends 131 minutes in front of the set. Yet, as if
that isn't enough, the Du Mont Laboratories are working on
a device that will permit a single TV set to receive two programs at the same time.

John Mason Brown has said, "People who deny themselves
television deny themselves participation in life today. . . .
They are self-exiled from the world." John P. Cunningham,
chairman of the Cunningham & Walsh advertising agency,

said, "Television has become a firmly established member of the American family. It ranks with the automobile (and even with the home itself) in terms of family concern." Neither Mr. Brown nor Mr. Cunningham is an unbiased commentator. Mr. Brown has had a television program of his own and Mr. Cunningham has lots of them. But no one can dispute the accuracy of their observations.

In a sense television is even responsible for the government, for there is scarcely an elected official who did not campaign via TV. Former President Eisenhower said, "In many ways the effect of television in swaying public opinion particularly about burning issues of the moment may be even greater than the press. You introduce personality as well as cold fact."

Sig Mickelson, president of CBS News, has written:

"Television's ability to create national figures almost overnight means that the choice of candidates does not have to be largely limited, as in the past, to the very few hopefuls who had achieved some kind of national status in a period of years. In that sense, television has made our electoral processes more democratic; it has brought high political office within reach of a larger segment of qualified persons."

TV has certainly produced great political problems. Congress passed a Solomonish law guaranteeing political opponents equal time on TV, but not even this assured everyone of a fair shake. A candidate for the Texas legislature, William H. Brigham, complained that *his* opponent, Jack Woods, was on TV *every night*. This was true. Woods was the KWTX-TV weather forecaster and he was also running for office. Brigham conceded that the weather forecast was nonpolitical, but he maintained that Woods was so charming on television that his appearances on the weather show gave him a political advantage. Brigham demanded as compensation a fifteen-minute program of his own every night, but the Federal Court ruled that this was going a bit too far, and rejected his appeal for equal time. (The law proved so unwieldy that eventually it was repealed.)

The impact of television on the mind of America has created many difficulties. One is in maintaining proper court procedure. Municipal Court Judge Carl D. Kessler said in Dayton, Ohio, that jurors who watch courtroom dramas week after week come into a real courtroom convinced they are experts. It is getting increasingly difficult, he said, to find jurors "who will listen to the judge's instructions in order to reach intelligent decisions." He was backed up in this by Supreme Court Justice William O. Douglas, who said TV is giving Americans a "distorted" view of how criminals are caught and tried.

Religion, too, has felt the impact. An Episcopal minister in Mississippi gave up the practice of making morning calls upon his parishioners because he found there was no time for talk, only time for sitting beside them as they watched vintage movies. "I might as well stay in the rectory and see the whole movie rather than miss parts of it traveling from one house to the other," he said. A priest in Philadelphia suggested quite seriously that members of his congregation give up TV for Lent. (None did, he reported.) Even the Pope had to reckon with TV, first by establishing a station in the Vatican and then by finding the Latin word for television. (He decided on *televisio*, which means "sight from afar.")

However, people still do go to church, leading ad man Cunningham to comment, "Watching TV is lowest on Sunday morning, and one can literally thank the Lord for that."

Television has affected education—not so much as one might hope, but there have been strides. An educational TV network films special programs for some fifty stations throughout the nation. Countless thousands have been rising with the sun (or before it) to listen to lectures on Elizabethan literature at the incredible hour of 6:30 A.M. Scarcely a school operates without a TV set today, and at least one educator envisions the time when a fifth-grade teacher will catch a boy surreptitiously doing math problems, and scold him with, "Johnny, what do you mean doing your homework when you should be watching TV with the rest of the class?"

TV has had a strange effect on the publishing world. Fewer people are reading more books. More people are reading fewer magazines and newspapers. Television eats into the time a person might allot for reading, yet the mere mention of a publication on TV will multiply its sales. Steve Allen recommended *Brotherhood of Evil* in a casual thirty-second spiel, and the very next morning four thousand copies were sold. The day after Alexander King appeared on "The Jack Paar Show," his *Mine Enemy Grows Older* sold out of the bookstores.

Libraries report that book borrowings have increased, not decreased, in the television age. However, the readers' tastes have been revolutionized. Once novels were the staple. Now the readers prefer nonfiction.

Even a city's water pressure is affected by television. In 1954 the New York City Engineer was baffled by sudden changes in the water pressure and began a massive study to locate the trouble. He finally found it in his own living room. He said: "At 10:00 A.M. the pressure went up like a rocket and stayed up until 11:00 A.M. I was puzzled for a while and then I discovered why. Arthur Godfrey's program went on at ten, and a hundred thousand housewives left their sinks and washtubs to watch it. When it was over at eleven they went back and turned on the water again. Now I can even tell when the commercials go on. Hundreds of thousands of people leave their TV sets during the commercials to get a drink or go to the bathroom, so of course the water pressure drops."

It is, of course, the entertainment industry which has suffered and benefited most from television. Within three years after TV sets reached mass production, the mammoth motion-picture industry was on its knees: Movie attendance tumbled by 30 per cent, thousands of theaters—fifty-five in New York City alone—closed their doors forever, and multiacre Hollywood studios surrendered their facilities to the infant giant. Within five years after TV became big business it owned the biggest hit on Broadway: *My Fair Lady* was financed by the

Columbia Broadcasting System on the grounds that it might eventually make a nice TV show.

Television killed small-club boxing and all but killed minor-league baseball. Television ate into anything and everything that required people to leave their living rooms. After the automobile industry's monumental effort to make America a nation of go-outs, television turned the tide and made it once again a nation of stay-at-homes. One writer was moved to call TV "America's modern fireside."

Is this good? The Anti-Saloon League says Yes and the Saloon Owners League says No. In between there are all ranges of opinion, some even medical. Doctors began worrying about TV spines for people who slumped motionless in front of the set for too many hours and TV eyes for people whose gaze seldom left the flickering screen from dusk to dawn. A Tokyo pediatrician even blamed an increase in bed-wetting on TV. In Los Angeles a woman was so entranced with a movie she was watching that she delivered her fifth baby without calling her husband from the next room.

TV can provide escape and even cure for the sick. A psychiatrist, Dr. Eugene D. Glynn, has written of therapeutic television: cases where the ignored child finds a substitute for mother love, where a hospital for schizophrenic adolescents finds the TV set the most practical tranquilizer in the institution, and even where an alcoholic found cure by substituting television for liquor.

It has become impossible even to poke fun at TV without surrendering to it. As *TV Guide Magazine* pointed out, the big laugh in Broadway's *Flower Drum Song* came when Miyoshi Umeki said her father could fall asleep in front of a TV set even when it was turned off. But, that gibe recorded, the show went on seriously to develop a plot in which the heroine learns how to get her man by watching a movie on television.

Yet TV can complicate romance. The National Union of Townswomen's Guilds in England passed a resolution deploring the fact that too many youngsters were staying home in front of the set instead of going out courting. "If there is no courting, there will be no marriage, no children and in the end—no nation," the Guild's resolution said.

As early as 1948 TV smashed a marriage. A New York woman got a separation on her complaint that her husband spent his evening hours in front of the set "oblivious to my presence." There have been many such cases since, some of them delayed in final settlement until it was determined who got custody of the family set. Some of these divorces have a desperate twist, such as the Chicago case in which the wife complained that her husband took the set to work with him every morning. (It was the only way he could be certain there'd be dinner prepared when he returned home, he said.)

On the other hand, Dr. Glynn wrote:

"Marriage after marriage is preserved by keeping it drugged on television; television is used quite consistently to prevent quarreling from breaking out by keeping people apart. This points up a somewhat less obvious side of watching television: its schizoid-fostering aspects. Television seems to be a social activity, an activity performed by many people together. Actually, though, it smothers contact, really inhibiting inter-personal exchange. A group watching television is frequently a group of isolated people, not in real exchange at all. Television viewers are given to solitary pleasures, not the social ones."

Dr. Clara T. Appell, a sociologist at Brooklyn College, made a survey of TV's effects on intimate family life. She was astounded by the results. Of the family members questioned, 60 per cent said their sleep patterns had been changed since the purchase of a TV set, and 55 per cent said their eating schedules were adjusted to fit the TV schedule. An astounding 78 per cent said that television was a physical help in family life—usually as an electronic baby sitter to keep the younger children out of mischief. Dr. Appell found that TV even had an effect on sex relations—it increased sexual intercourse, largely because both men and women said they were aroused by the romantic scenes they watched on the late movies.

Dr. Appell also found that even those who conceded they spent too much time at the set felt themselves powerless to combat the habit. She noted the case of one mother who lectured her young daughter about spending too much time watching TV. A few minutes later, disconcerted by the daughter's "What can I do?" nagging, the same mother blurted out, "Go watch TV and leave me alone."

The Brooklyn College sociologist also speculated about the result of late-night viewing. "One may wonder if this loss of sleep has any effect on the adequate functions of individuals the morning after," she wrote.

Another sociologist, Dr. Leo Bogart, wrote, "It is interesting that the bulk of disadvantages listed by the TV owners—'never get to bed . . . distracting from work'—reflect their inability to control themselves once the set has been installed in the house."

In London a parks commissioner became so convinced that TV viewing was an incurable malady that he proposed installing sets outdoors "to lure viewers into the fresh air."

A few hardy souls have fought back as the television madness swept the world, lonely Don Quixotes flailing at the windmill. It took a court injunction in Chicago to restrain Arthur Anderson from smashing his wife's third TV set after he had done mayhem to its two predecessors with an ax. And a sympathetic jury in Atlanta freed L. L. Crosby with a nod of understanding even though he admitted he fired a .22 caliber bullet into the set which his neighbor played full-volume every night until past midnight. But mostly the world has learned to live with TV, and a mineworkers union in England actually sought a pay raise for night-shift workers purely on the grounds that they missed all the good evening TV shows.

In addition to the TV that most of America sees, there is the lesser-known world of closed-circuit TV, that which transmits pictures only to authorized sets. Already these systems have caught bank robbers, demonstrated new operating techniques for surgeons, linked four cities for a single art auction, and become a bulletin board in the search for missing persons. The army uses TV for forward observation posts, and David Sarnoff, the chairman of the board of the Radio Corporation of America, has predicted that the next war will be telecast in its entirety (if it lasts long enough to get the cameras in position).

With its tight and massive grip on the time and attention of the people, it becomes obvious that television can be worked to do great good or great harm. In America, at least, it has done neither. And scarcely in the second decade of its existence, the U.S. television industry found itself beset by the bitterest of criticism for failing to become an instrument of uplift.

Typical of the assault was the speech made, not by an outsider, but by an advertising-agency president, Walter Guild, to the Western Radio and TV Conference. "Television," he said, "has proved abundantly that it cannot stand prosperity. Though born with a future unlimited, it has borrowed, plagiarized, stolen and cheated. Its basic menu is murder, as evidenced in the western and private eye shows, all stolen from grade B movies but not as good. Viewers look at them only because they are like the gambler who knows the wheel is crooked but who plays it because it is the only game in town."

The answer to this type of talk has come most frankly from Dr. Frank Stanton, president of the Columbia Broadcasting System. In testimony to Congress he said:

"If I am correct in my definition of the basic nature of television, we must face the fact that it is a major part of our function to try to appeal to most of the people most of the time. Some of the criticism, at least, is really a quarrel with the fact that television is a mass medium. It is not an elite medium. We can help education, but we cannot be education. We can give the pulpit a wider range, but we cannot be religion. We can help the American home, but we cannot be parents. This is not to say that we cannot at times lead or make contributions to society. But it is to say that the very nature of our being a mass medium operating in a society which is as we find it places some real limits on what we can do to improve society, to elevate tastes and to change the face of the world. We cannot force people to like what they don't like, to want what they don't want."

In other words, television will give its mass audiences what it deserves, no less and certainly no more.

IT TOOK 131 YEARS

The twentieth century marvel called television dates back to 1817. There was a working set as early as 1884. Yet it took 131 years to trudge from the first basic discovery to the sale of mass-produced sets.

There is no single inventor of television, no Robert Fulton, Samuel Morse, or Alexander Graham Bell. Rather, television is the product of widely spaced discoveries by many men from many nations. Some of the busiest pioneers actually hampered progress because they dramatically trumpeted new discoveries that turned out to be barks up the wrong tree.

In 1817 a Swedish professor named Jöns Berzelius discovered that selenium, a substance coming from sulphur, could conduct electricity. In 1873 a British telegrapher named May discovered that selenium could be used to transmit light by electricity. In 1884 a German named Paul Nipkow made the first TV set, using what he called a scanning disc: a disc that picked up the picture bit by bit through peepholes and re-etched it to a light-sensitive tube.

The race for TV was on. Six years after Nipkow first trans-mitted his crude shadows, two other Germans, Julius Elster and Hans Geitel, built the first photoelectric cells which were the key to TV cameras. In 1907 a Russian, Boris Rosing, and an Englishman, A. A. Campbell-Swinton, working unaware of each other, both came up with a tube in which to store light for the camera.

This should have put the world on the brink of practical television, but it didn't. Not wise enough to move from the world of mechanics and the mechanical disc to the world of electronics and the cathode tube, the scientists continued to fiddle and fumble with the basic principle they inherited from Kipkow.

But the 1920's brought the turning point. The decade was important to TV in several ways. For one thing, it saw the search for television—and for other scientific progress—move from the shack laboratory of the penniless inventor into the bosom of wealthy companies like the Radio Corporation of America and General Electric. For another, it determined who would operate television once it was developed.

Had the motion-picture companies taken it upon themselves to perfect television, TV today probably would be a substitute for the movies as we now see them in theaters. Had the Broad-way impresarios perfected television, the medium might today be basically a means of transmitting plays from the New York stage to theaters in other cities throughout the nation. But it was the radio industry that took upon itself the task of making television work, and so it became inevitable that TV, when developed, would operate within the image of commercial radio.

There were numerous attempts to commercialize TV pre-maturely. A young Scot named John Baird received consider-able financing in England by promising imminent TV on sets using the Nipkow mechanical-disc principle. Charles F. Jenkins did the same in the United States. They even put some sets on sale in the late 1920's, but their pictures, usually orange and black instead of black and white, were much too small and reception much too uneven for any kind of success.

It was a Russian immigrant to the United States, Dr. Vladimir Zworykin, who was responsible for the major breakthrough that guaranteed a successful future for television. Doing research for Westinghouse Electric, he picked up the old Campbell-Swinton cathode-tube principle, moved on after some improvements by Philo T. Farnsworth, and in the latter 1920's patented the iconoscope. Furthermore, he switched his allegiance from Westinghouse to the Radio Corporation of America. Television at last was nearing the living room.

The nation's first major telecast was not, however, put on by RCA, General Electric, or Westinghouse, despite their pioneering. It was staged by the American Telephone & Telegraph Company. On April 7, 1927, Herbert Hoover, then Secretary of Commerce, made a speech that was telecast from Washington over two hundred miles of AT&T facilities to New York.

The first voice on American television outside the experimental laboratories was that of J. J. McCarty, an AT&T vice president who spoke from Washington. His immortal words were: "I am instructed to make a little conversation while they are getting the loudspeaker ready. They are having a little power trouble."

In New York Walter Gifford, the AT&T president, replied by saying: "You screen well. You look more handsome over the wire."

"Does it flatter me much?" McCarty asked, and thus he set the pattern for all TV performers who would ever follow him. TV produces more hams than Armour's.

After the power trouble was remedied, Secretary Hoover spoke briefly on his pride in participating in such a historic occasion. The scene then switched to a studio in Whippany, New Jersey, and from there a comedian, recorded for history only as A. Dolan, provided TV's first actual entertainment: he told stories in dialect.

This was all an exhibition for AT&T's invited guests, and even the telephone-company hosts admitted they didn't have the slightest idea what commercial use could be made of the new wonder. "I'll just have to leave that to your imagination," Gifford said.

Most of the people at Bell were thinking mostly in terms of TV telephones. They frequently thereafter invited celebrities to make experimental calls for the publicity. They always got assurances, prominently published, that the world yearned for such a convenience. ("There are still some husbands who'd like to call up their wives and see them, too," said Fannie Hurst on the occasion of her visit to the TV-phone booth.)

The business world watched the development of TV with other ideas in mind. As early as 1931 the H&W Corset Company conducted the first closed-circuit TV experiment, using telephone-company equipment. H&W displayed its models before the cameras in the Bell Laboratories in downtown New York while a buyer for Franklin Simon & Company viewed them at receiving sets two miles uptown. The buyer bought $5,000 worth and said it was a fine way to shop. At least two large department stores immediately applied for TV operating licenses on the theory that eventually people would shop the electronic way rather than visit the stores in person.

As early as 1926 the William Morris Agency made the first show-business use of television. A cumbersome set was built for use as a vaudeville act. It was strictly a stunt, sending the picture from one side of the stage to the other for the amazement of the audience. The act went over big, but so did the set: it was so heavy that one day it plunged of its own weight through the floor of a Baltimore theater. No one bothered to rebuild it, although the Morris agency remained a pioneer show-business believer in TV and has since made millions of dollars representing performers in the medium.

However, for all these guessing games about the future of

TV, the men in commercial radio knew that the baby eventually would grow up to support *them*. For example, Edgar H. Felix of the staff of Radio Station WEAF wrote in the late 1920's:

"Television will find a complete structure ready to commercialize it. Broadcasting stations have organized personnel and established contacts in the advertising field, the advertising agencies have specialists in handling radio programs for their clients and the advertiser is already accustomed to radio and a medium of approach to the public. Consequently there will be no long period of adjustment and development. Advertising will be ready for the visual medium before the medium is ready for advertising."

These tantalizing forecasts began to intrigue the public, and in the late 1920's and early 1930's the subject of television became regular fare in the newspaper Sunday supplements. Sometimes the headlines would read "Television Is Just Around the Corner" and sometimes they would read "Television for the Home Will Never Be Practical," but seldom a month went by that some story didn't find its way into print. Most people thought the age of TV would be magnificent, but there were exceptions. The bishop of St. Alban's, Dr. M. B. Furse, wailed that his bath was the only private thing remaining in the world and that TV would soon take care of that. "I view with great trepidation the coming of the day when my morning ablutions will be reflected on the screens of New York for the entertainment of the American public," he said. This never came to pass. He died before the launching of the Ed Sullivan Show.

In 1928 TV got its first play, a one-act spy melodrama, *The Queen's Messenger,* presented by General Electric's experimental station in Schenectady, New York. Amateur TV bugs, an advanced version of the radio ham, reported receiving the performance as far away as the Pacific Coast. The picture received was three by three inches, but Dr. E. F. W. Alexanderson, consulting engineer for both GE and RCA, promised a twelve-by-twelve enlargement in the near future.

Only two actors appeared in the play, Izetta Jewel, a re-
tired stage star, and Maurice Randall, a contract actor for
GE's Schenectady radio station. Because of the small screen,
there were no full-length shots—only closeups of the heads,
hands or props. WGY staged the play with three cameras, one
for Miss Jewel, one for Randall, and the third for all the other
shots.

In 1930 TV took a big step out of the laboratory when the
National Broadcasting Company inherited the experimental
station from its parent company, RCA, and installed it at the
New Amsterdam Theater in New York City. NBC's first performer was "Felix the Cat," a bug-eyed wooden doll mounted
on a phonograph turntable so engineers could trace his movements on their screens. (A lady in New Jersey received this
picture on her husband's ham set and wrote NBC asking why
Felix didn't do anything more interesting than twirl. This was
the first of many millions of letters NBC was to receive about
Felix and some of his more highly paid successors. The original
question hasn't changed much.)

In 1936 the British Broadcasting Corporation, heir to Baird's
floundering attempts at commercial TV, began the world's first
regular television service. The programs went on three times
a day, for a total of three hours; the picture was ten by twelve
inches, received on sets which amateurs built for themselves.
The Americans sniffed huffily that the British were going into
business too soon, and time seemed to prove them right. By
1938 British TV-set manufacturers, who were producing sets to
sell at about $300, were ready to call it quits. They had sold
only 3,000 sets in two years.

Many had become convinced that TV was for the theaters,
not the homes.

The BBC urged them to hang on, promising that the thing
would fly eventually. Surely the fare had been enticing during
the limited hours of telecasting: the BBC had shown the coro-
nation in 1927, the Wimbledon tennis matches, the opera, top
plays, newsreels.

In the United States, $10,000,000 had been spent on experimentation with still no regular telecasting in sight, and David Sarnoff of RCA said there would be no regular TV until 1939. He was right. The experiments continued, once even inadvertently telecasting a suicide. (An experimental camera, on the air, happened to be pointed at an eleventh floor window from which a young woman took her last leap.)

But it was the predicted 1939 before America got regular TV. That's when NBC's W2XBS went on the air on a scheduled basis, beginning on April 30th with President Franklin D. Roosevelt's dedication of the New York World's Fair. On the same day RCA put its first sets on sale to the public; the prices ranged from $199.50 for the smallest set to $600 for the ten-by-twelve-inch screen. Three days later regular studio programs began with Fred Waring and his Pennsylvanians presenting the opening show. Waring said after the broadcast: "There is nothing very new about television showmanship. It's just the same old showmanship in a new setting."

From that point TV started a slow grind. Only 400 sets were sold in New York the first five months RCA offered them. In 1940 the prices were cut as much as $200 per set, bringing the range to $100 to $395, but the public remained wary.

The bright lights required for these pioneer TV shows made for brutal working conditions. An actor in a TV play reached for a bottle of cool beer as per the script, and then dropped it immediately; the lights overhead had made it too hot to hold. A woman giving a cooking demonstration couldn't understand why the studio crew wouldn't taste her goodies after the show went off the air; she didn't realize the men had seen her perspiration cascading down onto each cookie. The studio temperature was never less than 92 degrees.

On July 1, 1941, NBC's W2XBS, renamed WNBT for the occasion, and CBS's WCBW went commercial. NBC's first program was a Brooklyn Dodgers-Philadelphia Phillies baseball game. Its first commercial was a Bulova clock showing the time. Its first sponsor was the Sun Oil Company, which presented Lowell Thomas with fifteen minutes of news.

There was considerable adventure to staging these early TV shows. Gilbert Seldes, who headed CBS programming from 1937 to 1945 and was the entire programming department for a good portion of that time, recalls such mishaps as the sudden appearance of a microphone on "a deserted desert island" during a drama of the South Seas. He recalls, too, that closeups of the actors had to be planned hours in advance because it took so long to move the heavy and cumbersome cameras.

Many top performers were entranced by the possibilities of TV, however, and donated their services for the experiment. Jimmy Durante dropped in on one CBS show just for the fun of it and put on a hilarious impromptu performance for free—just the kind of performance that cost NBC thousands of dollars a few years later. One tragedy is that these early TV shows were not preserved, because there still was no kinescope to record them for posterity.

These TV pioneers were willing to try anything. On the day after the Japanese bombed Pearl Harbor there came the rumor that German planes were on their way across the Atlantic to bomb New York. Did the CBS-TV boys flee to the safety of the hills? They did not. They laboriously hauled a camera over to the window and prepared to televise the bombers as they came in over Park Avenue. "Then it occurred to us," recalls Seldes, "that a transmitter is like a beacon. The bombers could use this beacon to zero in and raid New York. We were only twenty minutes before program time but we loyally scuttled this big spectacular. And a little while after our decision we got the word that the raid rumor was false."

World War II was an important time for TV. While ostensibly all experimentation stopped, actually the great progress made in radar was also progress for TV. Wartime radar work, as a matter of fact, hastened the arrival of practical home TV by about five years. Thus when the Japanese surrendered, the broadcasting industry made immediate preparations to shift from sound to sight.

Only New York, Chicago, Los Angeles, Philadelphia, and Schenectady had stations in operation on VJ Day and these could be received by but 7,000 sets (5,500 of them in New York). However, a manufacturers' survey turned up 4,000,000 families which said they were ready to buy a set sight unseen. Hearn's Department Store in New York offered a few sets showing a postcard-sized picture late in 1945, and these were sold out at $100 each within a few days. The public was ready. The great rush was on. The networks began to form when the coaxial cable first went into operation in 1946.

In 1947 the big programs began going on the air—"Kraft Television Theater," "Meet the Press," and "Howdy Doody," to name three. But most of the TV industry considers 1948 the year that big-time TV was born. Some twenty-five new stations began operation throughout the nation that year. The manufacturers reached the point where they were turning out 140,-000 sets a month and selling all of them. The coaxial cable worked its way halfway across the country. And Milton Berle went on the air.

Berle was the first big-time entertainer to appear on TV regularly, and for a number of years he indeed *was* television. There had been something like this in radio: During their heyday in the 1930's Amos 'n' Andy held the American public in such a grip that it was possible to hear their entire program simply by walking down a quiet residential street and catching the broadcast from each house passed. Now the same was true of Berle.

The TV stations had operated heavily in the red as experiments. The advertisers had no hope of return because of the small audiences. But in 1948 TV got down to business literally as well as figuratively. As the audience size leaped, so did the fees for time. Some stations raised their rates as much as 50 per cent that year. The Federal Communications Commission was engulfed with applications for television-station licenses even though the number of channels was sharply limited, and CBS President Frank Stanton warned, "You can't pay for television transmitters with jellybeans."

By 1950 there were 100 stations operating, playing to 4,000,-000 sets. Many of these were in saloons as customer lures, and Henny Youngman came up with the gag advertisement: "Bartender Wanted. Must Be Able To Fix TV Set." There were four networks now, the American Broadcasting Company and Du Mont having joined the NBC and CBS pioneers. But most performers were working purely for the experience. An ABC program called "Hollywood Screen Test" paid such fees as $51.85 for Grace Kelly, $175 for Faye Emerson, and $60 for Teresa Brewer, Kim Stanley, and Anne Bancroft. Daytime TV became important because of a former Washington news announcer named Arthur Godfrey.

Since the 1930's everyone had foreseen great world events as a major TV attraction. In 1951 as the coaxial cable reached California the American public got its first taste of this somewhat by surprise. The Kefauver Hearings were launched, and, more with a why-not? attitude than anything else, the TV cameras were permitted within the hearing room. It was days before Senator Kefauver and his public-relations people knew what had hit them, or what they had hit. Suddenly the nation was staring at the hands of Frank Costello. A year later the Democratic and Republican national conventions were televised; these were not the first, for NBC experimentally had telecast a convention as far back as 1940; but these were the first to be seen by a large audience. No convention was ever to be the same again. The political parties knew that thereafter they must embrace show business, and must concentrate their major activities during the prime viewing hours of the evening when the family was gathered around the living-room set.

In 1948 CBS announced it had developed a system for color television, and in 1949 NBC announced it had developed a *better* system for color television. They engaged in a long, bitter, and costly struggle, with the FCC as referee. CBS won.

In a way this fight was history repeating itself. The NBC color system was based on the mechanical-disc principle. The CBS system was based on an electronic tube. Furthermore, only the CBS system was compatible—that is, CBS color transmissions could be received in black and white on existing sets. It was inevitable that the CBS system would prevail, but the plodding FCC did not endorse this method until 1953.

TV's only direction seemed up. There were setbacks, to be sure. The Du Mont network folded in 1955 for lack of outlets. And scandal hit in 1959, first with the exposé of phony quiz programs and later with gamy accounts of bribery and false advertising. But there was no indication that these dimmed the viewers' relish for TV. The medium had become one of the most compelling forces in American life.

1144818

THE HEART OF GOLD

There are some 530 television stations in the United States, housed in conspicuous local studios which run from cutely colonial to handball-court modern. But the great majority of these are only amplifiers for the networks. Their basic needs are a transmission tower and a bookkeeper; the rest is ginger-bread.

TV is a big business, and only the national networks are big enough to cope with it. The theory behind the network is obvious: Station AAA-TV in Sioux City could never marshal the money and facilities to produce a Perry Como show, so it joins a hundred or so other stations in a network which is capable of supplying such a show. But the practice of a network operation is something else: Station AAA-TV has precious little to say about what program it airs. It takes what the network offers, and that's that.

Yet AAA-TV is perfectly happy with the arrangement. The

network has become the heart of TV, but it is a heart of gold. AAA-TV is paid (about 30 per cent of its normal time charges) by the network to transmit the program. The station also has the right to sell spot announcements between the network shows. The production and transmission of the show was financed by the network and costs AAA-TV nothing. The production of the spot announcement was financed by an advertising agency or a sponsor and costs AAA-TV nothing. So the station's income from the network show and the in-between spots is almost all profit.

For this reason, affiliation with a network is the individual station's most valuable asset. A Milwaukee station that sold for $700,000 when it had no network tie resold for $5,000,000 when it acquired a Columbia Broadcasting System affiliation. On the other hand, a Charleston station that sold for $1,000,000 when it had CBS went for $650,000 after it lost CBS.

The network contract with the local station has one key clause. This involves "option time." Under the agreement, the station signs away to the network the option to use ten hours a day of the station's broadcast time for network programs. This leaves, of course, very little time for the station to present anything like a balanced schedule of local programs. Furthermore, the Justice Department said in 1959 that it considered the option-time clause a direct violation of the Sherman Antitrust Act.

Nevertheless, the FCC has recognized the contention that there could be no networks without option time. The networks insist that these firm commitments from the local stations are necessary to assure a sponsor that he can get the coverage he desires each week his program is on the air. Were the stations not tied down by the option-time obligation, they say, the sponsor might find his show carried by two hundred stations one week and twenty the next.

Actually, the loudest objection to option time does not come from those who would force the individual stations into more extensive local programing. It comes instead from the producers of syndicated shows who can find little market for their product as long as the individual stations are tied up by the networks for the greater part of the broadcasting day.

The FCC did cut the maximum amount of option time in 1960. It divided the broadcasting day into four segments (morning, afternoon, evening, and late-night) and ruled that a station could not option more than two and a half hours per segment to a network. This totaled ten hours a day, two hours less than the networks had been pre-empting.

The FCC also broadened the station's authority in taking option-time programs. In the past, for example, a station could reject an unsuitable network series before the series started— but could not eliminate the series once it had began carrying it; now a station can cease carrying a series any time it chooses. In the past the local station had to present a mighty good reason for substituting a special local show for a network show; now the station can make the substitution any time it wishes.

All of this may give the impression that the FCC has loosened an oppressive yoke on the necks of the local stations, but this, in practice, is not true. Most stations are perfectly content to take the network programs and sell spot announcements in between. As a matter of fact, many stations will subscribe to any network program, whether it is obligatory under the option-time clause or whether it is an extra offering presented by the network outside the option-time schedule.

The same option-time agreements were written into the radio contracts, but radio stations produced far more local programing than their TV counterparts. The reason is cost. A radio station in, say, Barrington, Vermont, could produce eight hours of local programing a day with a stack of records, a wire-service news ticker, and a $150-a-week disc jockey. A TV station in Barrington would need twenty times that outlay to produce local programs.

NBC and CBS, surveying the nation in 1951, decided that stations in 77 cities would cover two-thirds of the nation's families. They picked the 55 most important as "basic," and the TV stations in these areas make up the basic network. In addition, there's a second group of 53 areas which are "desirable" because they add important buying strength. Last, there are an additional 80 areas—small communities mostly—that the advertiser might want to buy to make certain that his message blankets virtually the entire nation.

Thus the size of the network will vary from program to program. CBS, for example, carried "The Danny Thomas Show" on 202 stations and "Have Gun, Will Travel" on only 163—although it was the same network, the same season. The difference was what the advertiser wanted to buy.

Although most of these stations are "affiliates," independently owned and associated with the network only by contract, the three networks each own five—the maximum allowed by the Federal Communications Commission. These, naturally, are in the biggest and richest cities. NBC's O&O stations (so called because they are owned and operated by the network) are in New York, Los Angeles, Washington, San Francisco, and Hartford; the CBS O&Os are in New York, Chicago, Philadelphia, Los Angeles, and St. Louis. The ABC stations are in New York, Chicago, Los Angeles, San Francisco, and Detroit.

The general conception of the TV network executive is that of a show producer. This is far from the truth. The network people generally are not show people and they are not advertising people, either. The network people are facility men. They have, over the years, looked upon their network as a hall to be rented. The trend is somewhat in the other direction now. The networks have come to the view that their business will profit most if they own the show as well as the hall. But this still does not make them show producers. They are becoming show buyers. Then they lease the combination—the show and the hall—to the advertiser.

The granddaddy of the networks is the National Broadcasting Company. It's the oldest, but neither the biggest nor the best.

NBC is a wholly owned subsidiary of the Radio Corporation of America. Anyone can buy stock in RCA, and its board of directors includes all its key executives. But there's one real boss—David Sarnoff, who has been a guiding genius of the mammoth company since it was formed to break the Marconi Wireless Telegraph Company's monopoly on radio communications during World War I.

The Sarnoff story is one of those legends too corny for Hollywood. He arrived by steerage from Minsk, Russia, when he was nine years old, and within two days he was selling newspapers on the streets of New York. He went to work for the Marconi Company as an office boy and worked his way up to wireless operator. He was the man on duty in 1912 when the *Titanic* SOS filtered in feebly over the Atlantic. Young David Sarnoff stuck to his key for seventy-two hours relaying disaster messages.

In the days just before and during World War I, radio was considered purely a communications medium, and not too good a one at that because there was no way to keep the messages private. It was as the twenty-five-year-old assistant traffic manager of Marconi that Sarnoff, in 1916, wrote a memo that opened up a new vista for radio and also set the pattern for television.

He wrote: "I have in mind a plan of development which would make a radio a household utility in the same sense as the piano or the phonograph. The idea is to bring music into the home by wireless. The same principle can be extended to numerous other fields, as, for example, receiving lectures at home, which can be simultaneously announced and received. Baseball scores could be transmitted in the air."

When RCA was formed and David Sarnoff became its manager, he set out to put his grandiose plan into practice. Originally he had no intention of selling advertising on the radio stations. As a matter of fact, he was against the idea. He conceived radio programs as the means of inducing people to buy radio sets from RCA.

It is from the Sarnoff memo that modern TV and radio stems. And today David Sarnoff still runs NBC. He sits in a glorious office on the fifty-third floor of the RCA Building in Radio City (with a complete private barbershop in an anteroom) and permits the NBC executives of the moment to function as they see fit only as long as things are going well. However, the moment there's trouble, financial or otherwise, the voice of David Sarnoff is the only one heard at NBC.

NBC's big move, when TV went big time, was to bring in Sylvester (Pat) Weaver as its president. In the days of radio the advertising agencies ran all network programing. The networks were true to their theory that they were nothing but hall renters. The advertising agency, on behalf of the sponsor, put together the show, hired the performers, bought time from the network, and then staged the show. This made for strict formula programing. There was little adventure in radio because the ad agencies did not dare take risks with the sponsors' money.

Pat Weaver, as chief of radio programs for the Young & Rubicam agency, realized this. He was determined that, as president of NBC, he would not surrender TV to the ad agencies. As he puts it today: "I brought in some of the top ad-agency programing men to help me at NBC and I told them, 'Look, we ruined radio. Let's not let it happen to television. Let's stage our own programs and just sell advertising time to the agencies.'"

Weaver had grandiose ideas for TV. As an inveterate writer of long and flowery memos, he saturated his fellow NBC executives with these ideas. Weaver determined early in the game that the costs of television would be so great that no single sponsor could carry a full show. He determined that the networks would have to go into show business, and he signed many of the top stars to long, high-paying contracts without knowing for certain what use he would make of them. He coined the word "spectacular" as a means of describing a single big TV show, staged with no relationship to what was

presented last week or what might come up next week. He
forecast that excessive control of TV by sponsors would lead
to trouble.

Weaver wound up as a prophet with honor but without a
job. Sarnoff eventually fired him. For one thing, the aging boss
of RCA realized that Weaver was gambling—he was signing
stars and putting on shows without any guarantee of return.
In the radio days NBC didn't gamble. All the bills were paid
by the ad agency before the show went on the air. For another thing, Weaver's lavish programing department was showing a smaller percentage of profit even when the shows were
sold. And when the shows turned out as flops, the loss was
staggering.

At first Sarnoff gave Weaver an opportunity to "straighten
things out." Robert Sarnoff, David's son, thirty-seven years old
at the time, was named president of NBC, in charge of operating the company generally, and Weaver was appointed chairman of the board. He actually was chairman of himself. He
was given time to trim the fat and make his ideas conform to
what David Sarnoff considered efficient, but within a matter of
months he was out.

NBC brought in Robert Kintner, who had been fired from
his job as president of the American Broadcasting Company
in a fight over "management procedures," to serve under Bob
Sarnoff. Eventually Kintner was named president of NBC and
Bob Sarnoff chairman of the board.

Kintner is a salesman, not a creator in the Weaver sense.
His experience at ABC put him much more in the old radio
mold, although eventually television has learned that Pat
Weaver was much more right than wrong. Sitting in his office
today as head of the McCann-Erickson Inc., advertising
agency's international division, Weaver says his big mistake at
NBC was not ousting more of the radio holdovers. "Except for
a few key men, I built on that radio inheritance," he says.
"They never understood what I was trying to do and never
agreed with it."

Many of Weaver's innovations nevertheless remain. He started the "Today" show, for example, and it is one of NBC's biggest moneymakers, grossing about $7,000,000 a year. He first advocated the magazine concept: Where once a sponsor could buy only a fifteen-, thirty-, or sixty-minute segment on network radio, today he can buy anything from ten seconds to two hours on the TV network.

There are always reports that the younger men gradually are wresting control from David Sarnoff at RCA, and sometimes there are reports that NBC will soon be sold to a major motion-picture company or the like. But the man in nominal command is Bob Sarnoff, eldest of David's two sons. Harvard-educated and trained originally as an advertising man with a Des Moines agency and with *Look* Magazine, Bob Sarnoff went to work for NBC in 1948. By 1951 he was executive vice president and by 1953 he was president. "Obviously, I'm well aware I got to the top in quick time," he said. "The burden has been on me to show I could do the job."

Actually, even if he is the boss' son, young Sarnoff's rise is not so phenomenal as it seems. NBC is like that. A man who left his job as a press agent to take a menial position with the network was a vice president within four years. And vice presidents (Fred Allen said NBC even has a vice president in charge of saying "Don't open the window") have become menials in even less time.

The Columbia Broadcasting System appears a much less frantic organization. Although it is younger than NBC, it often appears more staid, more conscious of its likes and dislikes, more consistent in its actions. It makes more money than NBC, has 242 affiliates to NBC's 196, and claims the largest viewing audience in the world.

Yet if NBC began life with RCA as its rich papa, CBS was born on the wrong side of the tracks. Two months after NBC first went on the air, a pioneer radio announcer, Major Andrew S. White, began forming his own network. It emerged in 1927

as the United Independent Broadcasters. On the verge of
going broke, White sold out to the Columbia Phonograph
Record Company, which renamed the network the Columbia
Phonograph Broadcasting Company. The red ink still flowed,
and Columbia Phonograph sold to a Philadelphia dentist, Dr.
Leon Levy, who took on the fledgling company as a hobby.

Levy's in-laws were the Paley family who operated a cigar
factory in Philadelphia. As cigarettes caught favor, the sale of
cigars went down. The anxious Paleys did something desperate.
They bought time on the Levy radio network, presenting Kate
Smith, then unknown, as the star of their show. The sale of
cigars went up from 40,000 a day to 100,000 a day. This was
enough to startle William S. Paley, then twenty-seven, whose
father and uncle operated the cigar factory. To make certain
there'd always be time on the network for La Palina Cigars,
young Paley bought it and, on September 26, 1928, became its
new president. In less than two years his Columbia Broadcasting System began showing a profit.

Young Paley lost all interest in manufacturing cigars. He
moved to New York to run his network full time. Like Sarnoff
of RCA, he worked ten and twelve hours a day, six and seven
days a week. Sometimes he'd call the network in the middle
of the night with a program suggestion.

As radio reached its heyday in the mid-1930s, a young Ohio
State University psychology professor, Frank Stanton, became
fascinated with the industry. He made great study of "radio
listening behavior" and he forwarded copies of his scholarly
papers to the CBS executives. Then he wrote an article that
purported to prove that advertising directed at the ear was far
more effective than advertising directed at the eye. CBS hired
him immediately as its director of research.

Stanton, the Ph.D. egghead of network radio, immediately
launched a search for the common denominator. He even devised a machine, the Program Analyzer, which was supposed
to record the effects of a radio program on as many as one
hundred persons at a time. "CBS now can check a show at its

dress rehearsal, and tighten up the loose ends before the broadcast," glowed one trade magazine.

The Program Analyzer did not dispense with flops, but it did help make Stanton the president of CBS when Paley decided to step up to become Chairman of the Board. One Madison Avenue legend is that Stanton himself spread the rumor that he was the personal choice of Charles Luckman, then head of Lever Brothers, one of the biggest advertising accounts of all. Luckman, so the story goes, was asked by Paley if Stanton was his choice. Taken aback, Luckman wouldn't say Yes or No. Paley took this to be yes, and Stanton became CBS president.

When TV went big time, CBS played around with the Pat Weaver ideas by making Hubbell Robinson, who shared many of Weaver's views, as head of its operation. But Robinson left to go in the production business for himself, and Stanton brought in Louis G. Cowan.

Cowan had produced TV shows independently with some success, but he hit the jackpot when he conceived "The $64,000 Question." For a period this was the most successful of TV shows, and Stanton reckoned that the man who could produce such a bonanza might well be the man to evaluate all shows on CBS. Cowan became executive vice president. When the quiz scandals rocked the industry, Stanton just as coldly fired Cowan for the very same reasons that he was hired: Cowan was the daddy of "The $64,000 Question."

He had, he said, divested himself of any interest in the program long before the scandals (although his wife had retained an interest in the producing company). He had not, he said, any connection with the fixing of the quiz shows.

Stanton, however, was the most noble-sounding of all TV executives in the public breast-beating that followed the scandals. He even banned ersatz laughter on filmed shows, even though comedians insisted that these laugh breaks were an absolute necessity to their timing. (Stanton eventually gave up on this one.)

Despite the summary dismissal of Cowan without any face-saving pretense of "resignation for reasons of health" usually granted such a mogul, CBS is considered the best employer among the TV networks. One reason for this is that CBS is more likely to promote its executives from within the ranks rather than bring in for a key job an outsider who in turn brings in his own outsiders. Mostly the stability depends upon two men, Paley and Stanton, who will set policies and then stick to them.

The American Broadcasting Company is the youngest of the networks, and also the brashest. It began as a floundering follower and has emerged as a clattering trail blazer, revolutionizing many aspects of network operation.

ABC began life as NBC's country cousin. In the 1930's NBC got so rich that it cut itself into two pieces in order to make twice as much money. It operated two radio networks, the Red and the Blue. But the federal government stepped in with anti-trust action and ordered RCA to sell one of the networks.

Naturally, all the good features were lumped into the Red network and retained by RCA. The Blue Network, containing the leftovers, was sold.

Rechristened the American Broadcasting Company, the new company was last to enter television, and consequently could sign up only those stations which had been by-passed by NBC and CBS. When United Paramount Theatres, Inc., headed by Leonard H. Goldenson, bought the network from Edward J. Noble in 1951, the greatest asset was the office aspirin supply.

The network dared say little about what type of program the advertisers brought to ABC. A buck was a buck, and not one could be spurned. Even when something good appeared on ABC it didn't stay long. As Goldenson subsequently testified to Congress, "When a strong show developed on ABC, typically it was moved to one of the other networks as time periods opened up." ABC lost the United States Steel Hour and the Pulitzer Prize Playhouse, to name two, in this fashion.

Furthermore, because the Federal Communications Commission had exhausted the number of channels it was willing to assign, there was scant hope of ABC growing as a network. In many markets that were required by advertisers, the FCC had authorized only two stations, and they were sewed up by NBC and CBS.

So, in desperation, ABC decided to strike out on its own. It rid itself of all the advertiser-owned shows and began to buy its own. ABC did not develop programs. It simply shopped around among the package producers for the best. To this day ABC, now fabulously successful, originates few programs. Its program director, Thomas Moore, essentially is a buyer, not a creator.

ABC needed some rash steps to make itself noticed. To get Walt Disney on its network, ABC put up the money to build Disney's dream, Disneyland Park, in Anaheim, California (a not unfortunate decision, since the network subsequently sold its interest back to Disney at a profit of 1,400 per cent). To get the best film-show techniques, ABC induced first Warner Brothers and then M-G-M and 20th Century Fox, the big motion-picture studios which had ignored TV, to go into TV-show production. To get Frank Sinatra, Goldenson personally sat down with the crooner and figured out a deal that would pay for itself with income-tax savings.

ABC turned the television world topsy-turvy. Where once it was considered good business to have the advertiser bring in a paid-up show, now it was considered bad business. ABC figured that if it owned the show and sold it to the advertiser only, then the sponsor could never cart the show off to a bigger network. Where once a network balanced its rival's hit comedy show with what presumably was a better comedy show, ABC developed the theory of counterprograming: if NBC was showing comedy at 8:30 Monday night, then ABC would deliberately avoid comedy and plan a drama or a western instead. This, at least, would capture those in the audience who didn't want to see a comedy show.

The whole idea was to get away from the tyranny of the advertisers because the advertisers had no loyalty.

Goldenson explained it this way:

"We made up our minds we would not wait for the advertisers to come to ABC. They brought us only their poor programs. They took their best ones to the other two networks, and when a good one developed at ABC they took that away, too. So we simply took control of the programs."

ABC decided to make a definite appeal to the younger married families of the nation. It refused to follow the lead of the other networks in paying lip service to intellectual programing. The other networks actually do little more than ABC to break away from lowest-common-denominator programing, but they issue flowery statements indicating their concern for the eggheads. Not so Goldenson. "TV is a mass medium," he says frankly. "These minority groups—these eggheads—are not big TV watchers anyway. TV is a mass medium, and we don't want to lose this status."

His network has produced some splendid documentaries in recent seasons, but this is only occasional fare. ABC has never lost sight of the mass audience.

As a result, ABC has developed a formula of half-hour and one-hour pattern programs—situation comedies, westerns, adventure shows—that largely follow the plan of network radio. The only difference is durability. The hit radio shows lasted for years. ABC watches these hit TV shows carefully, and the moment they start slipping they are bounced off the air for something new.

Now, Goldenson and his crew have made a castle of the shambles. Oliver Treyz, the president of ABC, is not a showman at all. He is a supersalesman. It's his job to dash to a big sponsor and sell him on the spot the moment that Tom Moore's window shopping discovers a show that appears to have promise. ABC is, in a sense, exactly the opposite of what Pat Weaver wanted NBC to be in the days he was exhorting his minions with those brave-new-world memos. Weaver wanted an adventurous TV, constantly striking out in new directions in an effort to produce delightful surprises. ABC developed a safe TV, seldom veering from the beaten path, and never jolting the viewer with something he doesn't expect.

The emergence of ABC as a powerful network created supercompetition among the three big chains. The rivalry became bitter despite the fact that all three usually could sell out almost all, if not indeed all, of their time.

CBS issued a bulletin which sniffed haughtily that ABC's improvement in ratings was based purely on "action" shows, which is the network way of saying that ABC was murdering more people per night than CBS. At one broadcasters' convention a rival network's men were circulating among the station owners, whispering that the affiliates that took a new ABC blockbuster had to agree to forego being paid for a full season; this ABC hotly denied. ABC also was accused of rate cutting, that is, making itself look good with big sales from advertisers who were sometimes getting reduced rates. ABC denied this, too.

NBC and CBS battle each other in pretty much the same way. The competitive spirit is so great that *Variety* reports that sometimes network men sneak into the cutting room of a rival chain after hours in order to scoop up the discarded film from the wastebasket; they can subsequently view this and determine what new type of program the rival is preparing.

The heavy competition makes things tough on the producers of shows. They get scant attention when they beg for "one more chance" for a slipping program. The network ditches the show as quickly as possible in order to prevent a rival network from luring away viewers who might never return. Consequently a McCann-Erickson study showed that of 421 new shows which went on the air between 1948 and 1957, only 31 remained in 1959. And of these 31, several were casualties by 1960.

Even when they were under the greatest stress, during the

first outbreak of the TV-quiz scandals, the networks found
they were unable to cast aside their rivalry for united action.
CBS banned quiz shows and President Stanton was quick to
sneer at NBC when that network refused to follow suit. The
heads of the three networks did finally get together for one
meeting to debate a common course to combat the scandals.
They met and talked for four and a half hours and left the
hotel room as they entered, in complete disagreement.

By and large, of course, this is all to the good. A combine of
the three networks would automatically mean a monopoly in
television broadcasting, even though there remained three
distinct ownerships. But it is surprising to see that three companies under fire cannot stop scrapping among themselves long
enough to face a common enemy.

Broadcasting magazine recently made a survey of the networks' customers—the advertising agencies—to determine what
they thought of the networks. In summarizing the answers,
Broadcasting said this:

"If buyers invested their money according to program 'quality,' management reliability and integrity, they would buy CBS.

"If mass appeal and low cost-per-thousand were the criterion,
they would go for ABC.

"If they were looking for originality, flexibility and initiative
in a network, they would buy NBC."

CBS, the report said, "is sometimes considered stuffy." NBC
"juggles its brass too much . . . an air of instability comes from
frequent realignment of top executives." ABC is "hard to pin
down on a deal—you'd better have your lawyer along."

Nevertheless, all three networks are tremendous moneymakers. The National Broadcasting Company TV network
went into the red $643,000 its first year of operation, and NBC
had lost $5,459,000 on TV by 1953. But then the tables turned.
By 1955 NBC had earned back all of this $5,459,000 it had
previously spent and was, in addition $2,315,000 ahead.

By 1959 NBC was earning about 25 per cent of all the
parent RCA's $40,000,000 profit after taxes. Rich CBS showed

an even bigger profit, $25,000,000 in 1959. ABC made about $10,000,000. The top management of these networks is drawing salaries on the average of $150,000 a year, plus stock dividends.

NBC's financial position is the most difficult for the outsider to assess because of its corporate setup: It is merely a division of RCA, and therefore its profit-and-loss figures are published only as part of the RCA totals. Columnist John Crosby got into a public hassle with the NBC management when he contended that the network actually was making more money back in Pat Weaver's uplift days than it is now that NBC is a follower of the ABC-formula programing. NBC contended that Crosby was wrong and that its profits are higher than ever.

It would take an accountant, and an NBC accountant at that, to resolve that argument. But there is no doubt that the over-all financial health of all TV is robust.

Actually, the stations owned by the networks do so well that the networks themselves sometimes appear to be the satellites on the ledger. In 1959, according to the FCC, network-owned stations earned only 23.9 per cent of television's total revenue, yet showed 63.9 per cent of the profits.

Television does well everywhere, however. Generally business in the United States has been concerned with the fact that expenses are going up faster than profits. But this is not true in TV. In 1959 TV expenses went up only 9.7 per cent over 1958 while profits before taxes went up 29.3 per cent. More than 20 per cent of the nation's stations grossed more than a million dollars in 1959.

Good business has meant a changed business for the networks. Following ABC's lead, NBC and CBS have taken control of their programs from advertising agencies. As in the case with ABC, most of these are produced by outside packagers and then sold to the network. In some cases the network puts up a portion of the money to finance the "pilot" show—the introductory show that will be used as a lure for prospective sponsors. Even when they don't put up money, however, the networks may collect a refund from the show they buy by charging for "creative counseling" or some such.

This policy of the networks in buying shows first and then offering them for sale to sponsors has created something of a crisis on Madison Avenue. The once all-powerful sponsor can still keep a show or cancel it, but he can no longer change it or move it. Relishing this new-found power and security, the networks refuse to take on a show owned by an ad agency even if it is a good show. They seem very highhanded to sponsors and agencies which yearn for the old way of doing things, but the networks can afford to be highhanded. TV is so profitable for advertisers that if one sponsor won't buy a show, the next one surely will.

George Abrams, former president of Richard Hudnut products, put his plight this way: "The networks chase ratings more than anything else because that's what their rates are pegged to—the higher the audience, the more money they are entitled to charge. So they will refuse your program even if it is a good one and even if you're willing to pay for it, on the grounds that it might hurt their ratings for the night. I don't see any change coming. I think things will stay like this for some time. And it can be tough. I took a show, a somewhat different show, to CBS with the money to sponsor it, and I was told, 'It's good but it's different and we won't stick our necks out.' They just wouldn't risk even a good show because their judgment could be wrong and their rating for the night would be lowered."

As a result, ad agencies are now calling for a fourth network to open up more time on television. But they know that such a call will go unheeded for some time. To begin with, there are not enough major market stations for even three networks— ABC is frozen out of several key cities and a fourth network would lack outlets in these plus many more.

The owner of a documentary called "The Race for Space" did put together something of a network of his own by selling his film to individual stations in 1960 after the three major networks refused it. But this was a hit-or-miss proposition that would not interest any major advertisers on a regular basis because it is too undependable and inefficient.

It is much more likely that the networks will continue to operate as they are for some years to come. They want formula programs, put on film or tape, for these are their best assurance of high ratings and, in turn, of high time charges and consistent sponsorship. Pat Weaver pointed out the reason for the network control of a show: "The advertiser is interested only in the cost per thousand persons reached. His low cost could mean a bad show. But when the bad show loses its audience, the advertiser has only to withdraw his sponsorship. The network is stuck with the time, and the need to replace the show."

On the other hand, if the network itself presents a show that will pull a big audience, it need not be so concerned with the support of a single sponsor. If he pulls out because of costs or other reasons, the network still has the show and can peddle it to someone else.

Thus the broadcasters think they have now found the perfect method of operating. An independent producer dreams up and creates the show. If it's good enough, the network will buy it from him and resell it to the advertiser. The independent producer has taken the initial risk. The advertiser pays the bills. The network can hardly escape making a profit on every such program it carries. The advertisers don't like this system, but they are told by the networks to take it or leave it. They take it. That's why there are no hungry networks today.

PACKAGES, SURPRISE AND OTHERWISE

The packager is the showman of TV. He has the unenviable job of trying to please all of the people all of the time: he must satisfy the network that his show will produce high ratings; he must satisfy the advertising agency and sponsor that his show will sell soap; he must satisfy the star that his show will further a theatrical career; and he must satisfy his wife that the tremendous financial risk will not mean moving from a Beverly Hills mansion to a Lower East Side walk-up.

Anyone with an idea can become a TV packager. Some are stars with only their own talents to sell. Some are hand-to-mouth scroungers dreaming up mammoth ideas in matchbox offices. And some are the masters of the sprawling Hollywood studios which can grind out TV shows with the same soulless automation that produces the sponsor's cigarettes.

The stars were among the first packagers. They were not in-dulging in the American dream of owning their own business but rather in the American nightmare of paying their own taxes. They learned they could wind up with more cash in the bank at the end of the year as business-owning producers than they could as salaried performers. Thus the Bob Hopes and the Perry Comos formed corporations designed solely to produce a Bob Hope or a Perry Como show. They were soon followed by the professional producers like David Susskind. The promise of cash was so enticing that Hubbell Robinson quit the relative security of a six-figure salary as head of CBS television to assume the risks of an independent producer.

These risks are great. The packager must put together a sample show—called a pilot—before he can begin peddling it. These pilots can cost as much as $100,000, and the whole outlay can be a total loss. He may not find a sponsor or, most heartbreaking of all, he may find a sponsor and yet be told by the networks that they have no time available for the new show.

Quite often the packager does not make a dime even when the network buys his show. A survey of twenty-three packaged TV shows made by economist Irving Bernstein for the Screen Actors Guild records that only five of these were sold for an immediate profit. However, weep no tears for the beleagured packager. His silver lining comes in television's re-run policy. Granted he may have recouped only 85 to 95 per cent of his costs in his original sale to the network, but he still can look forward to a whopping fee when the show is run the second time. And that second fee is almost all profit. It will shove him 'way over the top on the total operation. Consequently, Bernstein reports, "There seems to be a rule of thumb in Hollywood that the producer tries to sell his network show on the first run for the price it cost him to produce." After that he simply awaits the re-run money, known to the trade as residuals.

One of the packager's problems is the fixed costs of a TV show. His budget is divided into two sections, "above the line" and "below the line." His "above the line" costs are artistic— writers, stars, actors, directors. His "below the line" costs are mechanical—the camera crews, the studio rent, the truck drivers, and the administrative overhead. His show succeeds or fails on the artistic efforts of his "above the line" people.

His costs in that section of the budget, though, are only one-third to one-half what they are in the other section. Each weekly episode in a typical half-hour series costs from $30,000 to $50,000. The star of such a show draws from $750 to $7,500, and the remainder of the cast will collect a total of $3,000 to $9,000.

Because the packagers of the big dramatic or variety shows do not have the re-run possibilities enjoyed by the series producers, they must make their money on the original sale. However, they are less likely to be floored by the total loss that a series producer suffers when he finds there is no sale for his idea. No one makes Bob Hope or Perry Como turn out a pilot film before deciding to sponsor their shows.

These stars have found such success in the production business that many have expanded their one-show corporations into full production companies. In addition to this, a number of motion-picture stars have turned to TV packaging as a means of investing the money they made on the larger screen.

The biggest of the packagers, however, is the huge Music Corporation of America, which entered television by the service entrance and has remained to become the lord of the manor. MCA spreads through show business to such an extent that it is known to the trade as "The Octupus." Originally an agent and booking service for orchestras, MCA developed high-pressure tactics into a fine art. Once it had corralled all the major orchestras into its stable, hotels and ballrooms found it impossible to book these top attractions unless they dealt with MCA bands exclusively. From representing orchestras, MCA expanded to representing singers, then actors, then writers, producers, and directors.

Ultimately it went into the production end of the business. This presented a ticklish situation. MCA represented the actors and writers, and now MCA had become the employer of the same artists and writers. The conflict of interest was obvious.

Ordinarily the theatrical unions do not permit agents to hire their own clients, but, as one Screen Actors Guild official put it, MCA is so big and powerful "that we had to face reality and also to recognize the fact that this meant many more jobs for actors and everyone else in show business." MCA was given a waiver on the union ban.

Operating under the trade name of Revue Productions, MCA soon was one of the most successful of all TV packagers. Some of the shows were owned outright by MCA. Others were put together by other packagers and then sold by MCA at a 10 per cent commission. Still others were independent shows in which MCA, retaining its original business as actors' agent, represented the star performers.

MCA is careful not to charge a commission to its actor clients when it sells their services to Revue. And despite all the cocktail-lounge tattlers in Hollywood, it is impossible to turn up a concrete case in which Revue underpaid an MCA client. In other words, everyone in Hollywood suspects MCA of the most foul skulduggery in its dual role of producer and agent, yet no one has been able to prove a single instance. The unions, including those representing actors, say, however, that they get more grievances against MCA than against any other established studio.

MCA has enjoyed such success as a TV-series producer that it purchased the Universal-International movie lot in California and now also serves as landlord to independent producers who want to rent studio facilities by the day. MCA's income from TV production is almost six times what it is from the original occupation of artists' representation. Its total income is about $30,000,000 a year; the net profit after taxes is about $2,500,000.

MCA, built to success by luxury-loving Jules Stein, today is directed by dour, close-mouthed Lew Wasserman, a man who works six days a week and thinks about work on the seventh day. Its TV policy is to produce shows safely in the mold: "Markham," "M Squad," "Johnny Midnight," "Laramie,"

"Wagon Train," "Johnny Staccato." There is very little pretension here, and very little red ink, either. Using the number of
series shows on the air as a measure, MCA is the leading package producer in Hollywood.

Fortune magazine estimated that MCA gets some sort of cut
from "no less than 45 per cent of all TV evening hours." It told
of one network president who drew up the nucleus of his fall
schedule and then handed the chart to MCA with the instructions, "You fill in the blank spots."

The Justice Department has spent considerable time and
manpower investigating this octopus, seeking some provable
violation of the antitrust laws. There have been no discernible
results.

Despite MCA's successes, its next-in-line competitor in the
artists' representation business, the William Morris Agency,
has not gone into actual TV production. For one thing, it
doesn't have the power or resources of MCA. For another, it
wonders about the federal antitrust threat to a company that
is representing artists and hiring them at the same time.

Nevertheless, William Morris does sell entire shows as well
as the services of individual performers. It is exclusive selling
agent for one of Hollywood's largest packagers, Four Star
Productions; as such it does not share ownership of Four Star
shows, but does collect a 10 per cent commission on each program sold. William Morris has encouraged the packagers to cut
in the top writers and actors as part owners of the shows in
order to lure away from MCA some valuable talent. However
MCA is quite willing to cut in the actors, too, if it means
clinching an especially good deal.

The story of MCA's rise is written largely on ledgers. A
much more human tale is the story of Desilu, one of MCA's
principal rivals. This is the case of a mammoth company rising
out of one show.

Lucille Ball and Desi Arnaz were second-rung performers
at best when their "I Love Lucy" TV show hit the top. It
became the most popular show of its time. Eventually it faded

into the oblivion which is the fate of all TV shows, but before
that time Arnaz and his wife had bought the RKO motion-
picture studios where once they had worked as contract actors.
They converted it into one of the nation's busiest TV factories.
Their Desilu Studios produces some 750 hours of TV film a
year, the equivalent of 600 full-length movies—far more than
RKO ever dreamed of assembling in the halcyon day of the
B picture.

Furthermore, Desilu was a pioneer in the making of movies
for TV. It devised many of the speed-up techniques which en-
able Hollywood actors and technicians to produce in a week
the hour-long film that once required a month.

The major motion-picture studios were ridiculously slow to
recognize the impact of television on the American entertainment industry, and they were equally slow to join the force
they couldn't lick. Now the trend has been reversed, and the
big studios are all TV packagers.

Oddly, the studio operated by the last of the old-line movie
tycoons was the first to see the handwriting on the screen and
get into TV. That was Columbia Pictures Corporation. It was
headed by the late Harry Cohn, who might have been created
by Arthur Kober had he not actually lived. Harry Cohn was
the man who, in all seriousness, shouted down the hall of his
writers' building, "Write faster!" if the click of the typewriters
wasn't rapid enough to satisfy him. Harry Cohn was the man
who listened to the outline of a proposed movie on General
Doolittle's air raid on Tokyo and then asked only one question,
"Where's the girl?" Harry Cohn believed in the old formulas,
yet when the TV age came he alone among the big Hollywood
producers moved immediately to meet the challenge.

He formed an organization called Pioneer Telefilms to make
TV commercials and to experiment with TV films. And after a
two-year study of the field, Cohn in 1949 wrote a fifty-page
memo that was the charter for Screen Gems, the TV-producing
subsidiary of his Columbia Pictures. Screen Gems blazed the
trail for the other film packagers. Once it was the leading

producer in the business; it has since been overtaken by rivals, but it still grosses about $40,000,000 a year and still ranks near the top.

Eventually firms like Warner Brothers, 20th Century-Fox, and Metro-Goldwyn-Mayer followed Columbia into the TV business. Warner Brothers enjoyed especial success. It has fed so much of its product to the American Broadcasting Company that it is known as "one-third of a network." The Warner technique has been to sign young actors, struggling and desperate for any chance to make good, for comparatively low salaries on long-term blanket contracts that permit the studio to use the performer in either TV films, theater films, or both. When the young actor becomes a star he screams for more money—money commensurate with his new fame—and he gets a deaf ear from the studio. Warner's can even collect the guest-star fees the actor may earn. This has resulted in a lot of bitterness, and also a few one-man strikes. It has also resulted in a good profit for Warner Brothers.

Following the Warner success, two other big movie companies went into TV. United Artists simply bought its way in by purchasing Ziv TV Programs, Inc., a pioneer in the packaging business. 20th Century-Fox tried another approach; it hired as its TV head an advertising-agency man, George Levathes of Young & Rubicam, under the theory that an ad-agency man would be the best judge of what programs ad agencies would buy for their clients. M-G-M has had the least success. "They haven't taken the business seriously enough," says American Broadcasting Company Chairman Leonard Goldenson. "They treat TV as a secondary sideline—and it's not."

All of these film-show packagers produce the same type of product—the half-hour and hour series show which has become the staple of TV just as it was the staple of radio. But there are other specialists.

The firm directed by Mark Goodson and Bill Todman in New York has made several fortunes by producing quiz and panel shows. Goodson and Todman go back to the days of radio. They seldom concern themselves with scripts (or, at least, they don't own up to scripts) or dramatic stars, but rather with gimmick ideas. They invent shows like "What's My Line?", "I've Got a Secret," and "The Price is Right." Anyone who has watched any of these shows will see that they all share a common heritage—the guessing games of childhood. Yet they have been parlayed into one of the richest packaging firms in TV. The risk is small, the expenses almost nil, and the public's endurance seemingly unlimited.

Yet even Goodson and Todman know the packager's nightmare—the sponsor's cancellation. "It was different in radio," Goodson says. "In radio if the show seemed promising the sponsor might suggest it be tried for a year to see how it caught on. Today the sponsor looks at you the second week and says, 'You didn't beat the opposition yet.' "

Or things can work the other way. The panel show is being seen in 15,000,000 homes according to the rating service. Everyone is happy. Then along comes another show, which is seen in 16,000,000 homes. As Todman puts it: "You've still got 15,000,000, but the other guy has sixteen, so the sponsor is hoarse with panic when he asks, 'Fellas, what are we going to do with the show?' "

Goodson and Todman shows survived the TV-quiz scandals unmarked and unmolested. On the other hand, a rival panel and quiz packager, Entertainment Productions, Inc., grew to prosperity with its "$64,000 Question" only to suffer liquidation when that show was thrown off the air in the wake of exposure.

The packager's biggest problem is the small market. He can sell only to three networks. Once a program has been rejected by all three, it almost always is abandoned. In theory the packager could begin peddling this rejected show to the individual stations around the country for local use. This type of syndication once was a major part of packaging. But because today the networks consume almost all the decent time the local stations have to offer, the syndication business is all but dead.

One reason is the price the packager must charge for his

show. He needs about $4,000 from a New York station and $2,000 from a Chicago station on to $450 from a New Orleans station to break even. Yet these stations cannot pay such prices for a show that will be seen at ten o'clock in the morning. To get their money back, they would have to spot the show during the prime evening hours. And they can't, because those hours are taken up by network shows.

Because of this, the TV syndicators mounted their assault on the networks' "option time" clause. They were reluctant dragons, however. A packager naturally is shy about offending these networks because of the grudge which might hang over to the next time he offered a program for sale.

The TV-station managers have their complaint, too. They maintain—and rightly so—that the show they are offered by syndicators is simply a show that's not good enough for the network. They'd rather devote their extra time to re-runs of old network series or the full-length Hollywood movies which have always been a standby of the local station when it is not being fed by the network.

Because of the packager's great desperation to land his show on a network, spring is his aspirin season. It is in the spring that the networks and the ad agencies make their plans for the following fall season. And so it is in the spring that the packagers make the rounds with their pilots.

In an average spring the networks figure that, combined, they have enough room coming up for 30 to 50 new shows. They will be shown about 200 pilot films, all candidates for these time slots.

The tragedy of wasted effort was best explained by C. Terence Clyne, the McCann-Erickson advertising agency's top TV executive. He told *TV Digest:*

"We screened 220 pilots last season. Of these, about 40 actually got on the air, because we bought them or somebody else did. Of that 40, only 20 were renewed the following season. This means that only 10 per cent of all new pilots actually became TV shows that are renewed at the network level."

The other 90 per cent—costing about $50,000 each—are waste.

The program-buying season is so frantic that at its peak the advertising and network executives will see as many as nine or ten shows in a single day, and then weigh them. They reject those that are too lavish as phonies that cannot be maintained all season. They reject those that are too skimpy as hopeless from the beginning and certain to get worse. They look, instead, for something in between—a promising show that is not so good that a general level of quality cannot be maintained.

"I'd rather have a fair show every week than a great show one week and an awful show the next week," says one agency executive.

Even if an agency likes a show, however, it must first be certain that the network will carry it. And the networks today are interested only in shows that they can control. To some extent, they are assuring control by advancing money to make the pilot. Sometimes, too, an advertiser will finance a pilot if he is particularly interested in the show. The idea is to make certain that no competitor will get first crack at buying this program. Many packagers, in turn, are eager to give the sponsor a part ownership in the show, figuring that the sponsor will be reluctant to cast away a program in which he has sunk money. But this anchor to windward does not always achieve its objective. General Foods spent $100,000 making a pilot of "Father of the Bride," and yet the show never got on the air. Likewise the Young & Rubicam advertising agency put almost as much into a show called "Rob Roy," and this, too, was scrapped before it ever got on the air.

By the same token, the independent packager is quite willing to cut in the network for a share of his program because he knows that the network is then more likely to give him time on the air. Though the networks sometimes put up cash for a pilot, sometimes they simply level a fee for "consultation" and take the fee out in trade—part ownership of the show. The value of this ownership, as with all of these packaged shows, lies in the re-runs when the profits are high.

Some producers have sought to minimize the loss in unsold shows by putting a group of pilots together into an anthology dramatic series. This has worked in a couple of instances, but not many.

There has been some criticism of the networks for accepting shows from packagers under any circumstance. The objection is that the networks are deserting their function of creating TV programs. But Robert Sarnoff of NBC testified before Congress that he felt the responsibility of the networks was to air the best shows they could find, with no concern for where or how they found them.

At any rate, the packager is now an integral part of the TV industry—the man who will supply the entertainment while others in the industry concern themselves with more prosaic matters. The packager's risks are great. His rewards can be greater. He balances forever on a precipice.

THE MAN FROM MADISON AVENUE

Television has been called the twentieth century medicine show. There could scarcely be a more apt description. The idea behind television is not to entertain, but to sell sponsors' products. The entertainment is only the lure, and in the final judgment a program rises or falls not on the applause it draws but on the sales it produces. Pat Weaver, when president of NBC, told his staff in no uncertain terms, "We are first of all in the advertising business, for that is where our revenue comes from."

The result is a continual clash between the show-business people who put on the entertainment and the advertising men who pay for it. Every TV program is watched over by the man from Madison Avenue, the representative of the advertising agency that is, in turn, the representative of the sponsor who foots the bill.

Show people quite often turn bitter at the interference.

Comedienne Betty Hutton said, "Ad men know nothing about our business, yet they're running a fantastic medium. Their agencies are destroying this wonderful field." Movie director William Wyler says he avoids casting in his films any actor who has appeared in a TV commercial because the actor has degraded himself publicly. Yet neither Miss Hutton nor Wyler (nor anyone else) has suggested another means of financing free television. And when actor Tony Randall was asked if he'd be so disdainful of advertising agency men if he had a regular TV show of his own, he replied, "Certainly not. I may be a hypocrite but I'm not a fool."

The advertising agency is hired by the manufacturer to prepare and supervise all his advertising. The manufacturer pays the agency nothing. Instead, the agency collects a 15 per cent commission on the space or time rates of every newspaper, magazine, radio station, and television network with which it places an ad. But although it is the newspaper or TV network that pays the agency, the agency's only loyalty is to the manufacturer. The big accounts are worth millions of dollars in commissions each year, and for every agency with such an account there are ten competitors lurking nearby with promises of shrewder ads and brighter ideas.

For this reason the agencies hover with nervous nellyism over the programs they buy, constantly on guard for things they fear might work against the sponsor's best interests. Quite often, of course, these agency men become overzealous. The late Fred Allen defined an advertising agency vice president as "a fellow who comes to his office at nine in the morning, finds on his desk a pile of molehills and has until five P.M. to make a mountain out of them."

The agency men are not deliberate destroyers of art. The evil, if any, is not in their deeds but rather in the system that makes advertising TV's only source of revenue. Many of these agency men are themselves trained in show business and they are shrewd judges of what the public wants to see on the home screen.

TV advertising is, of course, a heritage from radio. Yet in radio's first days a station that carried commercials was considered in very poor taste.

Commercial radio first began to consider advertising in the early 1920's. There were immediate objections to the idea. Secretary of Commerce Herbert Hoover said it was "inconceivable that we should allow so great a possibility for service, for news, for entertainment, for education to be drowned out in advertising chatter." However, as an experiment, an actor and lecturer named Bruce Reynolds bought up fifteen-minute segments on station WEAF in New York for $100 each and resold them for what he could get. WEAF kicked him off the air because too many listeners complained. Reynolds moved over to WAAM in Newark, where the station owner would take his cash but no checks because he didn't want written evidence he was selling time on his station.

By 1925, however, it was obvious that someone had to pay for the radio entertainment—and only the advertiser volunteered. The advertising agencies moved in and became radio-show experts. As early as 1939 the National Broadcasting Company was issuing booklets on the prospects for TV advertising. When TV went big time ten years later, advertising— and the advertising agencies—were ready.

It is the job of the agency to buy for its client, not necessarily the best show available, but rather the show that will best sell the product. One ad man, for example, will not consider a show starring a woman because he thinks women select the channel most of the time; he prefers a "sexy male type" as the star of his shows. Another won't even look at a pilot unless he can also see three additional scripts and six additional story lines; he wants to know the subject matter of the drama, which he considers more important than the actors or the quality of the performance.

But the real measure of buying and maintaining a TV show is the "cost per thousand." This is the byword of commercial TV. It is a means of determining what it costs the sponsor to reach each 1,000 viewers with his sales message. On the cost-per-thousand theory, a show that costs $50,000 and reaches 5,000,000 viewers is a better buy than a show that costs $350,-000 and reaches 25,000,000 despite the vast difference in the size of audiences.

Once the TV show is bought, the agency's job is only beginning. It must then prepare the commercials that will run on the purchased show and also as spot announcements on local stations throughout the nation. These commercials are of the greatest importance. After all, the only purpose in buying the show in the first place was to provide audience for the sales pitch.

The advertising industry itself is of several minds as to what constitutes a good commercial and what constitutes a bad one. There are rules of thumb, of course. One advertising man says, "The really effective commercial sets up a problem, settles it quickly through use of the product and then ends quickly."

This is the basis of the hard sell—the pitch being that the viewer dare not go another moment without purchasing the product in question. There is also the soft sell, based largely on humorous commercials, designed to convey the idea that the sponsor is a pretty nice guy and so obviously his product must be nice and, what the hell, why not buy it?

One of the big problems with TV commercials is good taste. What is it? Nobody knows, but everyone thinks he knows. One advertising executive says that the problem with TV is its very power as a selling medium. "You see a one-inch truss ad on page 38 of a newspaper and you think nothing of it because the ad is not very powerful," he says. "But if you see a 20-second truss ad on a local station at 11:00 P.M.—and that's the TV equivalent of a one-inch newspaper ad on page 38—and it seems in horrible taste. That's only because the TV ad automatically has more impact than the newspaper ad."

Other TV and advertising men also complain that everyday things suddenly swell 'way out of proportion when seen on TV. Stockton Helffrich of NBC noted that there was a howl of protest over a TV brassiere ad, yet anyone walking through any shopping center will nonchalantly pass dozens of bras in show windows. (And besides, Helffrich added, "How about some credit for the ad man who found a way of getting a 40-inch bosom on a 17-inch screen?")

However, there is no doubt that TV ads are sometimes in terrible taste. They can actually be frightening. Two days after south Texas was ripped by a hurricane, one advertiser was booming over the airwaves: "There's another hurricane coming. (*Pause.*) A hurricane of values at—" His ad did, of course, attract the attention of the jittery community. He's lucky it didn't also attract a lynch mob.

Commercials that go overboard can backfire. They fail to sell the product. With one out of every three commercials considered a flop each year, *Printers' Ink* magazine asked the Schwerin Research Corporation to determine what makes a *bad* commercial. One of the factors Schwerin discovered was "scare psychology." It decided that excessive threats of social ostracism are more likely to drive a viewer away from a product in disgust. It decided also that claims which are too extravagant also drive the prospective customer away. To be successful, the commercial must be believable and it must in some way cause the viewer to associate himself with the product or with the problem the product solves.

Schwerin is one of several firms now engaged in the business of testing TV commercials before they ever get on the air. The commercials are shown to an audience, then Schwerin checks back later to see which brand each person selected when next purchasing the product in question. They found that about 40 per cent of all commercials have no effect on which brand the viewer next buys. It found that some commercials even lead the viewer to switch from the advertised brand to another one.

There has been considerable publicity given in recent months to faked commercials: dropping Alka Seltzer into a glass of beer instead of water to give it more fizz, icing a cake with shaving cream to make it seem frostier, slicing the cake in advance and then gluing it back together so it will seem to cut perfectly, photographing the model's "after" hairdo first and then mussing it up for the "before" shot. "Dishonest advertising is here," wrote agency executive Fairfax Cone in a memo to his staff. "It is real. And whatever the percentage, it is large and is not diminishing"

Why this trickery? Are the products impossible to sell in an honest way? The fault almost always lies with the ad writer's anxiety to produce a different commercial, a more exciting commercial, a commercial that will be more arresting than the commercial for a rival product. When this trickery is exposed, the excuses are apt to be ludicrous.

An agency turned out a commercial to show how the Libby-Owens-Ford glass used in General Motors automobiles was so much clearer than the glass used in rival cars. It turned out that the window was rolled down—there was no glass at all—in the shot that showed Libby-Owens-Ford's "flawless glass." The excuse for this? By using no glass we saved money, the agency producer told the Federal Trade Commission.

Another agency turned out a commercial to show that Rise shaving cream always remained moist but that Brand X dried on the face. The FTC proved that Brand X wasn't a shaving cream at all, but a special compound made for the commercial so that it would certainly dry up on the face. The excuse for this? "The need to speed up the pictorial effect was necessitated by the time limit imposed by the length of the television commercial," Carter Products told the FCC.

Then, of course, there was the celebrated case involving the Colgate-Palmolive Company's manner of shaving sandpaper. The sandpaper turned out to be a mockup composed of glass or Plexiglass with sand applied.

So what? Who wants to shave sandpaper anyway? Why spend thousands of dollars for such a silly commercial? The Ted Bates & Company, Inc., agency which produced this TV commercial said it wasn't so silly—that men talk about having "a beard like sandpaper" and so it would only follow that a cream that would shave sandpaper would also shave a tough beard. Privately, a Ted Bates man added: "It's a matter of attracting attention. If you see a man shaving on TV you keep walking to the bathroom and never stop to hear the commercial. But if you see someone shaving a piece of sandpaper you stop and wonder what the hell, and then we've got you hooked —you'll hear our commercial."

Well, why didn't they shave real sandpaper if it's such a great idea?

"Too gooey," said the Bates man.

There are some in the advertising business who object to these rigged ads not only on moral and esthetic grounds but also on the grounds that they are too unrealistic to be convincing. W. D. Moore, who directs advertising for Dodge automobiles, told the Los Angeles Advertising Club:

"When television shows cars roaring up what seems or is purported to be a 60-degree incline, it's a very simple trick— just tilt the camera. But worse, it's an insult to our fine civil engineers, who don't build highways like that. So why show them?

"How many people walk into a dealer's showroom and say, 'Man, I want a car that can really climb'? It's bad enough for ads to be unbelievable and worse for them to be ridiculous.

"Let's toss out ads that show ecstatic housewives smelling their towels or caressing their two-ply, supersoft, double-strength, facial-quality, negligee-colored toilet paper. Let's treat toilet paper like nothing more, nor less, than what it really is—toilet paper. If my wife or your wife ever re-enacted in real life the TV commercial toilet-paper bit we'd probably call the wagon—or go on it."

These TV commercials, honest or otherwise, are expensive. It costs about $2,500 to produce a full-color advertisement for insertion in magazines, but it costs about $10,000 to produce a black-and-white TV commercial. And General Motors once spent as much as $35,000 on a single commercial: the first scene was in the snowy north and the final shot was in sunny Florida.

"You can never tell exactly what they'll cost," says Stuart Ludlum of the Kudner Agency. "We had an awful experience on a commercial featuring skiers. We went to one location and there was a thaw. We went to another and there was a thaw. We went to a third, and it rained. Finally we went to the studio and set it up. We should have done that in the first place."

Batten, Barton, Durstine & Osborne once needed the sound of a bloodhound baying, the idea being that the poor hound couldn't pick up the scent of a fugitive who had used Trig deodorant. They finally found an honest-to-gosh bloodhound pack at the New York State Police barracks in Hawthorne. They rushed up with their tape recorders, but the hounds wouldn't bay. "Of course not," explained a trooper. "We train them to keep silent so they won't warn their prey we're on the trail." The disconsolate BBD&O men packed up their equipment and were about to leave the scene, bayless, when suddenly there was the unmistakable howl from the kennel. One of the hounds was hungry. He bayed enough for six commercials, and the happy ad men headed home, triumphant in the cause of Trig.

The business of making TV commercials is so extensive that it has become an entirely new facet of show business. Young actors and actresses trying to break in find great experience in commercial work. The agencies employ full-time casting directors. And commercials have even developed their own stars, such as Betty Furness, who has made more than 2,000 advertisements for Westinghouse, and Julia Meade, who toils for several companies.

The TV commercial girl has become a little industry unto herself. She carries an agent, a lawyer, and tax adviser, she belongs to two or three unions, she pays as much as $1,000 a year to a hairdresser, she needs a telephone answering service to catch appointments, and she spends thousands per year on clothes. (The Internal Revenue Service has issued what it calls "the Dinah Shore ruling"—a dress can be deducted from income-tax returns as a business expense if it's too tight to sit down in.)

TV has produced all kinds of commercial specialists—technicians, directors, producers. It has even produced its own stunt man, a former University of New Hampshire physics instructor who now makes $100,000 a year driving bulldozers over automobiles and performing similar scientific wonders for the benefit of commercials.

The advertising agencies ran radio outright and once had control of television. Today their power has been somewhat pruned. They still have much to say about the content of the program they purchase, but they no longer are absolute masters of the TV industry.

Naturally they're unhappy. Kudner's Ludlum said: "Now we find we're sometimes buying what we don't really want. We bought a lousy Western for a client—we know it's lousy, but we bought it because the time was right and the day of the week was right for this client's product. We bought it, however, only because we couldn't put a better show in that spot. The network already was committed by contract to the Western's producer and for us it was a case of take it or leave it.

"The networks think too much in terms of ratings and not enough in terms of the product we have to sell. They offered me 'Dennis the Menace,' and that show is a big hit as far as the ratings are concerned. It has a tremendous audience. But we suspect that the audience is composed mostly of kids. That's fine for Kellogg's but I can't put Renault on there.

"I have five or six good ideas of my own for Renault. But I can't get them on the networks. They want their own shows —the ones they control—they don't want anybody else's shows.

"This also has taken from us the actual control of a program's editorial content, but we still fight to get the best out of our shows once we've bought them. For example, we bought a drama show from the pilot and I went to Hollywood to see the scripts. Some were just plain lousy. I sat down with the producer and urged him to do something. In the old days he would have had to listen to me. Now it's up to him. I could only try to convince him. In one case he took my suggestion. In another we compromised. And in a third he just ignored me. There was nothing I could do. I still had to have a show for my client. TV is so powerful an advertising medium that bad TV is better than no TV."

Partly because of the exposés by the Federal Trade Commission and partly because business is good enough to permit an independent attitude, the networks in 1959 tightened up their restrictions on commercial copy.

CBS took special pains to point out that a commercial that is acceptable for entertainment programs may not be acceptable in the more serious context of news programs. CBS also went into the area of good taste. It ruled that live models cannot display undergarments. It ruled that you must stress the pleasantness of relief and not the discomfort of the ailment when advertising cold and headache remedies. It took special pains to praise the commercials for bathroom tissue by saying they "have been a good example of the wisdom of dealing with the problem of product acceptability by recognition of the unique nature of television and consequent adherence to the highest standards of taste." There was no need to mention what sort of commercials might have resulted if the toilet-tissue people had not shown proper restraint.

NBC and ABC have taken generally the same attitude as CBS on the clearing of commercials, although CBS always has been the most finicky of the three networks.

The agencies have resisted these tighter standards. Some network officials reported that the agencies began playing one network against another, threatening to take their business "across the street" if a border-line commercial were not accepted. The networks have pretty much remained firm against this sort of pressure, secure to the knowledge that any commercial can be tailored to meet their standards. Some agency people think that the three networks should combine to open a commercial-clearing bureau. The present practice, however, is for the agency to submit the commercial idea to the individual network in advance if there's any doubt about whether it will be cleared for use on the air.

Grace Johnson of ABC, Joseph Ream at CBS, and James A. Stabile at NBC are the people who finally rule on the acceptance of ads. They are "continuity acceptance directors." They reject such commercials as one that compared the human colon to a railroad roundhouse (bad taste), one that maintained that a beer was noncaloric (not true), one that showed too much of the model taking a shower (too risqué), and one that offered children a photo of a bosomy beauty as a premium (too educational).

Despite these minor setbacks, the ad agencies continue to prosper. The biggest in the nation, J. Walter Thompson, spent $110,500,000 of client money in TV alone in 1959 (and collected 15 per cent in commissions), McCann-Erickson spent $90,000,000, Young & Rubicam $89,000,000, BBD&O $73,000,-000, Ted Bates $90,000,000, Leo Burnett $55,700,000, Benton & Bowles $73,700,000, N. W. Ayer $35,800,000, Kenyon & Eckhardt $39,900,000, and Dancer-Fitzgerald-Sample $51,300,000.

All these agencies have huge TV departments (the Thompson office is headed by Dan Seymour, who once was better known, if poorer, as a top radio announcer), which reflects the industry's strange mixture of show business and advertising business. The agency men agree that the best combination is an ad man who learned a little about show business, rather than a show-business man who learned the advertising business. They get, of course, caustic arguments from the show-business side of this theory.

But, at any rate, they are there, poised with their snake oil after the crowd has formed to see, direct from the Casbah, Salome and her dance of the seven reinforced-fiber tear-proof veils. It may be a medicine show, but it's a living, a very good living indeed.

THE PATRONS OF THE ART

And now a message about our sponsors. They are the patrons of the television art. They are the medium's blessing in that they finance it and they are the medium's curse in that they prostitute it. They are perhaps the most maligned and also the most misunderstood people on earth.

The sponsor goes into television only to sell his merchandise. He does not consider TV a philanthropy. Many of these men who sponsor sordid private-eye shows or idiotic situation comedies also support civic operas and symphonies and art museums. One is business and the other is pleasure. Television is business.

TV can do a fantastic job of selling merchandise. Through the use of television commercials, the R. T. French Company was able to increase the sales of instant mashed potatoes by 670 per cent in New York. Through the use of television, Lestoil sales were hiked from 150,000 bottles a year to 100,000,000 bottles a year between 1953 and 1958.

Yet TV advertising is not a sure thing. Philip Morris cigarettes sponsored the "I Love Lucy" show when it was at the
peak of its popularity, and the sale of Philip Morris' went down,
not up, during that period.

What's the difference between these successes and failures?
No one can ever be sure. This is not an exact science. But in
the dozen or so years that television has been big time the
sponsors have slowly come to some theories about which type
of show will sell and which will not.

George Abrams, former president of Richard Hudnut beauty
products, says that angry people and unhappy people are not
in a buying frame of mind, no matter what the product. So
he avoids sponsoring TV shows that might make the viewer
angry or sad. "That's why situation comedies are best," he
says. "They make everyone feel good, and the audience is
more receptive to your commercial message." Of course, avoid-
ing sad dramas eliminates from Abrams' agenda some of the
great plays of modern literature, but Abrams buys TV time to
sell Richard Hudnut products; he goes to the theater when he
wants to see great drama.

A great deal depends, of course, upon the product that is for
sale. Dodge automobiles are bought by older people, so Dodge
for years sponsored Lawrence Welk's musical show; younger
folk laughed at Welk as "square" but the people who bought
Dodges loved his old-fashioned fox trots. Dodge dealers reported that these people frequently mentioned Welk when
they entered the showroom. Chevrolet, on the other hand, is
the young-family car. So Chevrolet sponsored Dinah Shore,
who appealed to them. A survey disclosed that only 20.5 per
cent of the persons buying Chevrolets had never seen the Dinah
Shore Show. Renault, on the other hand, presented still another problem: the little French car is sold largely on snob
appeal, so Renault's TV shows are more likely to be the big
specials, the Winter Olympics, for example, or a sophisticated
variety show.

The biggest mistake a sponsor can make is buying the wrong

show. One survey, for example, disclosed that a Western sponsored by a cigar company drew an audience that was largely composed of boys six to eleven years of age; very few smoked cigars. A wax and polish sponsored a Western that was viewed mostly by men; it's the woman of the house who buys and uses the wax. A cigarette sponsored a situation comedy that was viewed mostly by teenaged girls, a prospective market, perhaps, but not an immediate one.

How can the sponsor make such a ridiculous mistake? There are two possible reasons. One is that he misjudged the appeal the program might have when he first bought it. The other is that he bought blindly from ratings; he was assured that the program had a very large audience, and he did not pause to determine just what age groups and what sex dominated that impressive mass.

Then there is the matter of unqualified people selecting the TV show. One of the largest TV buyers, according to *Advertising Age,* is an engineer who is an expert in production lines. Another key buyer is a former district sales manager. Still another is a recruit from a small advertising agency which had never handled any radio or TV business.

Lewis Gruber, chairman of the board of the P. Lorillard Company which makes Kent and Old Gold cigarettes, told a stockholders' meeting of the pitfalls always lurking in the TV sponsor's path. "We avoid making long-term commitments in order to guard against being caught in an ebb tide of waning talent and program popularity," he said. "When we feel a program has served its purpose we seek a replacement. And may I remind you that high ratings are not necessarily indicative of magic selling ability. Many shows with moderate ratings do far better at the cash register."

For one thing, the Schwerin Research Corporation found that a TV show can be too good. If the audience gets too keyed up by the drama or the music, it will be too let down by the commercials and the sales message will be entirely lost. Jack Roberts, vice president of Schwerin, said: "Possibly the most difficult program type with which to work is the 'tense' show—the western, the mystery, the adventure show. The tense show creates an emotional involvement which often acts to wash over and engulf the commercial that interrupts it."

To prove his point he inserted for special audiences the same commercial in a mystery, an adventure, a western, and a situation comedy—three tense shows and one light show. Then he checked to see what effect the commercial had on each audience. Some 7 per cent of those who saw the commercial during the situation comedy changed to the brand that was advertised. None of those who saw the same commercial on the tense shows changed to the advertised brand.

This being the case, why do the advertisers buy these exciting shows to such a great extent? The reason is that these shows nevertheless produce the greatest audiences, and some sponsors will play the percentages—they'll take a crack at the 50,000,000 audience and gamble rather than take a 25,000,000 audience with a safer program.

More and more, however, the networks find the sponsor interested in factors other than the size of the audience alone. One thing that concerns the sponsor is product identification. Even if a man enjoys a TV show, the whole half-hour is wasted as far as the sponsor is concerned if the man can't identify the product an hour later. For this reason the sponsors are constantly laboring to make certain the viewer remembers the product. A favorite gimmick is to link the star and the product —it's "The Dinah Shore Chevvy Show," rather than just the "Dinah Shore Show" or "The Chevvy Show," and, going beyond that, many sponsors won't buy a show if the star doesn't agree to perform in the commercials.

There is in addition to actual retail sales a further benefit to be derived from TV sponsorship. It makes the local dealers happy, and it also makes them feel important. The manufacturer's salesmen always discuss the TV show with the dealers, taking special care to tip the dealer in advance when something new—such as a spectacular—is coming up. One cosmetic manufacturer said: "Our TV show is worth the money if only because it gives the salesman something to discuss with the dealer. Instead of starting the conversation with a crass selling spiel, they'll talk inside TV for a while and then ease into the sales talk as confiding friends."

The main point of the TV show, however, is to sell the brand to the consumer. And it is an intricate operation when the sponsor conducts a search for a new program to replace one he has just ditched. Sometimes the advertising agency does the work, simply submitting its decisions to the sponsor for approval. Sometimes the sponsor takes personal command. Either way the hunt is long and diligent.

Let's take a case history. Richard Hudnut, the cosmetics firm, needed a show and went shopping. NBC said that "This Is Your Life" would be available. The Hudnut people began their study. First they checked the show's rating. This indicated it was watched in 12,500,000 homes. This was good, but the figure had to be checked against the price of the show. Was the cost-per-thousand favorable? It was, and Hudnut pushed ahead with increasing interest.

"This Is Your Life" had been shown on Thursday nights. The people at Hudnut thought Sunday would be better. They asked NBC if there was a time slot available Sunday. The NBC man grinned sheepishly and said ten-thirty Sunday nights was open. This was supposed to be a big joke. The rival CBS showed "What's My Line?" at ten-thirty on Sundays, and other sponsors were reluctant to buck such a popular show.

But the Hudnut advertising manager had long felt the "What's My Line?" popularity was due to wane. He said he'd take that ten-thirty Sunday spot. "That was like asking the butcher for the steak with the big bone," he said later.

Hudnut had other reasons for wanting Sunday. For one thing, the advertising agency that handles Hudnut also handles the "Loretta Young Show" which was on at ten o'clock Sunday; by buying the ten-to-eleven full hour, the agency would get a discount and pass on part of this saving to Hudnut. For another thing, Hudnut figured that the type of viewer who tuned in to see "The Loretta Young Show" would stay tuned to "This Is Your Life." ("They're both soap operas really," said Hudnut's George Abrams.)

Hudnut next checked the sponsorship history of the show. It had been sponsored for four years by Hazel Bishop, a Hudnut competitor, and then four more years by Proctor & Gamble. That was good, too. The Hazel Bishop sponsorship proved the show could sell cosmetics. The four intervening years of Proctor & Gamble sponsorship was a buffer against the possibility that viewers would get Hazel Bishop and Hudnut products confused and buy the wrong brand.

The next step was a study of the audience. This produced the first alarming sign. The audience seemed to have too high a percentage of viewers who were women over forty. The Hudnut customers are more likely to be women in their twenties and thirties. Abrams told Ralph Edwards the show might attract younger viewers if it used younger guest stars—singers like Bobby Darin and actresses like Piper Laurie. Edwards agreed. So Hudnut sent NBC an order for the show.

But at the same time that Hudnut was making this investigation, other prospective sponsors were doing the same thing. And one, Alberto Carver, also a cosmetic firm and thus a competitor of Hudnut, had ordered "This Is Your Life" before Hudnut made its final decision.

NBC stepped in to mediate the two claims on the show. Carver had filed his claim first, so he was entitled to the show, but NBC remained a bit partial to Hudnut because it had offered to take that hard-to-sell 10:30 P.M. Sunday time slot. NBC induced Carver to take another show. Hudnut became the sponsor of "This Is Your Life."

Having gone through such an exhaustive investigation before buying a show, it is only natural that a firm like Hudnut, or any other company with such a heavy investment, would attempt to shepherd it over the air waves each week. Much has been said and written about sponsor interference with the

artistic or editorial side of television. Ford deleted a shot of
the New York skyline because it showed the Chrysler building.
A gas-company sponsor deleted all mention of gas ovens in a
show about Nazi war crimes. A breakfast-food sponsor deleted
the line "She eats too much" from a play because, as far as the
breakfast-food company was concerned, nobody could ever eat
too much. A cigarette sponsor forced an actor to stop tapping
his cigarette on the back of his hand because the gesture might
cause the audience to suspect the brand wasn't packed tightly
enough.

The basic rule in television is that the sponsor has a right to
determine "taste and policy" but not "program creativity."
However, these are mere words subject to any convenient
interpretation. Each show is different, with the strength and
determination of the sponsor pitted against the strength and
determination of the producer. The weaker soon capitulates;
and only rarely, in cases involving a star of such magnitude
that he can assume a take-it-or-leave-it attitude, does the sponsor turn out to be the weaker.

In an effort to head off trouble before it appears, the sponsor
will make known his needs and taboos as soon as he buys a
show. This permits a producer to guide his program around the
pitfalls. Sometimes these instructions are bland generalities
cautioning against any possible offense to potential customers.
At other times they are detailed documents touching upon
hundreds of specific potentialities.

When General Mills assumed sponsorship of a show called
Tales of the Texas Rangers, it sent the producers a 22-point
guide. This touched upon a moral code (it should be "synonymous with the moral code of the American middle class"),
ministers (they should "never be cast as villains"), the Civil
War (remain "mindful of the sensitiveness of the South"), and
grocery prices ("no reference should be made to any difference
in the price charged by supermarkets as compared to independents").

General Mills made it plain it intended to offend no one. It said:

"There will be no material for or against sharply drawn national or regional controversial issues. There will be nothing slurring any given type of occupation. There will be no ridicule of manners or fashions that may be peculiarly sectional. . . .

"There will be no material that may give offense either directly or by inference to any organized minority group, lodge or other organization, institutions' residents of any state or section of the country, or a commercial organization of any sort. This shall be taken to include political organizations, fraternal organizations, college and school groups, labor groups, industrial, business and professional organizations, religious orders, civil clubs, memorial and patriotic societies, philanthropic and reform societies (Anti-Tobacco League, for example), athletic organizations, women's groups, etc. which are in good standing."

Furthermore, General Mills said, never mention competing Western programs or heroes. And furthermore, the memorandum added, never mention "competitive horses" either.

Liggett & Meyers, the makers of Chesterfields, issues instructions peculiar to its business. For example it warns producers to "avoid shots of messy ashtrays crammed with cigarette butts," and presents this poser: "We don't want public criticism in encouraging the too young or 'too young looking' to smoke. On the other hand, the high school and college market is extremely important to Liggett & Meyers as future longtime customers."

The taboos seem to go on forever. Coca-Cola won't permit half-finished bottles or glasses of Coke on its shows (Coke is too good to put down) and Mars Candy Bars flipped its lid when the character on one of its shows gave a little girl a dollar to buy "ice cream and cookies."

This kind of thing—and more serious instances where entire plays were altered to meet the sponsor's objections—has produced some great howls of protest. Even an advertising-agency chairman, John P. Cunningham, said, "The television industry should immediately embark on a long-term study of whether the current method of sponsorship is in the public interest."

However, the sponsors have answered back. The Association of National Advertisers pointed out that it is the sponsor who is paying for the show and that therefore he has a right to pass judgment on what his money buys. CBS made a study of the matter and then flatly decreed, "The advertiser may object to a program or an element thereof, if he believes it is detrimental to his product or good will."

One of the most persnickety of the big-time TV sponsors is Du Pont. The company will permit offense to no one—not Negroes, not bigots, not even butterfly lovers or butterfly haters—in its shows. Du Pont is, ironically, all the more conspicuous for this policy because it deals with quality dramas and dramatists. ("We want controversial scripts for our programs, but we don't want to offend anyone," explained one Du Pont man.) Were the firm to sponsor a situation comedy written by a team of Hollywood hacks, no one would notice the restrictions. But since it involves high-level talent, these people—especially the writers—are inclined to scream out loud when they feel their art has been hampered by Du Pont's heavy hand. Yet Du Pont has stuck to its policy, and in answer to complaints that it was unjustly interfering with art the company presented this explanation:

"Our company and all 86,000 of us who comprise it are pretty careful about the quality of goods we put out bearing our label. If it's a Du Pont product you know that you can depend upon it and that the company is exercising all possible diligence to insure its reliability. Du Pont can hardly be any less attentive to the product it presents on your TV screen."

Advertising Age thereupon wondered in print what Du Pont executive had the necessary experience and education in writing, acting, and directing to make these judgments. Jack Gould of the *New York Times* pointed out the contrast between Du Pont and the Standard Oil Company of New Jersey, which had sponsored the far more controversial "Play of the Week" without touching the scripts.

Officially Du Pont remained silent after stating its position. But a Du Pont executive said privately: "All of these critics forget the point of the TV show—to bring in extra customers. If you alienate one prospective customer with your TV show, it's a flop commercially no matter how successful it is artistically. And our interest is frankly commercial. We are a manufacturing concern, not a cultural foundation."

The sponsors seem supersensitive to that one prospective customer who might be alienated. One bunch of wags began complaining to a sponsor about the "terrible incident" on his TV show, never mentioning the incident and not even having any particular thing in mind; they just wanted to see what reaction they would get. All received apologetic letters from the sponsor and one even got a telephone call asking if he'd please explain which incident on the show had so offended him.

"It's too awful to discuss," he said, and hung up.

Actually this control by sponsors is diminishing, not in any surrender to the arts but because more and more shows share two or more sponsors to cut the costs. Many advertisers feel they'd prefer half-sponsorship of two shows to full sponsorship of one show on the grounds that this spreads the same amount of money over a more varied audience. This greatly reduces a single sponsor's control over the context of a show.

Too, the networks which once catered to the individual sponsor now concern themselves with the big picture. They won't accept a show if it might produce a low rating. This is because the show before it and the show after it also will suffer and, in the long run, the entire network will suffer.

The classic example of the revolt of the networks against the sponsor is that of "The Firestone Hour." This was a radio staple and was carried over to TV by the Firestone Tire & Rubber Co. It was more than a commercial TV program, however. It was a family institution. Idabelle Firestone personally wrote the theme song. Elizabeth Firestone sometimes played her own composition on the piano.

When the show's ratings dipped too low for comfort, NBC booted it off the air even though the Firestones were willing to continue sponsorship. ABC, then in its struggling stage, eagerly grabbed the show just as it would have grabbed anything at the time. But then ABC struck it rich, and so it, too, wanted to ease the old show off its schedule.

It offered Firestone a better program, even Walt Disney, which at the time was the hottest show on the network. Firestone refused. ABC countered with the suggestion that "The Firestone Hour" then be moved to ten o'clock at night—out of the prime-hour period.

"No," said Firestone's advertising agency. "Harvey Firestone goes to bed at ten every night and he wouldn't get to see it then."

That was the end of "The Firestone Hour." ABC simply kicked it off the air. That also was the end, in a way, of the personal sponsor in TV.

Of course, television still has today dynamic meddlers like Charles Revson of Revlon who try to direct personally every show they sponsor. They are not running the programs for their personal likes or the likes of their wives.

Revlon's cosmetics sales increased 54 per cent in a single year during the sponsorship of the fabulously successful "$64,-000 Question." When scandal killed that show, Revson scooted off in frantic chase after a similar success. He has not yet found it. One of TV's top comedy writers, Goodman Ace, was signed by Revson to do a variety show called "The Big Party" but Ace walked out after six of the fifteen weeks for which he had contracted. Revson drove him batty, he said, editing dialogue and suggesting music and designing sets. "Someday," said Ace, "I'm going to write a Broadway revue based on what went on."

But Revson did have his reasons. His investment was great. The cosmetics industry to a large extent rises and falls on the success of its advertising. Some 15 per cent of each cosmetics firm's total income is poured back into advertising.

Advertising is so important and TV so costly that every brand-name manufacturer is continually increasing the amount he spends on ads. For example $23.63 for the sale of each Chevrolet goes into the advertising fund; $106.40 from the sale of each Lincoln also goes into advertising.

The nation's ten biggest advertisers are General Motors, Proctor & Gamble, Ford, General Foods, Lever Brothers, American Home Products Corporation, Colgate-Palmolive Company, Chrysler, R. J. Reynolds, and American Tobacco— all of them manufacturers of either automobiles, foods, soap, or cigarettes.

They are all heavy TV advertisers, naturally. But the fact that General Motors is the nation's biggest advertiser does not make it the nation's biggest TV advertiser. Actually it ranks only sixth. GM spends about $21,000,000 a year in TV, while Proctor & Gamble spends about $95,000,000.

There is a reason for this. The heavy, expensive products which require some family thought and discussion might attract interest on TV, but the manufacturers have learned that they must set the details down in print, in newspapers and magazines, where they can be pondered at leisure. GM spends $11,000,000 a year more in newspapers than on TV. Ford spends $3,000,000 more in newspapers than on TV.

The cheap brand-name products like soap and cigarettes and soft drinks are bought more on impulse or memory. For them TV is not only the ideal medium, but some manufacturers who deal in products of this type feel TV is the only medium they need.

Thus, although it may vary a bit from year to year, TV's top twenty advertisers are Proctor & Gamble, Lever Brothers, American Home Products, Colgate-Palmolive, General Foods, General Motors, R. J. Reynolds, Bristol-Myers, Adell Chemical, Brown & Williamson, P. Lorillard, Sterling Drug, Gillette Safety Razor Company, General Mills, Miles Laboratories,

Liggett & Myers, Kellogg, American Tobacco, Warner-Lambert, and Ford.

Combined, these twenty firms alone spend more than five billion dollars on television advertising each year.

That buys a lot of words from the sponsors. But it pays off. The same twenty firms are among the biggest moneymakers in the world.

GOVERNMENT: OF TV, BY TV, FOR TV

In Washington the television industry rides a sort of roller coaster. When things are going bad it is scolded and threatened and wheedled by the government. When things are going good it is patted and praised and, most of all, ignored by the government.

This inconsistency is the root of many problems. When the federal agent appears at the door, the TV station owner never knows whether the chap has come by to cadge a drink or to deliver a punch on the nose.

One reason for the confusion is the fact that the government never actually set up an agency to regulate TV. Instead, a series of bureaus gradually drifted into control of various phases of the industry with neither the proper preparation nor the proper facilities. The situation has been made worse by the political appointees who administer the bureaus: They lie dormant like contented housecats when no one is looking, but roar like offended lions when the public glances their way.

As early as 1866 Congress first touched upon government regulation of communications when it authorized the Postmaster General to fix some telegraph rates. In 1887 the Interstate Commerce Commission was given additional control of telegraph, and in 1927, when the commercial value of radio became obvious, Congress created the Federal Radio Commission primarily to issue licenses. The Federal Communications Commission came into being in 1934 as successor to the radio commission, with a far greater area of authority.

It is this FCC which is primarily in control of TV. Its basic power lies in its authority to award licenses to the applicant who appears most qualified, and to renew (or refuse to renew) these licenses on the basis of how the station has performed. The criterion is simple—the station is charged to operate "in the public interest." In theory this is ideal regulation of a public facility; all the FCC need do is follow old Andy Jackson's advice: "There are no necessary evils in government. Its evils exist only in its abuses. If it would confine itself to equal protection, and, as Heaven does its rains, shower its favors alike on the high and the low, the rich and the poor, it would be an unqualified blessing."

But in practice the regulation of television in this country has been haphazard at best, and at times those favors have not so much been showered indiscriminately as piped underground to the vineyard of a favored patron.

The FCC is charged with supervision of all radio, amateur and professional, marine and national defense; it is charged with supervision of all common carriers, telegraph, telephone, and cable; it is charged with supervision of all television. By law, it can scarcely make a move without first holding a public hearing and subsequently considering a daisy chain of appeals from its already overdelayed decisions.

To accomplish all this, the FCC has a staff of only 1,200, including office boys and stenographers. And of these, 25 per cent are engaged solely in field engineering.

Former Commissioner Charles King cited the hopelessness of the situation in a speech to the Michigan Association of Broadcasters. He said, "I haven't found out yet what the public interest means. Nothing says it. We do an off-the-cuff job on the commission. As a lawyer, I don't like it. I would much rather have it defined."

He told the broadcasters: "There is no question the FCC can't censor broadcasting and the commission has no right to interfere with free speech. Yet we do."

King said that the FCC, groping for some sort of rule about what was in the public interest, once decided that sustaining programs were all good and commercial programs were questionable. That theory soon crumbled under the weight of its own foolishness.

The power in the FCC rests in its seven commissioners, all appointed by the President for seven-year terms. It is a bi-partisan organization; only four commissioners can be members of any one political party.

Washington lawyers say off the record that the FCC generally has been among the weakest of the federal regulatory agencies. It became somewhat tough when scandal burst into the headlines, but how tough no one will know for some years. To announce a crackdown is one thing, and to enforce it consistently is another.

The Kennedy Administration went into office pledging long-range reforms rather than swift repairs. James Landis, who made a pre-Inauguration investigation into the federal agencies for President Kennedy, said in his report, "The Federal Communications Commission presents a somewhat extraordinary spectacle . . . It seems incapable of policy planning, of disposing within a reasonable period of time the business before it, of fashioning procedures that are effective to deal with its problems. The available evidence indicates that it, more than any other agency, has been susceptible to *ex parte* presentations, and that it has been subservient, far too subservient, to the subcommittees on communications of the Congress and its members. A strong suspicion also exists that far too great an influence is exercised over the Commission by the networks. The quality of its top personnel is, of course, primarily responsible for these defects."

The present Federal Communications Commission is made up of three lawyers, two engineers, a broadcasting executive, and a former FBI auditor. They are:

NEWTON MINOW, a 34-year-old Chicago attorney who was appointed chairman by Kennedy in 1961 and as such draws $20,500 a year, $500 more than the other commissioners. Minow's experience in broadcasting is confined to representing clients who sponsor or appear on TV shows. He says he believes the FCC should "protect the public interest," but that he prefers the industry to do "most of the job" of regulation "if they will do it."

Minow thinks that the FCC can have influence on networks in matters of programing. He feels the chief problem is the gap between the formula and the "egghead" shows.

FREDERICK W. FORD, a Republican of Bluefield, West Virginia, the former chairman of the commission who stepped down when Minow was named its chief. He is a lawyer, but quit private practice in 1939 to work for a series of federal agencies, one being the FCC. He was in the Justice Department as Assistant Deputy Attorney General in 1957 when President Eisenhower appointed him a commissioner. Ford has long believed that the FCC should be strict in its supervision of TV programs. His predecessors on the commission thought otherwise.

ROSEL H. HYDE, another Republican, another lawyer, is originally from Bannock County, Idaho, but he has been employed by the FCC since it was first formed in 1934. He was general counsel when appointed commissioner in 1946. In 1948 WBAL, owned by the Hearst interests, was specifically cited by the FCC as a radio station that had not met the commission's standards. Nevertheless, when a group of Baltimore businessmen sought to get the license, Hyde voted against them and for Hearst to retain it. After the TV scandals broke, he apparently changed his attitude and specifically suggested that interests desiring TV licenses should file applications for stations that hadn't operated "in the public interest."

ROBERT E. LEE, the fourth Republican, of Chicago, is the most controversial of the commissioners, largely because he was known as the late Senator Joseph McCarthy's man in the FBI. Lee became an FBI auditor in 1938, and he rose to become J. Edgar Hoover's administrative assistant. Through Hoover's help, he became director of surveys and investigations for the House Appropriations Committee, and in 1953 he was appointed to the FCC. His reappointment was confirmed in 1960 after considerable Senate opposition, more because of his relationship with Senator McCarthy than because of anything he had done or not done in the FCC. Lee has often spoken out against government regulation, but the TV scandals led him to warn of "harsh consequences" (unnamed at the time and unseen since).

ROBERT T. BARTLEY, a Democrat, is a nephew of House Speaker Sam Rayburn of Texas. He has been in various Washington government jobs for thirty years, becoming director of the FCC's telegraph division in 1934. During World War II he worked for the National Association of Broadcasters, and in 1952, while he was serving as Rayburn's assistant, he was appointed a commissioner. He said he is "a firm believer in self-restraint by the industry and self-regulation in programing practices."

JOHN S. CROSS, a Democrat, is an electrical engineer. He was assistant chief of the State Department's telecommunications division when appointed to the FCC in 1958. Cross has said he thinks stations should file a report on how they have met their community's TV needs and that these reports should be "spot checked" by the FCC before it renews licenses.

T. A. M. CRAVEN, the third Democrat and also an electrical engineer, is a Naval Academy graduate who quit the service and went into radio in 1930. He was appointed to the FCC in

1937, served one term, and then joined the National Association of Broadcasters. In 1956 he was appointed to the commission a second time, becoming the only man ever to be so recalled. He has said he does not believe the FCC should interfere with TV-station operations except in the case of outright violations of law.

The one absolutely necessary function of the FCC is that of assigning TV and radio stations certain places on the broadcast band and keeping them there. Otherwise any station could begin broadcasting at any frequency, and the result would be an unintelligible babble on your set. In order to enforce these assignments, the FCC must license the stations. On this the entire industry agrees.

But beyond this point there is disagreement. It is the public's air that the FCC is divvying up, and there are many Americans who feel it is the FCC's responsibility to make certain the air is in good hands. Yet because these radio and TV stations are commercial businesses, there is also pressure to avoid government interference with private enterprise.

In 1946 the FCC, anticipating the impending mushrooming of television, issued its Blue Book, "Public Service Responsibility of Broadcasting Licensees." This proposed "a more detailed review of broadcasting station performance when passing upon applications for license renewals." The FCC said it would compare "promises" with "performance." If there were any cheers at this attitude, they certainly were drowned out by the broadcasting industry's screams of protest. This was censorship. It was persecution. It was Communism. Because of the outcry, the Blue Book proposals were forgotten, although the law clearly gave the FCC the right to refuse license renewals to stations that were not measuring up.

The result was an FCC overladen with apathy. "There has never been revocation of a license in the hands of a responsible operator," former FCC chairman J. Lawrence Fly said.

The applicant for a TV license must state just what kind of programing he plans. Since these applicants are always in com-

petition with others seeking the same licenses, the promises
are grandiose—agricultural programs, educational programs,
local dramas. "But," said former Commissioner Clifford Durr,
"when the license comes up for renewal, you look at the existing programing and compare it to the proposed service, and
any relationship is coincidental to say the least. The man who
gets the station is often the man who is willing to stretch the
truth the farthest."

Yet no TV station has ever lost its license for failing to keep
its promises on programing. As a matter of fact, one Senate
wag said, a station can hold its license just as long as it doesn't
play "The Old Gray Mare" all day.

The FCC realizes that the stations don't have control over
the content of many programs. They are tied into the networks
for the greater part of the TV day and take just what the network decides to give them. This has led to proposals that the
networks also be licensed by the government. The networks
have replied that there is no mechanical reason to license them
—that the broadcast band doesn't limit networks as it does
stations—and so any federal regulation would amount to outright censorship. Fly thinks a law could be written that would
require minimum standards from the networks and still not
interfere with their basic freedom, but many authorities disagree. For one thing, you can use words like "public service,"
but who is to define them? A TV writer said, "Some people
think putting on the high-school band is a public service."

Besides, the networks produce the best TV programing, not
the worst, and they are always subject to pressure from the
affiliated stations, which are licensed by the FCC. Too, the
key stations that the networks themselves own are licensed.
An FCC push to force local stations to make good on programing promises would certainly be reflected in network fare.

But it is hard to imagine the FCC getting tough on license
renewals when you consider the manner in which some licenses
were issued originally.

Here was the true FCC scandal of 1958. The most celebrated

case was, of course, that involving Channel 7 in Miami and Commissioner Richard Mack, who was eventually indicted for accepting a "loan" from those who were successful applicants for the station. There were numerous other cases of undue influence cited, and still many more that never came to light. Furthermore, any public faith in the FCC must have been finally shattered when—in the very midst of the scandals—the then FCC chairman, Richard Doerfer, blithely took a free vacation on a broadcasting executive's yacht.

The real trouble is the lack of space on the air. Anyone with enough money can start a newspaper or publish a book. But only those with licenses can open a TV station.

The airwaves permit only twelve Very High Frequency (VHF) channels in a 190-mile area but would permit seventy Ultra High Frequency (UHF) channels. The VHF channels are undoubtedly the best, and the FCC assigned the first TV stations to these channels—with good intentions and bad foresight. It did not anticipate the great growth of TV or the great demand for licenses. By 1948 it had second thoughts and ordered a "freeze"—it would issue no more new licenses until it could determine whether it had made a mistake.

But if the start of new stations was frozen, the manufacturing of sets certainly was not. The factories were turning out sets by the millions, and these were not equipped to receive UHF stations. They could be converted, to be sure, but this would cost each set owner about $40.

In 1952 the FCC ended its freeze, and the FCC began licensing UHF stations as well as VHF. But by then it was too late. By then 16,000,000 non-UHF sets had been sold. The UHF stations that dared begin broadcasting went broke if they were competing with VHF stations, as most were. Some $50,000,000 has been lost by broadcasters trying to buck reality with UHF stations.

Thus of the 100 major cities in the United States, 19 have only one TV station, 32 have only two stations, and 26 have only three.

They could all have several more if TV operated on UHF. But by now there are perhaps 50,000,000 sets which can't receive these stations. Had the FCC not put in its freeze, had it either made the right decision in the first place or else reversed the wrong decision quickly enough, the manufacturers would have converted, too, and the public would enjoy the benefits.

Belatedly realizing the error of its ways, the FCC is trying to do something about UHF. It is encouraging new broadcasting tests, particularly in New York, and it is attacking the tough problem of what to do about the home sets.

One idea discussed by Commissioner Fred Ford is to forbid transportation in interstate commerce of sets that cannot receive both types of channel. This would force the manufacturers to convert new sets. Actually, Ford says, an all-channel set would cost "substantially the same" as the set that receives only VHF.

Such coercion on the manufacturers could force eventual acceptance of UHF, but it would take a long time. There would still be the problem of the high cost of converting the millions of existing sets to UHF. Obviously, dealers faced with the prospects of many new sales of all-channel sets will not be interested in a cheap way of salvaging obsolete VHF sets.

The FCC's blunders and its influence coddling and its apathetic attitude to lackadaisical programing promises to overshadow the truly grave problems it faces. There is no doubt that government licensing endangers freedom of the press, and TV certainly is a vital disseminator of news and opinion today. There is a delicate balance to be reached, and it can hardly be reached in the atmosphere the FCC has maintained during TV's first dozen years.

The FCC insisted for some years that it had grave doubts about its authority to control programing for this very reason. Yet when the public clamor came in the wake of scandal, the Justice Department issued a report saying the FCC was derelict, and so the commission suddenly reversed itself and decided to become a watchdog on programs. It announced creation of a new Complaints and Compliance Division to chase down specific complaints about programing, to monitor programs, and to needle stations (presumably under threat of the loss of license) to heed those complaints that seem justified.

Ford promptly released a summary of complaints the commission received over a three-month period. Most viewers who wrote objected to crime and horror shows, but some took outraged pen in outraged hand because Arlene Francis said anyone who disagreed with her about fluoridation was a "crackpot," and at least thirty-seven thought that substituting coverage of Premier Khrushchev's visit to the United States for soap operas was "bad programing."

Although the FCC is the agency directly charged with regulating television, the Federal Trade Commission is also deeply involved for the simple reason that the FTC regulates advertising and TV is the advertising business.

The FTC grew out of Woodrow Wilson's dream. Because he was convinced that the nation's businessmen had become hopelessly confused by the maze of laws and regulations that had crept onto the books over a quarter of a century, he proposed formation of a federal agency to which these businessmen could turn for advice, for interpretation, for suggestions.

Thus the Federal Trade Commission Act was passed in 1914. Although it provided for a Bureau of Consultation in deference to Wilson's idea, the commission also was charged with the elimination of unfair and deceptive practices in business. The FTC soon took this to include advertising. Subsequent amendments to the original act gave the commission the power of injunction in some cases and also the authority to combat monopolistic price fixing and mergers.

Like the FCC, the FTC has a broad field and a small staff. It would be impossible to estimate how many advertisements of various types are printed, painted, and broadcast in a single day, yet the entire FTC payroll totals 720.

At the top are five commissioners, all appointed by the President for seven-year terms. At present the commission consists of four attorneys and a former Congressman. They are:

PAUL RAND DIXON, a Democrat from Tennessee who was appointed chairman by President Kennedy. Dixon had served as counsel for the Senate anti-trust subcommittee. He directed its investigations into the drug, automobile and oil industries. He served the FTC as an attorney from 1938 until 1957.

PHILIP ELMAN, another lawyer and another Kennedy appointee. Elman is a Harvard Law School graduate who worked as law clerk for Supreme Court Justice Felix Frankfurter. Elman was assistant to the Solicitor General at the time he was appointed to the FTC.

SIGURD ANDERSON, who moved from Norway to South Dakota as an infant. An attorney, he was twice elected governor of his state and was appointed to the FTC in 1955.

WILLIAM C. KERN, a Harvard law school graduate who is a career man with the FTC. He joined it in 1940 and was appointed commissioner in 1955.

ROBERT T. SECREST, a former congressman from Ohio. He served on the House Interstate and Foreign Commerce Committee, the FTC's congressional "boss." He was appointed to the commission in 1954.

Ex-chairman Earl W. Kintner made the FTC an active force in the reform of TV advertising. The FTC was known as a stick-in-the-mud organization in Washington, forever in litigation with obscure snake-oil bottlers. When Kintner became chairman he chafed at the restrictions of tradition but had difficulty making the hired help move beyond the limits they had known for decades. When the TV scandals broke, Kintner found his excuse, and he has been shaking a big stick ever since.

Broadcasting magazine, as informed a source as any on the subject, reported that President Eisenhower had been unhappy with the FCC's inaction in the wake of the scandals and purposely unleashed Kintner to fill the void.

Whether that is true or not, it is a fact that the FTC, not the FCC, is the force that has shaken the TV industry in the past two years. It was the FTC that exposed the no-glass windshield commercial, the fake shaving cream, the sandpaper that wasn't sandpaper. It was the FTC that even warned that advertisers could go to jail for misleading commercials.

The FTC has a ticklish problem in trying to determine the difference between honest boasting, trick exaggeration, and outright fakery. It doesn't interfere with the boasting or even the exaggeration. It considers itself concerned only with fakery.

Take three examples:

A breakfast cereal will call itself the most delicious on the market. That's a matter of opinion and certainly no more than boasting. The FTC won't interfere.

An air line advertises the fastest flight from New York to New Orleans. That's O.K. too. It is true that any one of the competing lines will fly you there just as fast, but the FTC reasons that they *all* are running the fastest flight to New Orleans. (They'll beat a Piper Cub to hell and gone.) So it won't interfere here either, despite the trick exaggeration.

But an aluminum-foil manufacturer presents a commercial that demonstrates how his foil kept a ham fresh while Brand X foil permitted the ham to dry out. This is outright fakery. The fresh ham was fresh and the dried-out ham was dried out at the start of the commercial. The FTC does interfere, ordering the manufacturer to cease this type of advertising.

The FTC's greatest weapon actually is publicity. Although there are teeth in the law, the very value of the advertisement is eliminated the moment the FTC publicizes it as a fake. For this reason a manufacturer almost always responds in two ways to an FTC indictment: He denies that there has been a deliberate misrepresentation and then he announces he's discarding the claim anyway.

Like the FCC, the FTC is only as good as the diligence of its commissioners. It can chase down as many complaints as the small staff can process (usually a thousand at a time), or it can sink into apathy.

Another federal agency concerned somewhat with advertising is the Food and Drug Administration. This organization has jurisdiction only over the labeling and packed-in-the-box advertising, but it does affect TV to some extent in that any false claim on the label is apt to appear in the broadcast advertising. In addition, there are some four thousand state laws touching upon various modes of advertising; few of these affect TV directly.

But while these government agencies pose to regulate TV and its advertising, there is a hidden counterforce in Washington. It is the Congress itself. More than thirty congressmen are known to own all or sizable parts of TV stations. The FCC even admitted that it deliberately favors companies in which congressmen have stock when it chooses among rivals for a license. (They have the special qualification of being public leaders, the FCC explained.) In addition to these congressmen who actually own TV interests, there's scarcely a representative or senator who hasn't written the FCC a formal letter interceding for one faction or another in a competition for a channel.

These congressmen enjoy some strange advantages at times. The LBJ Company, which is headed by Mrs. Lyndon B. Johnson, owns the only TV station in Austin, Texas (population 132,000). It's true that Vice President Johnson is not a stockholder in the company, but his wife is, his two daughters are, his brother is, and so is his former administrative assistant. Furthermore, although the FCC has on file three bona-fide applications from qualified broadcasters, it has never got around to acting on them, giving the LBJ Company a monopoly in a city of nearly 150,000 which is not only the state capital but also the seat of the state university.

Senator William Proxmire of Wisconsin proposed legislation that would forbid anyone in or out of government putting pressure on the government regulatory agencies. But no sooner were his words out than it was revealed that he had interceded not once but twice when the FCC was debating transfer of a license in Wisconsin.

The power of a congressman's letter to a government agency can never be overestimated. It is from Congress that these agencies get their very pay checks, and it is through investigation by Congress that they can get their blackest black eyes. They heed what they know it is best to heed.

It has always been the broadcasting industry's position that it should regulate itself. These congressmen who own chunks of TV stock agree, of course, but they are not the only men in government who take that position. FCC Chairman Ford remarked at a luncheon, "I was asked the other day if I believed that the television industry could police itself, and I answered unequivocally and positively that it not only can, but will, and in fact is making progress in that area."

The broadcasting industry has chosen its own trade association, the National Association of Broadcasters, as the instrument of self-government. The NAB's chief efforts in the direction have been the assembly of a censorship code.

Otherwise, the NAB acts more as a lobby against government than as an instrument of industry government itself. Former Governor LeRoy Collins of Florida was hired (at $75,-000 a year plus $12,500 for expenses) as the NAB president in 1960—and the committee that selected him made a careful point of the fact that he was suited to stand up to any government attacks against the industry. Furthermore, in interviews before he was awarded the job he made it plain that he favored a firm stand by the industry against any outside pressures or attacks. In other words, the NAB really hired not so much a president as a Secretary of Defense.

This follows the pattern of the motion-picture industry. The movies launched the 1930's in a spirit of anything goes (and too often the starlet's clothes in the orgy scene were the first things to go). These excesses brought a threat of government censorship, but the movie industry begged for the opportunity to govern itself. Its Motion Picture Producers Association produced then what the broadcasters have produced now—a censorship code, and a hail-fellow president who could serve as lobbyist.

The NAB, which once opposed any FCC interference with programing, now concedes that the commission should examine the station's efforts to fulfill community needs and to keep the promises made in the original license application. But it still takes the position that to remain free, the broadcasting industry must largely provide its own regulation.

There is no doubt that this is the ideal solution. Is it the practical solution? Only a long-term trial can tell.

AS EASY AS ROLLING OFF A HORSE

Somewhere amid all these advertising men, network vice presidents, and federal commissioners you will find the actors. They are quite necessary, if only to introduce a brief message from their sponsor.

For all the ulterior motives that guide the men behind TV, the man in front of the set switches it on for only one reason—to be entertained. And for more than a dozen hours a day there are ingénues weeping over unrequited love, Indians tumbling off horses, and dopey fathers being outwitted by shrewd mothers in order to provide this entertainment.

Some of it is good and most of it is terrible but the whole of it keeps an awful lot of actors busy.

The classic dramatic actors of the stage are inclined to sniff haughtily at TV's routine fare, but they do perform in television's better plays. Helen Hayes summed up the feeling when she told an interviewer: "Technically TV is marvelous. But it does not bring out your soul the way theater does. One thing that TV can show well is violence, but that is not always good drama."

There are very few actors today who refuse to appear on TV. The reason, of course, is money. It's not that television salaries are so high, for both the stage and the movies pay more, but the TV pay is earned quickly and the work is comparatively easy. Greer Garson likes the one-shot appearance on shows such as the Hallmark Theater because they permit her to perform when she chooses and permit her to lay off as long as she chooses.

The actors trained on Broadway and in the movies found little difficulty adapting to television. There are two principal differences: the TV work must be done faster than in the movies and it must be done in a more natural manner than on the stage. The exaggerated motions of the stage actor, calculated to attract notice in the upper balcony, look ridiculous when magnified on the home screen.

In the world of TV these top-rung actors of stage and screen are a decided minority. The staple is the series program, and the majority of performers play the same characters week in and week out for twenty-six weeks of the year. They are the heritage of the B picture, schooled in the Hollywood system of wringing a single idea and a single characterization dry before turning to something new.

It is in the series that the actor finds his most comfortable work. For the hired hand it is steady work, a great rarity in the acting profession. For the true star it is a special financial bonanza. For either, it is the easiest of acting work, as easy, as Roy Rogers said, as rolling off a horse.

Charles Bickford, now in his seventies, has been an actor for fifty years. He has known all phases of show business, from burlesque to Broadway. And to Bickford there has been nothing that is so easy and so secure as acting in a TV series.

"It's the money mostly," he says. "Because of the tax system, if you act for a salary you act for practically nothing. But if you get a successful series and then sell it on a capital-gains basis you're rich.

"On top of that, you're much more famous if you're on TV. A few years ago I was on a show called 'The Man Behind the Badge.' I didn't do any acting at all. All I did was say, 'Good evening. Tonight's show is about such and such.' And then at the end I said, 'Next week's show is this or that.' I got more fan mail from that than I ever did from the movies.

"You have to work much faster on a TV series. In the movies you had eighteen to twenty weeks to do a picture sometimes. On a weekly half-hour TV show you have two days of rehearsal and then they film it the third day. It's not so exciting as the movies or Broadway or even live TV, but it is easier."

One great staple of TV is, of course, the Western. The craze began with the Lone Ranger in the earliest days and has never waned. Roy Rogers is now in his second decade on television, still going strong as he enthralls an entire new generation of fans. The somewhat more sophisticated Westerns, the so-called adult Westerns, are perhaps a little less durable, but there will be cowboys and Indians chasing each other across the TV screen as long as there is adventure in the young American's heart.

Some actors object to the type casting that a series show demands. Henry Fonda rejected offers for years because, he said: "These TV actors are better known by their character names than by their real names. Even when they appear as a guest of another show, doing something different, they're identified as the series characters." But like them all, Henry Fonda finally succumbed to the money and the security of the television series.

Apart from the usual show-business divisions of actors, singers, and comedians, television has produced a new type—the personality. These are men like Ed Sullivan and Dave Garroway and Arthur Godfrey and Jack Paar who don't really do anything outstanding. They just sit or stand and get famous.

How? Why? There are many explanations. The simplest

is that these men are believable, pleasant-appearing human beings and that their true vocation is salesmanship.

The success of Ed Sullivan has been the most surprising to the world of show business. He has no performing talent, nor does he exude the warmth of a Garroway or a Godfrey. Sullivan wanted to get in on the ground floor of television. As a Broadway gossip columnist, he was an intense rival of Walter Winchell. Although Sullivan's newspaper is considerably larger than Winchell's, it was Winchell who became most famous. Sullivan attributed this to Winchell's success on radio: Winchell got in on the ground floor and Sullivan didn't.

When TV was born, Ed Sullivan decided he wouldn't make the same mistake twice. He began looking for a show. It was given to him by Producer J. Worthington Miner, who was planning a variety program. "Ed was my choice for master of ceremonies," Miner said. "I based my theory on not wanting a performing emcee. I didn't think a performing emcee would last long, but that a nonperforming emcee would."

He was exactly right. Nonperforming Ed Sullivan is one of the most durable characters on TV. He feels that his success actually is not on the screen but off, in the selection of guest stars for the program. While most of show business is forever devoted to reproducing yesterday's hit, Sullivan constantly strains to produce something new. "It's my training as a newspaperman," he explained. "We are looking for news, for scoops, to show something different from yesterday."

On the other hand, Arthur Godfrey's success as a TV personality comes from another source. Godfrey never did anything different. All the shows were alike until illness forced him off the screen. Godfrey's success stemmed from his salesmanship—he sold himself and the sponsor's product simply by sounding sincere. "I had figured it all out twenty years ago," Godfrey told a *Variety* interviewer. "I had to be completely sold on a product. I had to be honest and think of some way to make the customer remember the product regardless of what he thought about my so-called talents. That's my whole technique."

What Garroway needed to make the grade was a chimpanzee. His warm personality, his obvious friendliness had attracted attention when he starred in a charming low-budget show out of Chicago in TV's earliest days, but when he first started on "Today" the show was a bust.

Executive producer Dick Pinkham later recalled, "We needed a device that would get the kids to turn on the set in the morning so the parents would watch. That device was a —————little chimpanzee that brought us $30,000,000 in revenue."

Within six months the chimp, J. Fred Muggs, hoisted the audience from 2,500,000 to 11,000,000. The advertisers flocked in. J. Fred Muggs got invitations to everything from Sugar Cane festivals to marriage. Garroway came to be famous. He also came to hate all chimpanzees, and J. Fred Muggs in particular. With the audience finally built up, J. Fred Muggs was sent back to his trees and Garroway stayed on to charm the audience this chimp had given him.

One phenomenon of this personality cult is that each of the major successes was developed by television on television. None came from the stage or the screen as proved stars. Furthermore, those motion-picture stars who attempted to match this success have invariably failed.

No one in TV can explain the how or why of this. Carl Lindemann, while in charge of day programing for NBC, tried for years to find a personality who could rival CBS's Godfrey. Money was no problem. Resources were unlimited. But Lindemann never could produce a formula, much less a man, to make the grade. He reached the desperate point where he would give an on-the-air audition to practically any likable male who walked into the RCA Building. "I found many who I thought would make it, but never one who did make it," he said. On the other hand, NBC threw in Paar, a perennial show-business flop, as host of its "Tonight" show in a gesture of desperation. Paar turned out to be an overwhelming success.

Though these personalities somehow must exude warmth, even forgetting all signs of talent, seeking a warm human being is hardly the answer to the search. Paar particularly is a cold fish personally, a worry wart who lives in terror of a poor program. Yet he comes through the screen as a warm lackadaisical sort of guy who just wants to have a little fun each evening.

And although these personalities have the least discernible talent, they are the most durable people on the air. Meanwhile the singers and comedians, the performers with the most obvious individual talent, die quickest. Perry Como and Dinah Shore and Jack Benny could go on forever, but they are exceptions. Generally, among the comedians, the bigger they were, the quicker they fell.

As a pioneer Milton Berle lasted seven years, but then even he was gone, not to return except as MC of a bowling program. Jerry Lester was once one of the biggest stars on television; today he plays small night clubs. Jackie Gleason, Lucy and Desi, Sid Caesar and Imogene Coca, George Gobel, Steve Allen all rode high and then fell off the bandwagon.

It is generally a matter of overexposure. The public just sees too much of them. At the start of Berle's seventh season on TV the advertising man behind the show, Myron T. Kirk, said: "As soon as I saw his first show I knew this was the last year. I got interested in Jackie Gleason." The comedian seems to wear out his welcome. Bob Hope remains a perennial simply by refusing to take the risk. He refuses to do weekly or even monthly shows. He appears only a few times a year, and his shows are taped a bit at a time, in leisurely fashion.

Veteran comedy director Leonard Stern says that the big comedy TV shows run in three stages as far as the viewer is concerned. "In the first stage the comedian's act is all new and the viewer is charmed. In the second stage there's a feeling of pleasant anticipation. The viewer knows what's coming next, but he's proud of it—he likes to tell his wife, 'Now watch him do so and so.' Then in the third stage there is only boredom, and that's the end of the road."

Stern, like all students of comedy, devotes considerable time trying to explain to himself and to others just why Jack Benny outlasts all the comedians and all the rules of thumb. After all, there has been the stage of pleasant anticipation on the Benny show for ten years. When does the boredom arrive?

Stern says: "Benny's success is basically due to the fact that he created a successful family—the regular supporting characters like Rochester—in the days of radio, and has kept the family intact ever since. The family is important. In television comedy the family is the distraction that keeps you from becoming bored with the star, it is the magician's left hand that diverts your attention for a moment. Red Skelton is good, too, because of the family—only, in his case he's his own family, playing various characters but, you'll notice, the same characters all the time."

This still does not answer the riddle of Jack Benny's durability. There are other "families": Gleason had one and Caesar had one and Steve Allen had one. These comedians, good ones all, eventually lost their TV shows.

Benny himself explains his success by saying he is simply a good editor. He says the star of a weekly comedy show must assign writers to specific jobs, and then edit their work to suit his talents. "At least 60 per cent of a show's effectiveness depends on this," he says.

All of TV's comedians work in this fashion—they're the editors supervising a staff of writers. They are not all good editors, however. Some TV people feel that the comedian should share this authority with a producer—a more objective judge of what will come off as funny and what will not. Jack Benny does. His producer, Parke Levy, had far more authority over the content of the program than do most producers of comedy shows.

Marlo Lewis, who saw many a comedian come and go when he was producer of the Ed Sullivan Show, says: "Comedians have a tendency to replay old jokes, old routines, because they went over once before. They don't see what you're doing when you change and fix and take new viewpoints."

The comedians themselves offer all sorts of reasons for the failure of comedy on TV. Imogene Coca thinks it's because the children have inherited the television set from the parents. Jerry Lester thinks it is because the comedy stars must concentrate on business—production costs, sponsor sales, and so on—and don't have the time to develop their humor. Louis Nye, a comic actor rather than a straight comedian like a Benny or a Hope, thinks there is too much talk and not enough accent on movement. "I remember," he recalls, "when I was on the Steve Allen Show I was supposed to tell Fred Astaire, 'You know, I'm the Fred Astaire of this group.' That might have got a laugh. But to make sure I worked out a ridiculous step, just one step, only a gesture really, and that insured the laugh."

Comedy writer Mel Tonkin blames the economics of the business. During a TV discussion on comedy, he said: "When the comedian first comes on, all he's interested in is being funny, in getting across as a comedian. Then he wants to produce a little. He wants to call the shots a little. He wants to write a little. They become head of corporations. The business of being funny becomes the least aspect of their careers. They're with lawyers, they're with accountants, they're with publicity people, and at the last minute someone comes up and says, 'Here's a script you're on tonight.' And they're not ready because they've been assiduously promoting. If it's Red Buttons or Jackie Gleason or whatever it is, they become huge corporations, and funniness is the least part of the operation."

Television is perfect for comedy and comedy is perfect for television. The advertisers like it because it's a happy show, a selling show. The audiences like it. But with comics dying off every season, the problem is how to replace them.

George Burns said that "there's no place for a comic to be a failure any more." TV has killed off the small night spots where comics once broke in, so a comedian must be either big time or unemployed. But still the fresh faces keep coming, quite often from the supporting casts: Nye, Tom Poston, and Art Carney are all products of "families."

TV has made show business easier to crash for those hopeful youngsters forever converging upon Hollywood and New York. The reason is the volume. Television chews up so many actors and so many scripts in a single day. It took Charlie Chaplin three decades to produce seventy-eight movies, scarcely enough for two years of TV as a regular program. But despite the never-ending need for talent, there is no open-door policy. Youngsters struggling for a chance to get experience are always told to come back when they have experience.

Sooner or later, though, they usually get that break. It's not a big one but it is a job. There are so many girls working in TV at salaries running $125 and up that Broadway and night-club producers have experienced a shortage of chorus girls. The youngsters just won't work those long night hours for $100 a week when they can get more pay and better hours on television.

Despite the good money in TV, however, the long-term contract is a thing of the past. Milton Berle was given a thirty-year contract by NBC. Eddie Fisher, Jimmy Durante, Jackie Gleason, and Martha Raye got contracts for fifteen to twenty years. They continue to draw the pay even when they're not on the air.

These contracts are mainly the result of a big talent raid that CBS radio staged on NBC radio back in the 1940's: it took away Jack Benny, Edgar Bergen, and Amos 'n' Andy in one swoop. When Pat Weaver took over NBC television, he was determined that the like would not happen again. He pinned down the stars to long-term agreements as soon as they made good. But he didn't anticipate the short life of a TV star, and today NBC and CBS are paying off many of these agreements long after the star has left the air waves.

Without the long-term contract, a star's big salary can shrink pretty rapidly. A pay check of $3,000 a week seems tremendous. But in the first place it is delivered, not to the actor, but to his agent. It has already been shorn of withholding tax and the other usual deductions, and the agent clips off another 10 per cent before sending the balance to the performer. The check is now down to $2,000. The withholding tax is not enough to account for the income tax on a salary this large, so to keep out of trouble later the actor has to put aside another few hundred dollars for payment to Uncle Sam at the end of the year. He still has over $1,000 a week left—but he doesn't work all year. At best he'll work twenty-six weeks. More often he'll work thirteen. This salary has to pay living expenses for the entire year.

The real money in TV is in those series residuals—the money paid for re-run shows. William Bendix stands to make $500,000 from the re-runs of "The Life of Riley" series because he shares ownership in the show.

When Ed Sullivan started his show in 1948, he paid Martin and Lewis $200 as the stars, and then shelled out $50 for Monica Lewis, $75 for Eugene Liszt, and $10 each for six dancers. Today Sullivan pays $3,500 for an average guest shot. Although he is known as a generous paymaster, Sullivan screamed when producer Leland Hayward paid out $20,000 to $50,000 to his guest stars for a single spectacular. Sullivan considered this unnecessarily inflationary.

The pay checks of the TV actors vary greatly, of course. In the dramatic shows the prices run from about $5,000 to $10,000 for the top stars, although June Allyson once got $50,000 for a single appearance. Dinah Shore pays her guests $10,000 tops.

The giants of TV like Bob Hope and Bing Crosby will get a flat fee of about $250,000 to put on a single one-hour show. They pay all expenses and salaries out of that and keep whatever is left. One way they save expenses is to swap guest appearances with one another for free. This is also a status symbol in television. Singer Bobby Darin was invited to be a guest on a Bob Hope show, and he was asked his price. He said he'd do it for free, but that Hope would have to make a return appearance on a Darin show. The agents for the two men dickered and finally came to this arrangement: since Hope is twice as important as Darin, Hope would appear once for free on Darin's show and Darin would appear twice for free on Hope's show.

The stars of the series shows who work strictly on salary average about $35,000 for the year. However, at one time Warner Brothers was paying James Garner as little as $200 a week to star in "Maverick" and Edd Byrnes as little as $300 for "77 Sunset Strip."

This is peanuts compared to the movies, where a Marlon Brando or a John Wayne will earn a million dollars from a single picture. But peanuts can be quite nutritious.

THE ANGRY YOUNG MEN

The television writer often appears to be the only Indian in a tribe of chiefs. Paranoia is an occupational disease.

The writer finds the producer demanding that he write better, his agent urging that he write faster, the advertising agencies insisting that he write safer, and the sponsor ordering that he write shorter. The producer wants to improve the show. The agent wants to finish this job so he can sign a contract for the next. The advertising agency doesn't want to offend any viewer. The sponsor wants time to insert one extra commercial.

Although there are many types of writer working on television, all have the same basic problems. Some learn to live contentedly with them and some never surrender.

The majority of TV's writers today work on series programs, sometimes under salary to the packager and sometimes on a perscript basis. There also is a handful of top TV playwrights who free-lance the major dramatic shows. There are, too, adapters, writers who take a book or a play and rewrite it into a television program, and there are the highly specialized writers of the comedy and variety shows.

Never is a series written by only one man. The series may employ a team of writers to take turns at installments, or it may work with several of the established free-lance men who are familiar with the needs of this particular show.

Either way the basic pattern of working is the same. The idea for an installment is discussed by the writer with the producer. The writer next does an outline, then a rough draft, then a finished script and, finally, revisions required by the producer. Well, not quite finally. Once the producer is satisfied with the script it must go for further approval to the network, the advertising agency of the sponsor, and sometimes the sponsor himself. Any one of these might junk the whole thing and demand a fresh start, but this seldom happens.

Under the Screen Writers Guild rules a writer cannot take an assignment on speculation. His idea must be bought before he writes a word. Usually the writer's agent will line up an appointment with the producer or story editor, and the writer will tell what he plans to do with the series' regular characters in the episode he proposes to write. He gets the go-ahead on the basis of his basic idea and, of course, his professional reputation.

The writer normally has about two weeks to do one half-hour series script, but many work much faster. They learn to think in the pattern of the shows for which they write, and work quickly in order to cram in as many scripts as possible during the course of a year. One of the top series writers in Hollywood is also one of the fastest. He is Sam Peeples, who operates like this:

"I'll get a call from someone who wants a script written and they'll give me an idea over the phone of what they have in mind. Maybe their last four episodes were set in the big city, so now they want one set in the desert. So I get in my car and on my way over to see them I think up some kind of situation, some kind of gimmick, that would make a story.

"Then I get there and tell them about it and we kick it around and make some changes, and then I go do the outline."

Peeples will write a half-hour TV script in two sittings of about four hours each. "But," he adds with a grin, "I won't turn it in for a week. I want the producer to think he's getting his money's worth."

Contrast this with the effort that writer Rod Serling put into the ninety-minute script *In the Presence of Mine Enemies*. "I got the idea of dramatizing a story based on the Warsaw Ghetto," he said. "I began reading up on the subject, and for twelve months, on and off, I researched it. Then I began to write. I spent four weeks on the first draft. As soon as I finished it, I started on the second draft, and that took about two weeks. This was sent to the network. By the time we were ready to start rehearsal there was a third draft—changes I wanted and also changes that had been suggested.

"The rehearsal period was three weeks. The play remained basically the same but there were minor rewrites, about three or four."

That's quite a contrast—the eight hours for the series show against fifteen months for the drama—but they both flashed on your screen as television shows. The difference is between TV's bread and butter, which is that fast series show, and TV's flossy dessert, which is the Serling play.

An odd development in series writing is the increase in women who write Westerns. This was once unthinkable, but one of the women who broke down the barrier, Fanya Lawrence, said: "When a producer first objected to my trying a Western I told him that he was after violence and that women have a greater sense of violence than men. After all, our emotions are constantly repressed. Writing Westerns gives us an opportunity to release our resentments against mankind by killing off people not just singly but in dozens."

Mrs. Lawrence, who now writes some of the top Westerns

on TV, has a special technique of adapting plots from the classics and converting them into cowboy-and-Indian dramas. Jean Holloway, another woman writer of Westerns, does the same thing. "Once I adapted a Jane Austen story for 'Wagon Train,'" she said.

The adapter's job can be very simple, merely penciling a Broadway play down to the size needed for TV, or it can be quite complicated, converting an involved novel into a one-hour television drama. There is a great trend toward adaptations of established works, partly because producers are more confident of success with a pretested book or play and partly because the book or play brings with it a sort of built-in fan club.

But the adapter does have his woes. Irve Tunick recalls being sent a book by a producer for adaptation. Tunick did the job and mailed off his script. Then he called to find out how the producer liked his handiwork.

"I didn't," said the producer.

"What's wrong with it?" asked Tunick.

"I don't like the story," replied the producer.

Obviously he had not read the book in the first place, or else it never occurred to him that an adapter might remain true to the original work rather than rewriting it completely, as is done far too often.

The most difficult of all writing is comedy, either situation comedy for a television series or straight comedy for the big comedians. Comic writers make the most money and have the most ulcers.

Bob Schiller and Bob Weiskopf, who worked as a team on the "I Love Lucy" situation comedies and now do others, are typical. They start out each episode with a straight story. "Most good comedy stories could be either dramatic or funny, depending on how they are handled," Schiller says.

From there they find the straight lines in their story and then begin thinking of the answers, the gags that will convert the playlet into humor. There is a great deal of difference between what is funny on paper and what is funny on the TV screen, and for that reason there will be many revisions during rehearsals.

"You can never tell," says Schiller. "Sometimes you put in a corny joke for a groaner—to make the people groan in anguish. But the audience will laugh at it. They will think it's really funny. It's hard to understand."

The greatest pressure is on the straight comedy writers—those who supply the laughs for men like Bob Hope and Steve Allen and the like. Hope has used as many as a dozen writers on a single show. Sometimes the writers work alone and sometimes in teams of two. For Hope, each would take on a small assignment—a blackout, a skit, maybe even just one part of the opening monologue—and work it out with no concern or contact with the other writers on the same show.

This is all put together at a script conference a week or so before the show goes on the air. The writers and the comedian sit around the conference table. Usually one writer is designated as "the reader." He's a man with more than a little ham in him, and hence will give the best delivery of the lines the writers are trying to sell to the comedian.

Pat Weaver, when at NBC, once thought it would be a great idea to have one of these sessions televised. He proposed that on a daytime show the writers would sit at their typewriters on camera and write; the emcee would wander along, examine their handiwork, and then read the funny gags over the air. This, happily, never came to pass.

The writers will wrangle and haggle over a punch line for hours and even days, sometimes right up until the moment the show goes on the air.

Take, for example, one case involving a skit on a Steve Allen show. The skit, featuring Diana Dors and Don Knotts, depicted what would happen if women completely assumed the predatory role and began taking the initiative to invite men on dates.

It was to end with Knotts, shocked at Diana's suggestion

that they adjourn to her apartment, stalking away from their night club table in a huff. So far so good, but what was to be the closing line?

One writer wanted Knotts to say, "Lucky I brought my mad money."

One wanted Diana to say, "And they told me he was a push-over."

One wanted her to shrug and then start the chase anew by asking a passing waiter, "Haven't we met somewhere before?"

For three days the writers tested these endings one by one. An hour before the show went on the air they were still in disagreement. They finally decided on "Men!"

They had failed to come up with a line funny in itself, but they had done the next best thing: they had produced a single word which, when spoken in the proper tone of exasperation, exactly summed up the point of their sketch.

On the other hand, another writer's problem is to find a single gag that must be a truly funny reply to a straight line. One of the classics, as far as the writers themselves are concerned, was one written for the Milton Berle show.

The straight line was said by Milton to his spinster-secretary Max: "Don't worry, honey. For every guy there's a girl and for every girl there's a guy."

The follow-up line, recited by soulful Max after a pause: "Well, somewhere tonight some girl has two guys."

A line such as this can take hours of thought, or it can pop from the writer's mind in a moment. Comedians are not usually very funny fellows when off the air. Comedy writers, on the other hand, are hilarious sitting around a night-club table. For one thing, they are always testing material on one another. The only way to write comedy, whether sitting in an office with your partner or guzzling in the saloon next to the studio, is to throw out the lines and see if anyone laughs.

But the comedy writers don't only write words. They also conceive sight gags—the pie in the face, the pratfall. And still another classic was the case of a writer who wrote only a silence into the script.

It was for Jack Benny. A stickup man said, "Your money or your life!"

There was a pause, a long pause, in dead silence. And the audience, seeing the stingy Benny pondering this difficult proposition, burst into one of the longest laughs in the history of radio or television.

It is difficult enough simply to sit down and write funny lines or to conceive a dramatic plot that is different from any one of the hundreds shown on TV last month or even last week. But television writers are handcuffed by a mass of restrictions that infuriate them.

A man can't be "lucky" because that's a brand of cigarettes. A character can't say "I'd prefer to fly" because the advertising agency has a railroad account. A little girl can't refuse her cereal because the next show is sponsored by a cereal.

These petty annoyances are bad enough. But the interference can go well beyond the alteration of a line here and there. It can submerge the whole point of a play. A classic case is Rod Serling's *Noon on Doomsday*.

This was a play based on the murder of the young Negro Emmett Till, in Mississippi. At the outset Serling was warned that he could not make this a play involving Negroes and whites. He wasn't too disturbed about that. There are other minorities. He made his victim Jewish, but set the play in a Southern town.

The advertising agency and the sponsor, U.S. Steel, refused to accept the script. First they made Serling change the locale, from a Southern town to New England, which made the whole thing ridiculous because mob violence has been unknown in New England since Salem. Then, to make certain, they even forced Serling to remove any reference to Coca-Cola because, they maintained, Coca-Cola is primarily a Southern drink.

By the time they were through with Serling's play about the

Emmett Till case, not even Emmett himself had he been around, would have recognized it.

The ad agencies make it plain they don't want to offend anyone, anyplace, any time—and that greatly restricts the possibilities of drama.

On the other hand, this fear of the public wrath—even the wrath of a crackpot minority—is apparently justified. After "The Philco Playhouse" put on a play starring Negro actor Sidney Poitier, several Southern dealers quit handling Philcos in favor of another make, and a petition with ten thousand names from Jackson, Mississippi, vowed a boycott on all Philco products.

Even when sales may not be involved—after all, who would boycott U.S. Steel because of the Serling play?—there are other problems. After a Negro girl won second prize in a TV beauty contest sponsored by the Ford Motor Company, Ford suddenly had labor trouble in one of its Southern assembly plants. The whites who had grudgingly agreed to work alongside Negro mechanics refused to continue.

The restrictions that hang like a dark cloud over television writers are not confined to the serious subjects of heavy drama. The comedy writers are also plagued by taboos. ("We can't offend teenagers on the Chevrolet show because, after all, they steal a lot of Chevvys," quipped one writer.)

Because comedy is critical, and tends to be destructive, comedy is taboo on such subjects as politics and race relations and all the thousand and one other things that are controversial today. A man like Bob Hope can get away with quips about Dwight Eisenhower's golf or John Kennedy's haircut because Hope is gentle and also because Hope is an American institution. But he is the exception, and not even Hope can put bite into his gags, although bite is necessary to much successful humor.

Playwright Paddy Chayefsky maintains that the howls about TV's restrictions are too loud. He wrote: "The taboos of television, though much is made out of them, are really no worse than those governing the movies or the slick magazine short story. Only on the Broadway stage or in the novel form is there any freedom of topic, and even the stage has produced little in the last ten years that could not have been done on television."

On the other hand, Chayefsky is much concerned about the prestige of the writer in television. He said: "In television the writer is treated with a peculiar lack of deference and outright contempt. He is rarely consulted about casting, his scripts are frequently mangled without his knowing about it, and he is certainly the most poorly paid person in the production. Some programs don't allow the writer to attend rehearsals of his own show. At the same time, he is granted the proud title of playwright, and in every respect but his work, he is treated with a dignity inherited from the stage."

The series writers are less likely to complain about their prestige in the industry because there is less pretension about their work. They are writers-for-hire and they know it. They are not creating a play, but only a story for a group of characters handed them in advance by the producer.

The comedy writers have their own peculiar problems. Goodman Ace, one of the best, says: "For the most part the comedy writers are considered a necessary but evil part of the television setup. There are some big comedy stars who never speak to comedy writers, some who rarely see them, some who, despite the fact that they depend on the writers to be witty, know deep in their hearts they could be much more clever about it if only they had the time to get it down on paper."

One of the troubles is that comedy writers are never sure of how much prestige they grant themselves. They are called writers, but they don't write whole books and seldom even whole pages. They write funny lines. Comedy director Leonard Stern maintains that this is one reason why comedy writers may lack prestige in their industry—they disparage themselves.

"They should take pride in working on TV," he said. "I wrote for the movies for years, and nothing I did then is up to what I do on TV. In the movies a writer was nothing. It was always 'Hello, boys' or 'Hello, kids,' in the studios.

"Once at Warner Brothers there was a team of writers known to Harry Warner only as 'the boys.' He always greeted them in the hall but he never bothered to learn their names. It was always, 'Hello, boys.' Then one day he was stuck. He was in the hall and he saw *only one of them.* He stopped for a minute and then he said, 'Hello, boy.' "

But for all Stern's cry of hold-your-head-high, the comedy writers have a prestige problem because of their relationship with their bosses, the comedians. There seems to be a natural enmity. One comic always greets any writer socially by saying, "Who are you working against these days?"

Writer Mel Brooks, discussing comedy writing with David Susskind, told of his experiences with Jerry Lewis. Once Lewis called in his writers and said that for the next show he didn't want a regular script. "I just want to go out there and I want something magic to happen."

"Get Mandrake," said Brooks.

But Lewis didn't get Mandrake and he did use a script. On television the comics need scripts written by first-rate writers, and sometimes not even this is enough to save a career. The good comedians, as Jack Benny said, are good editors of someone else's writing. They are also, of course, good actors.

The relationship between writer and comic varies from case to case, of course. The legend is that the writers for Jackie Gleason slipped their scripts in under his bedroom door and sometimes got them back in small pieces via the same route. Bob Hope, on the other hand, is known as a delightful boss. The more serious the comedian, the more closely he will work with his writers. Sid Caesar, the master of satire, was in constant conference with his writers. Steve Allen even permitted his writers to veto the choice of a guest star if they felt the star wouldn't fit the show.

Yet with all the headaches, there are many TV writers and many more persons trying to become TV writers. It is a difficult field to enter partly because few producers will read scripts or ideas not submitted by a recognized agent, and recognized agents won't take on inexperienced writers.

Serling, now a producer of his own series as well as a writer, remembers well the heartbreaks of getting started. He was batting out scripts in Ohio and on the brink of total discouragement when suddenly he was summoned to New York by producer Worthington Miner. Miner bought three of his scripts right on the spot. Serling dashed back to Ohio elated, for he had made the grade at last. He arrived home in a dead heat with a letter from Miner canceling the whole deal; Miner had withdrawn as the show's producer.

So when Serling became a producer in his own right he vowed to read every script submitted to him. "I do, and almost all are hopeless," he says. "About 90 per cent are written by rank amateurs with no knowledge of the medium, and the rest by hacks who don't grasp the basic idea of the series."

One problem is that there are no central points to which to send a script. The networks buy few, especially these days when most production is by outside packagers. The individual producers usually select their own story ideas, and the outsider has no idea which producers are looking for what ideas. Some writers, Marya Mannes for one, have suggested a central script agency where a hopeful writer could submit an idea and have it considered by a great many producers. This is not practical, however; the producers would commit mayhem, grabbing for the best ideas out of the central pool.

Robert Buckner, a top movie writer who also does TV work, blames the predominance of shoddy scripts on the small fees TV pays its writers. "The writers don't stop to think," he says. "They start writing right away. They do their thinking on the typewriter. This is because they are always in a hurry. They set up a target of a gross annual income at the start of the year and then begin writing as fast as they can to meet that figure."

But producer William Self insists that the amount of money paid does not affect the quality of the scripts. He says: "When

I was producer of the Schlitz Playhouse we had a low ceiling for scripts. The agents kept telling me that I'd have to raise the price to get some big-name writers and better stories. Finally once I did see the need for a top writer and I called the agents and told them I was prepared to go over our ceiling. They submitted some names—the very same names they had been submitting right along.

"All the shows have ceiling prices on scripts, depending upon their budgets. The writers know it, and so each writer demands the ceiling so that the maximum becomes the minimum, too. They just take the ceiling. A writer who'll do a script for $5,000 on a show that has a $5,000 ceiling won't do a show with a $10,000 ceiling for less than $10,000 even though it's the same writer putting out the same effort as he did for $5,000.

"The writers are always being pushed by their agents to forget quality. The writers are told to write faster so they can get the next show as well as this one. They are told to think up a gimmick for a series so they can own a part of the show instead of just their fee for a dramatic script."

The TV playwright who free-lances for the quality drama shows makes $25,000 to $30,000 a year. "Playhouse 90" has paid as much as $10,000 for a single script, but the average rate is about $5,000.

The series writer will get $1,500 to $3,000 for a half-hour show and perhaps as much as $4,500 for a one-hour show. The comedy writers are the highest paid of all. They will draw weekly salaries running from $3,000 to $5,000.

As in the case of actors, this is nothing compared to the pay from a Hollywood movie or the royalties from a Broadway stage hit. And this, undoubtedly, helps to make the angry young men even angrier. They moan over their lack of prestige and they groan over the restrictions that hamper them, but it is only for the Hollywood and Broadway gold that they ever desert the 17-inch screen.

BEHIND THE SCENES

A producer in television may be anything from a creative genius who controls the destiny of a dozen shows to a hen-pecked keeper of the budget with little more authority than the script girl.

It depends upon the man. It depends upon the program. It depends upon the organization.

Originally the producers were hired by the networks, given an idea and a budget, and told to bring back a show a week from Tuesday. Then, as television grew, the best of the producers branched out on their own, creating new shows and selling them to the network or advertising agency. Today, with the big production companies in Hollywood dominating the industry, the producer, with some notable exceptions, again is an organization man, hired as a straw boss.

Officially the producer is the man in charge of everything—from selecting the original story to buying the carpenter's

128

nails. But in cases where the show is ruled by a domineering star, the producer may be little more than a supersecretary responsible for all the minor decisions and none of the major ones.

Pat Weaver, in one of his famous NBC memos, set down the ground rules for when the star is most important to a show and when the producer takes control. He wrote: "When stars hit, the power of the star to deliver the audience is so great that the star is in control and form is not a major factor. But there comes a time when a new control over the audience must be gotten—from the creative brains. The star-makers, the producers, begin to take over."

The producer who works for either a network or a large packager is given the basic conception of the show, a budget, and usually a star. From there on he's on his own. His job is to produce the program.

He hires the writers to do the script, and then he confers with them as they develop it. He hires the set designers, and then he does battle with them to curtail their spending sprees. He hires the costume designers, and he then mediates between them and the fussy actors. He hires the director and he hires the cast and he serves as the liaison between all of these people and the front office.

He must know music in order to discuss it with his arranger, and he must know trucking charges, too, when the time comes to transfer scenery. He must make out rehearsal schedules and do so with an eye for efficiency, for every stagehand, every cameraman is drawing pay by the hour: an extra thirty minutes of rehearsal ordered by a pouting director could increase the show's costs by thousands of dollars.

There are a million mundane problems, and then there are some that are not so mundane. The producer may have to halt everything to explain to a guest comedian that he can't do a monologue on sports cars because the sponsor is Plymouth. He may have to console a blithering director who has just learned that the Hollywood sex kitten signed three months ago for a guest shot has arrived for duty twenty-two pounds over-weight.

The producer arises in the morning never knowing what problem he'll have to solve, but confident that there will be some problem by the time he reaches the office. (When Robert Alan Aurthur produced the story of Margaret Bourke-White's battle with Parkinson's disease, one of his problems was with Miss Bourke-White's doctor, who insisted that Marlon Brando play his role.)

At the Hollywood film factories the producer is able to draw on pools of scenery, pools of stagehands, pools of costumes, but his show is charged for all of them. Some of the charges seem ridiculous, like $35 for use of a kitchen stool any housewife can buy in a neighborhood hardware store for $8. But this is show business with its overpricing and also with its added-in overhead: no one paid the housewife to go buy that stool, but the studio has to hire people to purchase it, people to store it, people to cart it to the set and people to carry it back to the storeroom after the scene has been completed.

In the case of a variety show, the producer has a major problem of timing. From the booking agent he gets a list of guest stars. From the writers he gets a list of skits. From the singer he gets a list of songs. And from these he puts together a schedule, dubbing in the necessities—the commercials sent to him by the advertising agency, the opening and closing credits, and so on. This schedule lists, to the second, how much time each performer will have for each act.

The producer must also draw up a rehearsal schedule, taking care to have musicians on hand working when the musical numbers are to be rehearsed and not having musicians on hand loafing (but being paid) when they are not needed.

During the rehearsals the producer must watch to see that each act is staying within its prescribed time. Sometimes he must juggle and compromise. He is forever playing both boss and grievance-committee chairman at the same time.

The producer, because he is in charge of every detail and

every person on the show, keeps the longest hours. For a show that goes on the air at 8:00 P.M. Producer Deke Heyward starts work that day at 4:00 A.M., supervising the first construction of the set. He stays until the studio is emptied at 9:30 P.M. Once Marlo Lewis, producing the Ed Sullivan Show, was on the deck of a battleship in a broiling sun from dawn until 3:00 P.M. setting up that night's program. Sullivan finally asked him, "Why don't you go lie down a while?"

"A while?" protested Lewis. "If I lay down a while I'd never be able to get up."

In the case of a filmed series, the big job is getting it started. Once the first few episodes are shot, the producer can more or less work himself and his crew into a routine. But until then there's nothing but crisis.

William Self was hired by 20th Century-Fox to produce a half-hour weekly series called "Hong Kong." Self first assigned the project to a writer, Bob Buckner, and within a few weeks he got back an eleven-page memo outlining the general concept of the show and the story line for the pilot show, the one that would be used as the sample for the networks and advertising agencies.

Buckner, an ex-newspaperman, proposed to use a foreign correspondent as the central character in "Hong Kong." "And I want him to look like a newspaperman," the writer said. "Also, with a show like this we'll need a real actor, not just someone nice looking. The plots will be too involved to write around someone who can't act."

Self agreed, and together they began interviewing actor's agents. They decided on a young actor named Rod Taylor, and signed him. Selecting the remainder of the cast was easy, and at 8:30 A.M. on Tuesday, March 22nd, shooting began on the first episode.

At 9:00 A.M., a half-hour later, the phone rang in producer Self's office. It was Pete Levathes, the head of 20th Century-Fox TV. "I'm in Honolulu talking to Henry Kaiser," Levathes said. "I've just sold him 'Hong Kong' as an hour show."

"An hour show?" shrieked Self. "We're shooting the pilot now and it's a half-hour show—remember?"

"It's an hour show now," said Levathes, and hung up.

That was that. The production halted, and Buckner and Taylor went back to their script. Luckily, in this instance the original had been written too long. It was trimmed to fit it into the half-hour format. The trims were restored, a couple of extra scenes added, and within a few days "Hong Kong" was before the cameras as an hour show.

The few big producers who are remaining independent from the Hollywood factories—men like David Susskind, Hubbell Robinson, and Henry Jaffe—are apt to be the cream of the crop, but they are fighting a strong trend. Because they must turn out several shows at once to remain in business, they usually appear on your TV screen as "executive producer."

This can be a phony title. In the cases of Susskind, Robinson, and Jaffe it is not, but "sometimes," says Jaffe, "a producer will call himself the executive producer so he can have a man under him to blame for things that go wrong. If the show is no good he can replace the producer and then tell the ad agency or the network that he finally got rid of the bum who caused the trouble and that now the show will be great.

"But there is such a thing as a true executive producer. I'm our executive producer [Jaffe owns his own packaging company] in that I draw up a program schedule, I determine creative ideas, I engage the staff."

It's necessary to have an executive producer, Jaffe feels, to do the long-range creative thinking over the head of the show producer who is immersed in the day-to-day problems of each week's show. "Until a man is through with Show No. 1 he doesn't have time to think of Show No. 2," Jaffe says. "He doesn't see the forest for the trees. Or maybe he falls in love with an idea and begins to execute it without giving it sufficient thought."

Jaffe attends some production meetings of his shows and he does watch the progress of each show. But the individual producer actually bosses it. "While each producer is building the building, I am designing the whole real-estate development," he says. "I take a look every day to see that they are putting the ranch-type house where I want it and the gabled house where I want it."

One of the producer's main problems, Jaffe says, is casting. Once he decided to do Paul Bunyan, and sold the idea to Chevrolet. Then he began to cast. He decided that a burly folk singer would be perfect and, sure enough, the singer was available and eager. "He arrived with his wife, who announced that she would be co-producer," Jaffe says. "'She couldn't produce her way out of a peanut bag, so that was the end of him. I decided I'd get Charlton Heston. The writers said, 'He's no folk singer.' I had to explain to them that what we needed was an actor first and then a singer, not a singer first. They didn't understand that the part first of all had to be played. They were saying that the most important part of the yacht is the captain's uniform."

The executive producer works 'way ahead of the performance—sometimes eighteen months ahead. Nevertheless, changes are made right up until air time.

Jaffe thinks that a trend away from the individual producer is a trend away from quality. He cites the history of the movies, which became largely formula drivel when dominated by the mass-production studios but which took on true quality when independent producers inherited command with the advent of television.

"There is a delicate balance between the budget man and the creative man," he says. "You give it all to one side or the other and you go broke."

Although a producer must live with his show from the first idea until the last set is dismantled, the director has no duties until rehearsals begin. Then he becomes the most important man in a TV show. Television has often been called "the director's medium" because his work is so vital.

The director is a coach and he is a referee. He must coach the performers into playing their roles as life, and yet playing them within the logistics permitted by TV. He must referee between the writer, who thinks the actor is hired only to parrot his immortal words, and the actor, who thinks the script is just a series of suggestions awaiting his breath-taking interpretation.

The director is a delivery man. He must take this performance, which is pointless as long as it appears only on the studio stage, and deliver it to the home by way of the 17-inch screen. He must choose the camera shots to emphasize what must be emphasized, and he must pace his production so that it neither tires the viewer with frenzy nor bores him with sluggishness.

Writer Rod Serling said of the director: "He must know acting and actors, sets and designs, lighting and sounds, blocking and business, story and writer. And at that point where the legitimate play director quietly steals off into the darkness in the rear of the theater to entrust his work to the opening-night cast—this is when the TV director works the hardest in the most trying, frenetic, inhuman tension imaginable."

The TV director's job is greatest in the case of a live show. Then there is no room for mistakes, no allowance for retakes, no pause for pondering.

For a drama, the director begins by having his cast read the parts while sitting around a conference table. He lectures them on their roles, the emotions they must display, and then he leads them to the studio for a "blocking out." This is to show them where they will stand for each scene, how they will approach this spot (marked on the floor by chalk), and how they will leave it to reach the next spot. There are limitations as to how and when he can move his cameras. The actors must help. They must arrive at their stations on time.

As he does this, the director thinks out the camera angles he'll use—close-up, long shot, trick shot. Comes the day of dress rehearsal, some two weeks after that coffee klatsch around the conference table, and he gets to see these scenes as they'll be seen on the home screen. He sits in the control booth, a darkened room high above the studio, and watches two screens—one shows the scene that is on the air now, and the other shows the one that is going on the air next. Through this system he can make certain the second camera is ready before he orders the first turned off.

He gives his orders to the technical director, who, in turn, passes them on to the camera and sound and lighting crews. He tests lights and he checks scenery to see how it will show up on the home scene.

Then, eventually, all is in readiness for the on-the-air performance. He remains tense at his perch in the control room, ordering switches from camera to camera, following his script, praying that the scenes will be shifted on time and that the props will appear on time, and making split-second changes in camera shots when something does go wrong.

In the case of a variety show the director has less to do with the coaching of the actors, but more of a job in plotting his camera shots. The scenes change fast. And there is the tricky business of transferring musical numbers to the stage, following a dancer's routine, for example.

There is always a tendency on the part of the star to turn up with a "cast of thousands," to try to make up in quantity what may be lacking in quality. This was always the movie industry's answer. But in TV, even if the budget could stand it, the gimmick just won't work.

Director Bill Hobin says: "TV is an intimate medium. TV is intimacy and simplicity. It has to be, because of the smallness of the screen. That is why I aim for the uncluttered look, and intimacy. I can achieve these with a small cast and the use of camera close-ups."

Marlo Lewis explains the situation in more detail. "In the movies," he says, "there is a thing called an establishing shot. Wide vistas. Hillsides. Countrysides. Ghengis Khan's hordes. You wouldn't know what you were watching if you put this on the small screen. We deal in detail rather than in scope.

"In dances you've got to get depth, not width. We can pan about the set, and dolly the camera about, but it's still no vista."

In filmed shows, and to some extent in taped shows, the director is under less pressure. The mistakes can be corrected. For a filmed show each scene is shot apart, and then there's a break while everyone gets ready for the next scene. Tape is more like a live TV show, except that again there can be the pauses and the second tries when something goes wrong.

Nevertheless, most directors think they get their best performances from actors in the live shows. "It's the psychology," says one director. "As long as the actor knows the scene can be shot again, he's not on his toes, he is more lackadaisical, he is too full of what-the-hell attitudes. In live TV he knows it's now or never, and it's his reputation at stake."

Too, in filmed shows the director has trouble retaining the mood of the actors. Said one director, "The girl is about to be murdered, and she screams in terror. We cut and go gabbing to the commissary for lunch. We return and I say to her, 'Now, remember you were about to be murdered,' and we start the next scene. But how can she still be in the mood? We can get technical perfection in film shows but never acting brilliance."

MINK ON THE PICKET LINE

Just about everyone in network television, from the charwoman to the producer, belongs to a union. The result is a complicated maze of contracts and jurisdictional disputes that would cripple any other industry but seems to work out fairly satisfactorily in this one.

The networks have as many as 150 contracts with about 80 unions. They may have as many as 20 contracts with a single union, each dealing with a different situation.

Broadcasting magazine once ran a photograph of a scene being played for an NBC color spectacular. Over the picture was this caption, "How many unions are in this picture?"

The answer was 14. The cameras were maintained by one local. The stage manager was a member of the Directors Guild. The props were moved by the International Association of Theatrical and Stage Employees but constructed by the scenic designers union. The scenery also was made by the scenic designers, but the Teamsters carried it into the studio. The actors belonged to the American Federation of Television and Radio Artists. Their costumes were altered and fitted by the wardrobe attendants' union and their coiffures and make-up by the make-up union. The musicians belonged to their own union, of course. The script was written by a member of the Writers Guild. The wiring came under the jurisdiction of the electricians' union. The engineers in the control booth belonged to their union, the flip cards that tell the name of the show and the cast were done by members of the artists' local and, since it was so hot on the set, NBC employed members of the engineering union to operate air conditioning.

The pay scales are high: up to $246.10 minimum for scenic designers and well over $400 a week for the talent guilds. But this is a rich industry, and high minimum wages are not the headache. The big problem always is the maintenance of minimum crews and the scraps between the unions themselves over jurisdiction of borderline jobs.

The musicians, for example, insist upon a minimum quota whether you use the men or not. They say it's up to the network to find the work. Actually, the musicians themselves much prefer working to not working even though they get paid either way. They will not, however, do all musical work. For example, staff musicians won't provide background music for filmed commercials without extra pay even though the commercial may be made during their regular working day.

The stagehands insist that the studio maintain a basic crew on the five-day week. Often, because of the program schedule, the crew will be used only three days, and during odd hours at that. The men not only will get paid for the full five days, but will collect overtime for those odd hours.

The television unions have rigid job classifications and they do not permit crossing the line. Sometimes the network has to pay two men to do the job of one to satisfy both unions. For example, if a show needs a rear screen projection as background scenery, it must employ a technician to operate the projector but it must also retain a stagehand to stand by because this moving-picture background is classified as scenery. If a sound-effects record is to be played, a sound-effects man must be hired to play that record; it cannot be played by the engineer who would play all musical records on the show.

No one can touch a prop except a stagehand. No one can touch a piece of technical equipment except a member of the technicians' union. One New Year's Day Pat Boone planned a very informal program—he decided to put on a show using the cameras and other equipment as background. Immediately there was a furor. The stagehands maintained that since these cameras and microphones were to be seen by the audience, they were now props and must be moved only by stagehands. The technicians replied that this was their equipment off camera and so it remained their equipment on camera. Ultimately both won. In order to get the show on the air, the network had a stagehand *and* a technician push each piece of equipment seen on the screen.

Another network show called for a scenic artist to be painting a scene while the master of ceremonies talked in front of him. The American Federation of Television and Radio Artists said, "This man is now an actor; you'll have to pay him our scale." The scenic designers' union said, "Ridiculous, he has belonged to our union for years." The network asked the two unions to settle their own dispute, and the unions suggested that the man be paid both actor and designer fees for the same job. The network refused to go that far. Generally these disputes are compromised by paying the man the highest of the two or three fees to which he lays claim.

IATSE, the stagehands' union, frequently attempts to dictate to the networks how many men are needed on a show, and the demands smack of featherbedding. Yet this union is steeped in the tradition of "the show must go on," and its men will work like trojans through long hours without a bit of grumbling.

Sincere in these traditions, the television unions are much

more apt to settle their grievances off the set than many other unions; the slowdown is not a normal instrument of battle. However, there was one case where the Directors Guild and the technicians' union got into a jurisdictional dispute over whether cameramen could take orders directly from the director or whether these orders must be filtered through the technical director, who is a kind of crew boss.

To show how impractical it was to take orders only from the director, the cameramen at NBC suddenly lost their aim. During one show the audience suddenly found itself looking at a picture of the ceiling. During another the startled home viewer gaped at a row of midriffs instead of faces. At another time, in a similar dispute at NBC, the camera told to "pan left" kept whizzing around in complete circles; another camera told to "dolly in" kept going, going, going until it smashed right through the background scenery.

This was all deliberate, of course. The cameramen were merely demonstrating what kind of work the director could expect if he didn't co-operate with the union.

Because of the unusual nature of TV work, the contracts are especially long and complicated documents. The Writers Guild contract stipulates which rewrites can be required. AFTRA's contract covers such matters as extra pay for hazardous performances, insurance for actors who must fly to assignments, wardrobe hygiene, who must pay for the wigs (not the actor, of course), what kind of floor the dancers will use (always wood), and how many words constitute a line (more than ten). The Screen Actors Guild even gets around to airplane pilots: they get a minimum of $100 a day for flying or taxiing their plane for an airport scene.

And the stagehands have this clause:

"In the event that any soundman, electrician, propertyman, grip or shop craftsman is assigned work involving aerial flight, submarine diving or artificial air helmet diving, he shall be covered by a personal accident insurance policy, insuring against death and/or dismemberment in the amount of $20,000 and providing for weekly idemnity of $100 in the event of total disability, as such term is commonly understood in the insurance field, for a period of 52 weeks."

In the first days of television there was considerable confusion because no one knew which of the many competing unions would gain control of television. The principal duel was between the unions that had become established in radio and the old-line theatrical unions. Later the movie unions also joined the scramble.

Each wound up with a piece. The theatrical stagehands are in TV. The radio unions are in TV. And the motion-picture unions are becoming the most powerful of all.

Actors Equity, representative of the stage actors, first dabbled in television but found any union discipline difficult to maintain. An Equity official recalls that actors were so eager to get in on the ground floor of TV that they would work for any pay and under any conditions just to gain the experience. Many producers took advantage of this eagerness and chiseled every employee, stagehand, or actor as much as he could. Furthermore, the pressure to work "only for experience" continued even after TV grew into a position where it could afford decent wages.

The unions fought uphill, but they won. Today the minimums are high and are seldom if ever violated by secret deals.

It was the American Federation of Television and Radio Artists that first emerged with jurisdiction over the network performers, the announcers and sports broadcasters and newscasters as well as the actors and singers. But AFTRA's control was based on live television in the studio.

The moment the camera left the studio, someone else claimed jurisdiction. For example, when an NBC show invaded Radio City Music Hall to show a three-minute performance by the Rockettes, the American Guild of Variety Artists insisted upon negotiating for the chorus girls. It got them more than a week's pay for a three-minute appearance.

And when Ed Sullivan took his cameras into the Roxy

Theater to pick up the ice show, AGVA collected a week's salary for every person seen on stage.

Furthermore, AFTRA was barely established when TV began dabbling in filmed shows. These were made largely in Hollywood, and always with crews that belonged to the motion-picture unions. A series of jurisdictional disputes arose, and the Screen Actors Guild defeated AFTRA in 12 of 13 National Labor Relations Board elections.

The basic division now is the original division—AFTRA represents the performer on a live show and SAG on a filmed show. The actor must belong to both unions in order to work in TV.

To many in the industry the obvious solution was to merge these two unions into one big actors' guild. AFTRA seemed willing, but SAG, with the upper hand, maintained that despite the similarities of some problems it would be foolish to have the same union representing Clark Gable at M-G-M and an all-night disc jockey on a Manhattan, Kansas, radio station: they have nothing in common, SAG said.

Nevertheless, the pressure was so great that SAG and AFTRA agreed to hire an impartial arbiter, David L. Cole, to make a study of the situation. Cole issued a report strong for merger. He said:

"Over the years there has been an irrepressible and persistent demand by members that something be done to eliminate the requirement of multiple membership. Reasons for denying the memberships the merger must be good and valid reasons, and not reasons predicated on argumentation rather than fact. To do otherwise would be undemocratic."

Still SAG opposed the merger. It has now agreed to conduct joint negotiations alongside AFTRA as a sort of experimental step toward merger, but the organizations will remain separate for the time being at least. Meanwhile, a new problem looms. Television's technical advances are always 'way ahead of union thinking.

TV is headed for recording by tape. This is neither AFTRA's

live performance nor SAG's filmed performance. It's a little of both. To whom does it belong? It is likely that the in-between world of tape will produce a new joint union.

SAG's stubbornness is easily explained. Whereas once the union was concerned almost exclusively with actors whose movies were shown in theaters, today most of its members and half their income comes from television. In 1959 SAG members earned half their income from TV, $22,000,000 from shows, and another $11,000,000 from filmed commercials.

Too, salaries are just one concern of the talent guilds now. The magic word in any negotiation is "residuals," the pay for second and third runs of filmed and taped shows.

The actors, writers, and so on, have been collecting this extra money for some years. However, the scale upon which they will be paid is changing.

Under the old system they got 140 per cent of the union minimum for each re-run. The minimum for writers, for example, was $1,100 for a half-hour show and $2,000 for a full hour show. The minimum for actors ran about $285 a week.

The packagers maintained that this flat residual fee was unfair. They wanted a residual payment based, instead, on a percentage of what the re-run brought in. They won their point in 1960, but only after a Writers Guild 22-week strike that cost the industry some $5,000,000. Now the writers will continue to get that flat 140 per cent residual only until a royalty scale is worked out. They expect to wind up with something like 4 per cent of the gross price brought by each film's resale.

The writers also got a 10 per cent pay increase. The Screen Actors Guild has generally followed suit, hiking its salary minimums up to over $400 a week. It, too, maintains the 140 per cent residual but promises a study of the plan that probably will get the actors 8 per cent of the gross resale price.

The directors and producers will inherit the same type of deal.

But the Screen Actors Guild's interest in residuals does not stop at the filming of programs for TV now. It wants residual payments for actors who appear in those full-length movies which pop up on the Late, Late Show. It was this issue that caused another strike, a strike that halted work in the major Hollywood studios producing movies for theaters.

The argument was over films made since 1948 and not then released by the producers for TV. When they are released, SAG said, we want our people to be cut in on the money you make. The producers refused. The actors already have been paid for their work in these pictures, the producers said, and the pictures now belong to us. The man on the General Motors assembly line doesn't get repaid each time the car he made is resold on a used-car lot, the producers argued.

But SAG replied that its actors are not GM assembly-line workers. They are, in fact, placed in the position of competing against themselves in TV. They presented examples like this: Suppose Robert Taylor is appearing live on Channel 2 at the same time that an old Robert Taylor movie is being shown on Channel 4. Robert Taylor is in the position of competing against himself. If the Robert Taylor movie on Channel 4 takes viewers away from the live Robert Taylor on Channel 2, why should Robert Taylor not be paid for this draw?

The producers finally won. The actors traded a pension-fund contribution for their residual demands. However, new contracts with the motion-picture companies will call for residual payments to the actors when these films eventually are released to TV.

The TV industry generally operates as a closed shop. The biggest stars cart their mink coats and their Cadillacs to union meetings and strike headquarters with the same regularity as the teamsters. But there have been pinholes pierced in the armor.

The networks recently announced that they would hire directors who don't belong to the Directors Guild. This, the networks said, was not an attack on the guild as such, but a gesture of compassion. The initiation fee for the guild is $2,000, the result of a merger of the Screen Directors Guild and the

Radio & Television Directors Guild. The lower-paid directors, especially outside New York and Hollywood, cannot afford this high fee, which is based upon the lush salaries of Hollywood, the networks said.

The guild did not immediately fight this attitude on the part of the networks. The high initiation fee, a tradition of theatrical unions, is an embarrassment. However, the guild now faces the possibility that more and more directors will be hired from outside the union and that the whole authority of the union will thus be undermined.

Actually, television is strongly unionized only at the national level. The National Association of Broadcasters says that only 19 per cent of TV's total of 85,000 employees belong to the unions.

Too, the nature of the actor is such that the union must continually seek out those beginners who are so desperate for a chance in show business that they'll work for anything. The Screen Actors Guild has a special detective force that hunts out the surreptitious filming of nonunion movies and TV shows on the back roads of Hollywood. These fly-by-night productions pop up in garages, in vacant lots, behind a hill, anywhere they think they might escape detection.

The established producers, however, abide by the contracts they sign. In the making of TV shows time is money, and the producer avoids offending an actress to the point that she'll scoop up her maid, her hairdresser, her secretary, and her stand-in and march off to a meeting of the grievance committee.

PLEASING ALL OF THE PEOPLE
(SOME OF THE TIME)

In the heyday of radio every week was the same. The newspapers printed the program listings daily, but regular listeners never needed to consult them. Each show came on each week at the same time. When television arrived, the big question was whether to program it in the same fashion.

Frank Stanton, the president of CBS, was all for retaining the radio system. He said, "The public knows what's on, looks forward to it, plans around it, and makes a habit of the time period."

But NBC's Pat Weaver called this "robotry." Furthermore, he said, TV is too expensive for the sponsor and too exhausting for the actor and writer to permit an exclusive diet of daily and weekly shows in the old Amos 'n' Andy and Fred Allen radio tradition.

In the end both were right. TV has straddled the issue. It strives for weekly shows that will build up a viewers' habit, but at the same time it attempts to create new interest with a system of specials (or "spectaculars," as Weaver was delighted to call them).

TV has learned, for one thing, that its viewer is not so loyal as the radio listener. In the days of radio the set would be tuned to the same station for most if not all of the night; in TV there is much channel hopping as the viewer shops around not only between programs but even while programs are in progress.

But TV does build some loyalty, and the best bet in television buying is the series program. These are the most maligned by the critics; they are also the most profitable for the sponsor.

Despite the cry for more uplifting television programs, a Nielsen survey indicates that the audience still likes Westerns best and then action-adventure shows. As a result, the trend is not away from these programs but rather to making them longer—an hour instead of the traditional half-hour.

These are the shows that come from the Hollywood film factories. These are the shows that have replaced the old B movie as the opiate of the masses and, as a matter of fact, these are the shows that now employ the same writers, actors, and technicians who made those B pictures before TV emptied the theaters.

Hollywood is turning out Westerns for television to such an extent that there's actually a traffic jam of horses and stagecoaches. As many as three companies are on one location at the same time now, taking turns in the shooting so the wild whoops of an Indian attack in one film won't be heard during the hushed conspiracy of another. ("See that big rock over there?" says the producer of a Western. "It's been in every Western TV show in the past ten years.")

The cowboy shows and the adventure shows go heavily for violence. To criticism of this the TV people reply that it is the fault of the public taste. Under threat of censorship television will curtail the blood-and-thunder momentarily, but this must be a staple of the action shows over the long haul because it is what attracts the customers.

A poll of advertising men showed that 75 per cent think there is too much violence on TV, yet none presented any plan to curtail it. One thought it was not so much a matter of too much violence on a single program as it was the dovetailing of one such show after another, night after night.

These are the shows that predominate in TV because these are the safest shows to produce. The packagers say they have trouble enough getting acceptable scripts for programs on this level without having to round up twenty-six scripts a year for a show on a much higher level.

The basic virtue of the series is regularity—regularity of viewing, regularity of sponsorship, regularity of production. The series keeps generally the same cast (certainly the main characters) week after week, and the story line is basically the same. There is a special trick in TV of giving the leading characters distinctive mannerisms—"pieces of business," it's called—to make them especially memorable to the fickle and forgetful audience: Kookie's combing of his hair in "77 Sunset Strip" is an example.

"You can't find a story for a series," says Producer William Self. "You have to make it because you won't find in the *Saturday Evening Post* a short story with your characters in it." But the series story can contain more action than an ordinary play because the characters and locale need not be established. The viewer remembers who they are and where they are from last week's show.

Artistically the producers much prefer the anthology series—the series that has the same general theme but uses different stories and different characters each week. The stories can be better because they need not fit such a narrow mold, and the acting can be better because the cast can be selected with an eye only on this week's playlet. However, the audience doesn't form the attachment and familiarity with the anthology series that it does with the same familiar faces it sees each week in the straight series.

The networks agree that they are happiest with a highly rated situation-comedy program. If radio created an art form, this was it. Television has attempted to follow the lead, but too often the programs become tired and run out of both situations and comedy.

Yet a comedy series that clicks is such an asset that each year the networks are prepared to try out a few more. Situation comedy is gentle and can be anticipated. The viewer knows what's coming and he can feel superior when it comes. Too, these programs almost always are based on a family. This encourages a large viewing audience—the whole family will watch because the whole family will identify with the situation and, most important of all, will understand it. There is no greater dud than a comedy that goes over the heads of the audience.

The biggest bargain on TV—for the sponsor, not the viewer—was the quiz show. When these came into disrepute, the big shows disappeared and so did the name. But now, under the name "game shows," the quizzes are back, although not in such prominence. The audience-participation or panel show costs less than half of a filmed series to produce, yet its attraction can be as great. Quiz shows do better in the daytime because they are really little more than radio programs, and the housewife can follow them while performing her chores.

It is with the spectacular that TV breaks away from the radio mold. This was the brainchild of Pat Weaver. Actually, his first such show was on radio, back in 1933 when he was an advertising-agency man. He bought a full day of network radio to introduce Flying Red Horse gasoline.

When he came to TV he brought the idea with him. He wanted periodically to break the normal programing habit on NBC, pre-empting the time of regular shows to present something unusual, something special. He did so, and the other two networks adopted his policy.

The spectacular has a number of advantages. It will attract to TV those show-business greats who won't be committed to a regular show. It makes a place on TV for shows that just won't fit into a series—a ballet or a Broadway play or an original musical. It makes room, too, for news-in-depth programs that go far beyond the fifteen-minute news broadcasts of the regular telecasting day.

To the advertiser the spectacular has a special attraction because it provides him with a blockbuster to be used, for example, to introduce a new-model car. The spectacular can be cheaper, too. It costs Hallmark Greeting Cards less for a few top-quality shows a year than it would to sponsor a weekly half-hour series. The spectacular also permits seasonal advertising: a toy manufacturer can buy one big show during the Christmas season although he could never spend that sort of money every week throughout the entire season.

The network also gains from these specials. The spectacular can give it, for ninety minutes or an hour, a quality that could never be maintained regularly. The spectacular is the best hope of luring viewers away from another network once an opposition show has built a steady audience. And the spectaculars will get special publicity in newspapers and national magazines.

But if the theory of the special is glorious, the practice may be otherwise. Too often there has been nothing special about the specials. In the 1959 season there were three hundred of these shows, and most were flops. Too often the quality of the show was below, rather than above, that of the weekly shows. Why? This is where TV, for all its fractional ratings and sponsor sales charts, must face up to the unpredictability of show business. To hire a successful writer at a high fee does not guarantee a good script; the writer just may not click on this assignment. To hire an established star at a high fee does not guarantee that the star will succeed in this particular role.

The writers and directors, who ultimately are charged with the success or failure of the spectaculars, maintain that the casts are selected for box-office draw rather than because they belong in a particular show. "The result," said one writer, is "you get nineteen names that don't belong together. The rating will be high. Sure these people draw. But then the show will be lousy. Too often you wind up trying to make Helen Hayes dance on one show and Debbie Reynolds play Hamlet's mother on another just because the producers accepted these people for the box-office draw without any concern for the show we're producing."

Up to this point we've been discussing TV programing at night. In the daytime there are special problems—money problems, audience problems, attention problems. The television of daylight hours is not nearly so rich as nighttime TV. It has a limited list of sponsors—the soaps and the detergents are there, but the automobiles and cigarettes are not—because the audience is presumed to be mainly women and children. There is doubt, too, as to how much attention they are paying to the set even when it is on.

In TV's earliest days some network people thought there would be no daytime TV at all. They thought that the set would function as a radio until dusk, and then add its sight to sound. But the programing hours soon spread into the daytime, and stations now go on the air as early as six in the morning.

Within the trade television men concede that daytime TV is largely rubbish. Furthermore they see little hope for improvement. One NBC official said: "We made a real attempt to put on quality shows in the daytime. We tried 'Home,' and learned to our chagrin that the American housewife doesn't want to be improved—she doesn't want to be told how to cook better, how to dress better. We tried 'Matinee Theatre' and found that quality drama was just too expensive for the limited income that daytime TV has."

CBS has done better with the daylight. It is the home of the soap operas, and these, as on the radio, are a great draw on TV. But they are expensive to build. It takes one to two years to attract an audience. These audiences, once formed, are fiercely loyal, but there are no sponsors who now will pour money down the drain until the audience is large enough to pay off.

One of the embarrassments of daytime TV is its greatest success, "Queen for a Day." This is a program that commercializes human misery. Members of the audience are invited to tell their tales of woe, and the contestant who attracts the most sympathy gets a string of prizes.

This has been going on for seventeen years. There are no attempts to verify these pitiful tales, but the owner of the show, Jack Bailey, says that phonies "know they couldn't get away with it." The show does have some rules, however.

"No blind people and no cripples—no crutches," Bailey told an interviewer. "If you allow them on you might just as well throw away the other contestants. They would always win. So in fairness we don't pick them."

At times "Queen for a Day" was a little too strong even for NBC's stomach. It tested another show that also would present human misery as a form of entertainment, but on a somewhat higher plane. The show was to use domestic-relations cases— permitting real people to tell their marital woes to a real judge, a marriage counselor, and so on. The show was a flop. "Not low-down enough," explained an NBC executive.

Meanwhile "Queen" rolled on, moving from NBC to ABC but not spilling a tear in the transfer. This is in contrast to the usual ABC theory of featuring re-runs in the daytime.

The idea behind re-runs is, of course, that they are cheap and that there is a large audience that either missed them the first time or else would like to see them again. Nielsen checked 254 re-runs and found that the audience the second time was almost as large as the audience the first time. Furthermore, a study by Trendex showed that 72 per cent of a re-run's audience was unaware that the show was not an original one.

So the more successful night shows will be re-run to fill the daytime gaps and also to fill that time during the summer months when the networks presume a large part of their winter audience has gone to the beach. NBC paid Danny Thomas a whopping $7,000,000 for the films of his nighttime series so that it could be re-run in the daytime. The NBC plan was to show each of the 250 installments four times.

NBC got a bargain. This averaged about $7,000 a show, while the original Danny Thomas half-hours go for $56,000 each.

One tragedy of TV programing is that it will employ these re-runs to fill the summer months rather than use the time to experiment with original programing. It was during the summer that radio tried out its new ideas and its new stars, but TV is convinced that its audience shrivels too much to justify this expense.

A recent study by Nielsen of the summer versus winter audience backs up the networks. In the early evening hours, Nielsen said, the TV audience is 35 to 45 per cent less in the summer than in the winter. In the later evening hours the audience is 15 to 25 per cent smaller. The audience falls off less in the south and on the Pacific Coast because the weather in those areas is more consistent, and therefore the residents are less frantic about dashing to the beach before October's chill.

Nielsen also supported the networks and the advertisers in their choice of summer programs. Although the total number of viewers is smaller, a summer re-run will attract the same percentage of the surviving audience as a winter original. The people seem to stick with the shows they know. The few summer replacement shows, original shows designed to fill a hole left by a winter show that has temporarily left the air, attract far less viewers than the re-runs.

The few shows that remain all year, however, do best of all. Ed Sullivan attributes part of his success on TV to the fact that he continues to produce original shows all summer and thus does not have to reattract his following come September.

The summer re-run policy, in addition to filling the time with cheaper yet familiar shows, gives the packager the profit he was unable to get on his original sale. It also gives the network a gulf that separates last season's shows from the new ones.

The business of keeping a network schedule balanced and profitable is tricky. The programing vice presidents must always be prepared with a substitute when a new program flops. About one out of three new shows succeeds. When the other two fail, the programing department must move fast before the deserting audience slashes the ratings on the other programs the network is presenting that same night of the week.

Another factor in network programing is balance. The networks try to avoid an oversupply of any one type of program, first because it gets them in trouble with critics in government and out and, second, because it will oversaturate the audience. CBS released a summary of its programs and showed this balance: adventure 6 per cent, general drama 6 per cent, serials 21 per cent, situation comedies 11 per cent, variety 13 per cent, news 5 per cent, sports 7 per cent, western 6 per cent, talk 6 per cent, mystery 3 per cent, and the remainder miscellaneous.

The news and quiz programs are the cheapest. They run as little as $4,000 for the Douglas Edwards News show on CBS and $2,500 per 15-minute segments of many daytime quiz shows.

At the other end of the cost ladder are spectaculars, which run from $100,000 up. The record is $450,000 paid Leland Hayward to do the "Fabulous Fifties" special for General Electric in 1960. The Fred Astaire Specials, big successes, cost $290,000 each. Victor Borge costs an even $250,000.

The weekly shows generally cost about $50,000 for a half-hour and $90,000 for an hour. However, the Desilu Playhouse runs to $130,000, Ed Sullivan is budgeted at $100,000 a week, the Perry Como and Dinah Shore shows at $165,000, and the Bell Telephone Hour at $160,000.

These shows originally were live, as was all TV, but gradually film and tape have come to dominate the industry. Though this tends to give the shows a slicker technical appearance, it also deprives them of the sparkle that can only come from a live performance.

There's nothing new about film. It is the same process that has produced the movies for years. Magnetic tape is a TV-era invention, however.

The tape is about an inch wide, and records both picture and the sound through the regular TV cameras. Tape is much more expensive than film—a roll costs about six times as much. Tape also has two other disadvantages: because it is not a negative, duplicates are expensive to produce, and because the picture can't be seen on the tape itself it is very difficult to edit.

For this reason film is expected to predominate for some time. However, there is in the development stage a combination of film and tape: this is thermoplastic film that, like tape, can be played back immediately without chemical developing; but, like film, it can be edited by sight and can produce duplicate copies from the original negative.

The networks consider tape dangerous in the hands of an artist striving for perfection. Milton Berle ran $60,000 over his budget the first time he got a chance to use tape in a special; it was all in overtime as he kept reshooting scenes to make them better. He couldn't have done that on a live show. The networks try hard to curtail the practice of reshooting, but they don't have much success.

Film is more practical for this sort of work, yet the Hollywood technicians also must learn an entirely new pace when they switch from theater films to TV shows. A half-hour show is about one-fourth the length of a full-scale movie. Yet it can cost only one-tenth as much. The technicians had ninety days to shoot a movie but only three or four days to shoot a TV show. The sacrifice generally is in the technical quality of the picture: the lighting, the sound, the backgrounds are not nearly so good in the TV shows, but actually no outsider knows the difference.

Writer Bob Buckner, who works in both movies and TV, says: "I get a laugh now when I hear that a big studio is postponing the start of a movie because of cast or director problems. In TV we don't have that luxury. We just miscast when we have to. The show must go on—today. There's another one to shoot tomorrow."

The one type of show that simply won't adapt to film is the musical. Producer William Self blames Frank Sinatra's failure on the use of film. Sinatra insisted upon shooting the show with film and without a live audience, and the lack of spontaneity was too great, Self maintains. The show just didn't sparkle.

Therefore, the musicals will continue live or, upon occasion, on tape. Otherwise your television will come to you just like your pork and beans, right out of the can.

COMES A PAUSE IN THE DAY'S
OCCUPATION

The trouble with children's shows on television is that the advertisers don't want children's shows for children. They want children's shows for children *and* adults. They are convinced that it is commercially impractical to appeal only to children—and anything that is commercially impractical is not for TV.

Television even has difficulty defining a children's program. "Youth Wants To Know" is a discussion program featuring school-age youngsters, but the audience is definitely adult. On the other hand there are many blood-and-guts adventure stories that were designed for adults, yet appeal primarily to children.

But if a children's program is hard to define, can TV at least answer the question "What is a child?" At first television considered anyone under eighteen a child. It soon learned that a tot of four shares few interests with a boy of eight and that a boy of eight has little in common with a boy of fourteen. Now

157

it breaks down its programing into preschool age, school age, and teen age. But even here the spread is too wide. Is a teen-ager thirteen or nineteen? Millions of harassed parents are pre-pared to testify to the enormous difference between the two.

Frances Horwich, whose "Ding Dong School" is one of the more decorated children's programs on television, tried to de-fine the field for the Academy of Television Arts and Sciences. She said: "I'd say a children's program is one based on their interests, their needs *if* you know what children like. A chil-dren's program is not a hand-me-down re-run. It is not a family program. It is not one designed for such a wide age spread that it fits no one. This is the mistake of children's programs in the past. We didn't define them properly."

But Paul Tripp, another of TV's more appealing figures in his role of "Mr. I. Magination," replied: "I don't think the children make this distinction. As far as they are concerned, a children's program is any one they watch. Far too much of their time is taken up by programs that were not intended for children."

How do you design a program for children? The men at the networks who have worked long and sincerely over this pro-gram are forever baffled. One grand idea was to package a batch of old Shirley Temple films. The theory was that the chil-dren of today had never seen them and would love them. As it turned out, the program was a success but the theory was a flop. Children didn't especially go for the films but their nostalgic parents did.

It is this area of TV for children that most frustrates the individual network executive. These are educated men and they are honest men and, most important, they are almost all fathers. They will sit in their offices before an interviewer and sigh unconvincingly about the inevitability of pandering to the public taste on series programs, but they show genuine con-cern when the subject reaches the children.

Almost all of these network and advertising executives say that they limit their own children's television, both as to choice of programs and as to time spent before the set. They all think TV is technically and artistically capable of doing far better by the child. But they all say that the economics of the industry present an insurmountable barrier.

The advertisers, not villains but men who are putting money into TV only to sell products, are convinced that they must attract the parents as well as the children in order to make a sale. They take a dim view of a four-year-old's buying power. Therefore, with the exception of the few specialized products that can be sold directly to children, the sponsor's money usually goes into general programing—family-type situation comedies and the like—and is not available to pay the tab for quality children's programs.

Tom Moore, the programing director of ABC, says: "We're depending upon an action strip to get both the children and the adults. Children's shows as an economic force on TV are less than successful. The reason is that the child controls the knobs far out of proportion to his economic weight in the market place. Their shows get the ratings, but you can't sell over their shoulders. It's fine for Tootsie Roll and Bosco, which sells directly to the children—for productions in which the children have a definite say about purchasing. But children's shows can't sell soaps, detergents, and all those other things that are the backbone of television advertising."

There is no doubt, as Moore says, that the children's audience is there. Studies show youngsters watching the set for as much as three or four hours a day. (One survey turned up a tot in the midwest who views TV thirteen hours every day!)

Florence Brumbaugh asked 400 children between the ages of 6 and 12 to list as many advertised products as they could in 15 minutes. The youngest averaged about 20 items each; the 11-year-olds could list 50. Included were 15 brands of beer and 13 brands of cigarettes, not to mention various drugs and cosmetics. One detergent was mentioned 110 times. Almost all of the brand names were spelled correctly, an achievement that would no doubt startle the teachers of these children.

Almost daily the theory is advanced that the displays of violence on television programs encourage and even instruct children on a road to juvenile delinquency. J. Edgar Hoover has warned frequently of this, although he has also pointed out that movies and TV programs can be preventive weapons against crime, too.

The TV set comes in for so much blame that no one was particularly surprised when a university honor student in Iowa told police he got an "urge to kill" a mother and her daughter while he was watching Nikita Khrushchev on television, leading an NBC lawyer to comment wearily, "Chalk up two more for TV."

Actually, these theories that TV violence furthers real-life violence are theories, and nothing more. Professor Ithiel de Sola Poole of the Massachusetts Institute of Technology told an FCC hearing that seeing violence on television might actually be good for children. "Seeing violence acted out in dramatic form which they understand may purge children of similar feelings," he said.

Boston University's study of TV for children approached the same conclusion. Certainly, the report said, the child always has inclinations toward violence, and naturally he would enjoy seeing it on television, not only on Western and detective programs but also in other forms.

"Violence plays a large part in the formula for successful drama and the puppet show," the study said. "The humorous violence of the slapstick comedy can offset the child's awareness of his inadequacy by making others appear even more inadequate or absurd. His anger and dislike for the adult-imposed regulations, which he does not express directly, find expression in the cartoon comics and in the exaggerated violence of the puppet show. The obviousness and simplicity of the plot appeal to him."

The Boston study decided that television has had little effect on eyesight and health, achievement in school, and reading of library books. It has, on the other hand, considerable effect on keeping children off the street, on reducing their sleep, and on reducing their contact with other children. There is still no conclusive evidence of its effects on character development, moral behavior, fears and aggression and behavior patterns.

Except for the fact that schoolteachers sometimes must deal with sleepier children, most teachers say that the bright children remain bright and the dull ones remain dull in the age of TV. Those children who are interested by reading continue to read and those who would not read much anyway are more occupied by TV. All children who watch TV benefit through increased vocabularies and an awareness of a world outside their school and home.

Yet children's TV is constantly under attack. A nonprofit organization called the National Association for Better Radio and TV lists as many as ninety-five regular programs as "unacceptable for children."

However, those television executives who must answer for the fare they give our children generally are apt to be discouraged when they confer with Parent-Teachers Association groups and the like on complaints such as this. They find they listen to a cascade of clichés and little more. Stockton Helffrich, of the National Association of Broadcasters, who addresses many of these meetings because he is genuinely interested in them, said, "I arrive and they're sitting there grim-faced, just waiting to make trouble. 'That Monster in the Living Room' is the title they usually give me to speak on. And if I ask them about the few good children's programs on television they look blank. They've never heard of them."

Paul Tripp said he was interrupted at one such meeting by a lady who asked indignantly if he thought it was proper for a nine-year-old boy to be subjected to a TV scene in which a man hanged himself by his own necktie. Tripp asked the lady what time the program had been shown.

"Last night at ten-thirty," she said.

"Madam, what was your child doing out of bed at that hour?" he asked.

Sometimes the TV executives are as startled by praise as they are by complaint. Many scoff at the fact that these PTA-type organizations frequently list "Lassie" as one of the better programs for children. "Good Lord, have they ever seen it?" was Sonny Fox's question at a television academy discussion of children's TV. The principals of this show are forever being mired in quicksand or trapped in burning barns while awaiting Lassie's rescue, situations that could be very frightening to the small child.

A Columbia University psychiatrist blames, not the television networks, but the parents for any displeasure with what the child views. "These parents just won't take the time and effort to supervise their own children," he says. "They want the networks to do it for them. Do they want the book publishers to print only books suitable for eight-year-olds and do they want the newspapers to tailor the news for eight-year-olds? No, but they want to park the kids in front of the set where they'll stay quiet and then expect some announcer to step out and rear the youngsters properly."

But if the men in TV seem often to hide behind the fact that every set has an "off" knob, they have produced more improvement in children's programing than in any other department over the years.

The first big children's hit on television was Walt Disney. In 1954 he practically created the ABC network with his Davey Crockett craze. The measure of his success can be found in the fact that Crockett items grossed more than $30,000,000 in a year (and the cost of coontails rose from 25 cents a pound to $5 a pound).

But for a long time thereafter the staple of children's programs was the ancient animated cartoon, many of them made even before the talkies, and the creaky "Our Gang" comedies, which contained some frightful racial caricatures that would never be included in a present-day production. Cartoons remain important today. Almost every city has its local "Bozo the Clown" and similar masters of ceremonies who cavort with varying degrees of exaggerated good humor between films.

The new cartoons, made especially for TV, are witty and far more sophisticated than the old ones. Here the child is benefiting from that sponsor demand: many a parent shares with his child the satire of "Huckleberry Hound" and "Quick Draw McGraw."

These are extremely expensive to make. In animation there must be 16 individual drawings for each second of action. One cartoon will contain some 2,500 drawings. The children's market is much smaller than the adult market, yet the children's programs cost as much or more to produce.

On the other hand, the children's market is alway replenished. As fast as one generation outgrows Popeye, there is a new one sitting before the set to replace it. The makers of these expensive cartoons are much more likely to get their money back than the packager of a Western or an adventure program.

The programs generally considered the best for children include CBS's "Captain Kangaroo," NBC's "Hi, Mom!" and Miss Horwich's syndicated "Ding Dong School." These best programs have had the worst time trying to remain on the air because they don't attract sponsors. (Even when they do get sponsors they may rebel. Miss Horwich was aghast, she said, when she learned that "Ding Dong School" had attracted a gun manufacturer as a client; she was almost as shocked when a brassiere manufacturer bought time on the show.)

George Heinemann, one of the creators of "Hi, Mom!" at NBC, told its history. He said the network knew it had to develop something that would attract the mother and child at the same time. They recruited Shari Lewis as the mistress of ceremonies and began training her in vocabulary and facial expressions that would hold the child yet not drive away the mother.

"Next we had to get a name for the show," Heinemann said. "We picked, 'Hi, Mom!' In a way it's revolting, but it was something a little child could say: 'I want to see the "Hi, Mom show." ' "

Next Heinemann attacked the NBC Sales Department. "We told them we were getting an audience of 60 per cent children and 40 per cent adults."

Slowly the customers dipped their toes into the water. "Hi, Mom!" still does not draw the ratings that rival network shows draw, nor does it attract the audience that NBC could get with something more mundane in that time slot. But because the network wants at least one good children's show in the morning, it maintains this one.

At the same time, however, NBC cut loose "Ding Dong School," although it had many awards. In this show Mrs. Horwich, who has a Ph.D. in child development and education, conducts a kindergarten of the air, giving the tot something to do as well as something to see. NBC dropped it because of low ratings. It was subsequently sold to more than eighty stations independently, and now thrives in this manner.

Yet if a few good shows do appear on the air, the fact remains that much more could be done. Sonny Fox asked: "Where is a news show for children? Why not a children's Play of the Week? Why only four Leonard Bernstein shows a year? Why aren't there variety shows for children? Science programs?"

Walt Disney tried something of this sort with his "Mickey Mouse Club." As an hour-a-day program on ABC, it contained travelogues, adventure stories, news background, and variety especially tailored for children. The kids loved it enough to make the theme song something of a national anthem, junior grade; but because it couldn't attract commercial sponsors it was cut to a half-hour, then fifteen minutes, and finally, over Disney's bitter protests, dropped by ABC altogether.

One of the problems is that no one will sponsor a variety show for children as long as the children are already watching an adult variety show. And the surveys all indicate that until nine o'clock at night children are watching everything their parents watch. As a matter of fact, there is considerable indication that the children pick the programs their parents watch.

This was even an issue with the start of the daily Dick Clark program. It would seem obvious today that anyone who wanted to sell anything to teenagers would utilize a TV program that features popular music and teen dancing. Yet ABC had difficulty selling sponsors on the Clark show even after the rating services showed that the program attracted a huge audience. The sponsors had to be shown that adults watched this show, too.

Today there are two or three of this kind of program in every major city in the nation. Teenagers gather in basements to dance to the music. "It has even done something for their social status," says Mrs. Horwich. It has also done something for the sale of chewing gum, phonograph records, potato chips, and similar products which have a mammoth teenage market.

The next question, after the Clark success, was whether a higher type of show might not appeal to teenagers and still sell them merchandise. There was one definite attempt with a program called "Spotlight on Youth." This show equaled the Clark rating at least three times—with shows on teenage marriage, teenage dating, and a discussion of a "teenage bill of rights." Beyond that, however, it could not dent the huge edge Clark maintained in that duel of the ratings.

Some TV men say that if a "Spotlight on Youth" can equal Clark's audience three times, it has only itself to blame if it cannot do so more often. "Showmanship—that's what they lack," says one TV executive. "If the people who dream up these so-called uplift programs could inject into them the showmanship it takes to make them a success, we'd gladly buy them."

There are some sponsors waiting for good children's television shows, even those shows that don't attract adult audiences. These people, however, make highly specialized products. For all the quality of his program, "Captain Kangaroo" need never expect sponsorship from a thinking man's cigarette, but he certainly is the answer to "Colorform's" prayers. Here is a product, a paste-on toy, which must be sold to and for pre-school-aged children. What magazine should contain such an ad? What newspaper? None, of course, because the child can't read, but "Captain Kangaroo" is the perfect advertising medium for "Colorform."

Where children's TV programs do succeed for advertisers, they succeed with glory. Television, for one thing, has made brand-name buyers of children. What boy of fifteen years ago had the slightest idea who manufactured his cap pistol? Today he knows it's made "swell" by Mattel. What girl of ten years ago questioned the origin of her new doll? Today it's got to be Remco or take it back, Daddy.

Through the use of television advertising, Mattel, which is a firm launched in a garage workshop twenty years ago, pushed its sales from $4,000,000 in 1954 to $22,000,000 in 1960. Remco entered television in 1955, and by 1958, despite a major plant expansion, it was unable to fill 40 per cent of the orders received. Maypo even conquered the child's traditional opposition to his oatmeal through the use of TV commercials that insisted humorously that "cowboys like Maypo."

Television actually has revolutionized the toy business. Everything once was geared to Christmas, and the year tailed off into incidental sales after that. Today the toys are advertised all year round and consequently they are sold all year round.

Children's programs, furthermore, belong to the local stations, the one area where syndication still outstrips the networks, and will continue to do so for some time, if not forever.

Although the same cartoons are visible in the hours about dusk from coast to coast, there's always a local master of ceremonies and usually a local studio audience operating out of the local station. This permits local advertisers to cut in on a field that presents lush rewards to the limited products that can be sold to this audience.

Another factor is that this is the one time of the day when the networks still have not pushed out local programing with an increase in option time. It is a time of day when Mother is fixing dinner, Father isn't home yet, and Big Brother is playing baseball. Only Junior is left.

As they get past the cartoon-show age, children tend to leave the television sets during the earlier hours. They don't return in full force until they are married. The smallest percentage of TV viewers in America is the college students, and the next smallest is the high-school student.

But before reaching high school the youngsters are reared by TV. It is the most familiar baby sitter they know. As far as they are concerned, the "pause in the day's occupation" is brought to them by courtesy of Crunchies.

THE INTELLECTUAL GHETTO

The Metropolitan Opera House has a maximum seating capacity of 3,390 for a single performance. But what if this opera was presented on television? The audience might be 4,000,000. Wouldn't that be wonderful?

"It would be awful," gasps an advertising-agency man. "Only 4,000,000? The sponsor would blow a gasket. We'd lose the account."

Such is television's numbers game. The audiences run 20,-000,000 and up for the important shows, and anything as paltry as 4,000,000 signals a devastating flop.

When the developers of TV were tinkering in their laboratories, they had visions of the medium bringing opera, concerts, and lectures into the home. They had the foresight to produce the cathode tube but not the foresight to predict "Queen for a Day."

Yet partly because of a tiny conscience, but mostly because

of the gnawing fear of government intervention, the networks do cater to the minority that wants something more serious on TV. They do so on Sunday when, they presume, most of America is out driving or playing golf anyway. This bracket of discussion, serious musical and experimental drama programs is known to the trade as "the intellectual ghetto."

The networks seriously reconsidered this restrictive policy in the wake of the quiz-show scandals. Ironically, they were forced to these second thoughts only after the first salable intellectual they had ever produced, Charles Van Doren, turned out to be a fake. They did increase their public-service programing somewhat as a gesture of good faith, but this timorous meandering from the beaten path only convinced them that they had chosen the right road in the first place. Egghead programs don't sell.

It is all very well for CBS to conduct English literature and art lectures at 6:30 A.M., or for NBC to throw in an occasional news-in-depth program that will set the critics singing. But this cannot be a regular thing as long as "cost-per-thousand" remains the motto on television's coat of arms.

There have been rebels in TV's ranks. Pat Weaver, in one of those all-hands-on-deck memos he wrote while president of NBC, said: "NBC-TV, as a communications and information medium reaching nearly all of the television homes consistently, will make the average man interested in current events, will give him orientation and education to place current events in perspective. It will make him acquainted with his leadership in all fields, and their actions allegedly in his behalf. It will hold his attention while the basic issues of our times are analyzed and related to his own future, so that he may understand the alternatives clearly. In the entertainment pattern that attracts his viewing most of the time, he will find exposure to informational as well as cultural experiences which should make his leisure time gradually veer toward the more rewarding activities."

That statement could have been a bill of rights for a higher level of TV, but actually it did little more than produce snickers among the more realistic members of the staff. They knew that television doesn't work this way.

The classic battle for a more uplifting TV was fought in New York over "The Play of the Week."

This was not a network show, but rather a superattraction planned in desperation by Station WNTA. WNTA had no network affiliation, and for years it floundered trying to buck the network stations with a dreary run of old Western movies and syndicated rejects. This policy produced nothing but red ink, so WNTA pulled a complete switch. It decided for purely commercial reasons to cater to that articulate minority that was forever bemoaning the infantile network diet.

"The Play of the Week" was the big test. Top actors were lured from the legitimate stage for union-scale wages on the promise of daring and meaty roles never before available on TV. Top plays were promised. Subjects that were too adult, too offbeat, too intellectual for network television were to become standard fare on this program.

"The Play of the Week" attracted surprising attention. Partly because of their personal hunger for fare of this quality, the newspaper critics gave special kudos and considerable space to the program. Furthermore, an estimated 1,000,000 homes a week were tuning in. WABC, the American Broadcasting Company's New York outlet and hence a direct competitor of WNTA, became alarmed and sought to quiet any restiveness on Madison Avenue. It distributed this written report:

"It is now more than two months since WNTA premiered 'Play of the Week.' During this two-month interval the Channel 13 dramatic entry has shown a basic inability to achieve anything approaching creditable audience dimensions, from the standpoint of the usual media yardsticks.

"There may be other plusses attached to sponsorship or of participation within 'Play of the Week.' It is obvious from the following table, however, that these 'plusses' must outweigh what currently shapes up as one of the poorest media and/or cost efficiency values in the New York television market."

The report next listed the New York ratings, and there, for the advertising-agency man, was the moment of truth. Sure, all the fellows on the 5:27 to Westport were talking about the grand shows on 'Play of the Week.' But look at the cost-per-thousand. It would cost the advertiser from $3.50 to $5 to reach each 1,000 homes when buying a $3,500 chunk of "Play of the Week." But "Million Dollar Movie" would cost only $2 per thousand homes and "Highway Patrol" only $1.20.

So "Play of the Week" began to die, despite the cheers of the critics and the grateful applause of a fiercely loyal audience.

Jack Gould, the TV critic of the *New York Times*, began publicizing what he clearly thought was an outrage. And something happened. More than 20,000 persons wrote to WNTA pledging support to this unusual program. The Standard Oil Company announced it would sponsor "Play of the Week" *in toto* and furthermore that it would design special commercials that would not offend the presumably more sensitive ears of "Play of the Week's" select audience. A number of stations around the nation, reading of the furor in the trade press, asked for syndication of the show. "The Play of the Week" survived.

It would be nice to conclude with the revelation that this incident marked the dawn of the new era and that the soap companies began competing with Standard Oil for the rights to fine drama. But that, alas, is not true. The cost-per-thousand on "Play of the Week" remained deterrent and, furthermore, the *avant-garde* spirit did not prevent the program from frequently falling below the quality of many commercial network shows.

By restricting itself to several performances a year, for example, the Hallmark Theatre maintains a consistent quality on NBC above that of the "Play of the Week." Furthermore, Hallmark's audience never dipped below 14,000,000 and once it reached 21,000,000 for five presentations of Shakespeare.

This would indicate that the problem is not the intellectual content of the programs but rather the showmanship involved. If Hallmark can make the grade with Shakespeare even by the harsh cost-per-thousand measurement, does the "Play of the Week" or any similar venture deserve special exemption from Madison Avenue's rule?

The TV networks for years thought they could get away with a gesture of intellectual content by a brace of Sunday programs which comprised the "Intellectual Ghetto." There are all kinds of professors talking to other professors on panel shows all Sunday afternoon, and there are politicians to be interviewed as long as the interviewers can dredge up a question. But with a few notable exceptions, these programs became great bores as soon as the novelty wore off. By and large professors belong in classrooms or in books. They are not a monumental contribution to show business. On TV they talk half an hour to say what they can (and do) say much better in four pages of a well-written, well-edited book.

TV needs showmanship, whether at 8:00 P.M. when Ed Sullivan is on or at 8:00 A.M. when half the Columbia University faculty is on. Showmanship costs money to hire, and it requires more money for the sets and scripts that are its instruments of production. The networks are not prepared to supply this money. They are prepared to supply only the Sunday time, and this only as long as no paying customer wants it.

Leonard Goldenson, the chairman of the board of the American Broadcasting Company, maintains that there is no justification for demanding large amounts of highbrow programing on TV. "That type of person wouldn't spend much time watching television no matter what was on," he said. He feels that the existing networks should give some attention to an intellectual minority, just as it would to any minority, but that they must always remember, "We are a mass medium—we were created to be a mass medium and that is what we must remain."

When NBC called a conference of advertising men to determine how much support it could expect for increased public-service programing, the response was hardly heartening. Newman McEvoy, senior vice president of the Cunningham and Walsh agency, said, for example, "As a result of minority pressure we're going to get some minority viewing. Now, if that's in the best interest of the viewing community I'm dead wrong." He continued:

"I think it is rather unrealistic to suggest that a station can maintain a competitive position in the minds of agencies and devote a really significant percentage of its total programing time, particularly in the prime hours, to editorial material. WQXR [New York's good-music radio station] does a superb job and, in the halls of Washington, it is undoubtedly regarded as the ideal in broadcasting. But it is unrealistic to think a format of that sort should be foisted on a television station. Up and down Madison Avenue its image would deteriorate quickly—except for those advertisers intending to reach a limited sector of the market."

The advertising men agreed that the station or the network might gain prestige from better programing, even if the program cannot attract sponsors. Here they reveal the one ray of hope. Must the networks and stations make a profit on every moment of time at their disposal? Don't newspapers use up space that could otherwise be sold so that they can present the news? Don't these newspapers pay the reporters and columnists and editors out of their operating expense? Wouldn't you consider it outrageous if your local newspaper announced that it would not cover the state legislature this session because it had lost its sponsor? Or because a survey showed that the legislature stories received only 3.1 percentage of readership while Dick Tracy was getting 42.7?

This is the way TV works now, with, of course, some exceptions. The sustaining program, the program financed by the station or network in the absence of a sponsor, is rare. Judging from their multimillion dollar profits, the networks certainly could afford to put on some high-quality programs even if the audiences were smaller. Yet it is both human nature and corporate nature to avoid this extra expenditure. America's decision must be whether to legislate itself into this kind of programing. There are undoubtedly two sides to the question. On one hand, these are private corporations. On the other, they are using the public's wave lengths.

The Federal Communications Commission made provision for higher-quality programing when it first allocated channels. It reserved space on the dial for the sole use of educational stations, and today there are fifty such stations in operation. They have, furthermore, something of their own network: It is not hooked together for simultaneous broadcasting, but it does serve as a national distributor for programs. The network gets 60 per cent of its programs from its member stations, many of them run by universities, on a swap basis. It also produces some original programs and it buys certain shows from both the American and foreign networks.

The National Educational Television and Radio Center, as it is called, has given its stations such programs as four two-hour dramas acquired from the BBC, nine studies in depth on the segregation problem, seven concerts of the Boston Symphony Orchestra, and some extremely good experimental programs for children.

The educational network and its stations, however, must face up to the economic facts of life in their industry. They compete with commercial TV both for ideas and for personnel. Furthermore, as one station manager conceded: "Commercial TV certainly doesn't have a monopoly on dull TV. Our problem usually is showmanship."

One of the more interesting state experiments with educational television is conducted by the New York Board of Regents. The board made a deal with a commercial station, WPIX in New York City, to carry its classroom educational programs during the dull day hours.

James McAndrew, the director of the project, says the result is encouraging. The program consists of 65 shows a week, 43 of them live instruction. "It's austerity TV," McAndrew says. "We have no fancy props or scenery. But we found immediate acceptance at the start." The audience was composed of house-wives and night workers who wanted to learn French, Spanish, or mathematics. In addition, it was piped into 20,000 school children a week.

Yet McAndrew is not wholly satisfied with what he can do on such a limited budget. "Our problem really is what we're not doing," he says. "We talk about a Shakespeare play rather than doing a Shakespeare play. We talk about science rather than demonstrating science. I fear we have quantity instead of quality."

Furthermore, educational TV is subject to the same audience pressures that plague commercial TV. One Queens housewife wrote demanding that the Columbia professors be replaced by New York University professors.

The men in educational TV are not sure exactly what they want to do. They don't know whether to concentrate on high-quality programs for a general viewing audience, classroom-type instruction for the run-of-the-mill viewer who wants to learn something, adult education for credit, or supplementary instruction designed to be watched right in the schoolroom.

There's something to be said for each, of course. The Ford Foundation used part of its educational TV fund to launch "Omnibus" on a commercial TV network, and the program proved a success. Not only was the show good for general consumption, but eventually it was also able to finance itself through sponsorship.

Regular classroom instruction on TV whether for credit or not, could educate more persons in a month than all of the night schools in the nation could educate in a year. This instruction, furthermore, need not be confined to the three R's. Political science taught in the light of the day's news, art appreciation, musical appreciation, and languages, for example, could open a new world to many a routine-benumbed house-wife.

But in a time of increased enrollment and decreased teacher

supply, perhaps the greatest possibilities for educational TV are in the field of direct classroom instruction.

The gain here would be in quality. Many a classroom is presided over today by a teacher who knows little more of complex subjects and languages than do his students. TV could whisk into these same classrooms the finest professors from Harvard and Columbia. It could also bring into the classroom— into thousands of classrooms at the same time—practicing physicists and research chemists who might bring new inspiration as well as new understanding to students drugged by the drone of third-rate teachers.

Less than 600 of the nation's 45,000 school districts are engaged in any such direct classroom TV now. And of those that have tried it, some could not conquer the human element: students who were restive and inattentive before the screen and teachers who didn't co-operate because they resented the intrusion.

Yet it is a great vista—not without dangers, to be sure, for Dr. John Fischer of Columbia Teachers College warns of "mass production"—and one that would require far less money or industrial revolution than a law forcing the American Broadcasting Company to teach Chaucer once a week.

THE FIFTH ESTATE

There are some basic truths about television news coverage that can be stated quite simply. In presenting an adequate summary af all the day's important news, TV is bad. But in covering those particular events that especially lend themselves to the medium, TV is magnificent.

News is the one major commodity in television that does not belong exclusively to the networks. Throughout the nation there are stations that never attempt to produce local entertainment shows yet do a splendid job of covering the local news. On the other hand, the network news directors who plead for higher budgets are always reminded by the boss that they represent the tail, not the dog, and that television is primarily an entertainment medium. The news shows, like the movies' newsreels, are just an extra added attraction.

One reason for such good local news coverage is adequate sponsorship. The news broadcast is the most enticing buy offered to local advertisers. News is interesting. News is cheap. You don't have to pay the actors; you don't have to write scripts for them; and you don't have to build sets for them. People murder other people of their own volition on their own time in their own homes.

A local newscast can be anything from the bargain-basement format of one announcer reading wire-service dispatches to the ambitious round-the-world operations run by stations such as KWTV of Oklahoma City. Most stations choose a middle ground, depending upon the news services for world news but maintaining reporters and photographers for local news.

The man you see reading the news on television seldom knows any more about it than you do. His dispatches are written, edited, and selected by the behind-the-scenes news department, and his pictures were taken by the station photographer.

TV's news problem is the lack of adequate time. Except for special cases, television news shows run fifteen minutes. With time out for commercials, this is actually about twelve minutes. It is impossible, in this complex age, to tell the news of the day in twelve minutes.

As usual, TV has a stock answer to complaints about this: The audience won't sit still for any more news. And, as usual, it goes to the rating services as proof of this contention. When President Eisenhower went on television to report to the nation on the 1960 summit conference collapse, his share of the audience was far smaller than that of "Wagon Train." The top-rated network news shows attract an audience of little better than 7,000,000 a night.

When NBC launched the morning "Today" show, it was to be a gigantic, continuous news broadcast. This flopped. When "Today" switched its emphasis to a performing chimpanzee, entertainment, and lighthearted chitchat, it became a success.

And so TV will not break loose from its basic format of trying to tell all of the day's news in about twelve minutes.

In the early days of television the news broadcasts were further handicapped by an overemphasis of pictures. The TV newsmen were recruits from radio, and they were fascinated by the new dimension of sight. They preferred to show water skiers at Cypress Gardens to an announcer reading a dispatch from the Supreme Court. Eventually, however, they matured, and today almost all news editors are guided by the importance of the event rather than the availability of pictures.

Nevertheless, it is the film that can make TV news thrilling. William B. Monroe, who has worked for a newspaper, a news service, and now is news director of WDSU-TV in New Orleans, says: "Film can, and frequently does, tell a story in a way that is beyond the powers of a printed report. We have a film clip of a wild clash in the Louisiana Legislature between Governor Earl Long and Secretary of State Wade Martin—the finger-shakings, the attempts to outshout each other, the tones of voice, the attitudes of those nearby just couldn't be described in print the way it's presented in this two-minute piece of film. When people see this film they shake their heads, they make violent exclamations, they laugh. Even a skillful writer couldn't have put the scene across with such impact. The exotic-yet-seedy look of Arabian capitals, the flavor of a Presidential press conference, the grief of the mother of a school fire victim come across eloquently on film."

Yet for all this obvious advantage of news film for TV, there is a disadvantage. Monroe says: "The newspaper's advantages are the details of its stories and their permanence. Broadcast news doesn't stick with people like news they read themselves and reread if they want. People sometimes phone us about a news story they're interested in, and ask, 'What was that you said about so-and-so?'"

There is a constant war between the newspaper reporters and the TV reporters in the coverage of the news. Unfortunately, this comes out not as a race for scoops but as a dual of industrial jealousies. Reporters object to the presence of TV cameras in their press conference. They claim this makes them captive actors for the TV stations and that TV persists in filming these press conferences only because its own reporters don't have the experience and background to ask proper questions of their own. Los Angeles newspaper reporters boycott press conferences that permit TV cameras. Hank Osborne, the city editor of the *Los Angeles Mirror-News,* justifies the stand this way: "Newspapers send to press conferences the experts they developed—religion editors, education news, political writers. The TV stations don't have these experts, and so they seek to cash in on ours by filming our questions and the subject's answers."

On the other hand, many a press conference being filmed for television has been ruined by newspaper reporters who hog the floor in an uncharacteristic hamminess that can only be explained by the presence of the camera.

It is true that no TV operation, local or network, covers the news as thoroughly as a comparable newspaper. Even in New York, home of the networks as well as seven local stations, there are no full-time TV reporters covering police headquarters, city hall, or any other primary news source covered by newspapers around the clock.

Yet when the time comes for TV to shine, during a Khrushchev visit or a political convention or a Nixon-Khrushchev debate, the newspaper city desks are dutifully tuned in to the local TV station even though staff reporters are on the scene. There is no beating the speed or the experience of watching these events actually happen on TV.

Television coverage is at its best when the entire event takes place before the camera—Khrushchev's post-summit Paris press conference, for example, where the tone of voice, the grimaces, the fist banging are all there for the viewer to behold. Television coverage is at its worst when the news is complicated—the complex of committees and backroom deals of a state legislature or Congress, for example, where the off-the-record confidences and the fifteen or twenty sources the newspaper reporter will interview in a day can never be equaled by the three minutes a TV newscast devotes to the subject.

Television is excellent with its news-in-depth programs—the

one-hour studies of a single question that are the antidote to
the three-minute wrap-up of crisis in the Mideast. It is through
these news-in-depth programs that the TV networks seek to
discharge their "public service" obligation, but again they are
handicapped by the comparatively small audience these excellent programs attract.

The constant pressure for dramatic pictures to spice the
newscasts sometimes leads TV cameramen onto the dangerous
ground of the set-up picture and, next, the fake or near fake.
When Southern delegates angrily tore off their badges and
flung them onto a table in the 1948 Democratic National Convention, they did so at the suggestion of a TV man. As soon as
the cameras left them, the delegates were scrambling about
the table to retrieve their badges.

There was a classic example of this overzealous staging of
pictures while federal troops patroled Central High School in
Little Rock. This was several days after violence had been
quelled, and reporters and photographers were shifting from
foot to foot restlessly amid the calm that had set in. Along
came a group of ducktail-haircut toughs carrying, somewhat
sheepishly, an effigy of a Negro. The TV cameramen suddenly
saw their chance to produce a lively shot for the evening telecasts. "Burn it!" one photographer called to the youths.

The effigy was strung to a tree and touched off by a photographer's cigarette lighter. The young punks danced around
the flaming straw eagerly as the cameras ground and then,
carried away by their own enthusiasm, they cut loose with a
series of bloodcurdling shrieks that made for tingling viewing
that evening.

But this, in the final analysis, was a fake. The real news of
Little Rock that day was that calm had finally set in. The TV
viewer, on the other hand, saw only this harrowing scene
which could give but one impression—that the savages were
loose again.

The TV photographers, who were berated by their newspaper colleagues in drinking bouts that evening, defended

themselves hotly. They saw nothing wrong. All they did, they maintained, was to "get a little action into the picture."

Yet if the zeal of a bored photographer can produce near fakery in TV news, the honest action pictures these men take can become part of the news itself. The men arrested for mob violence at the school in Clinton, Tennessee, were identified largely from TV movies of the actual rioting.

The primary sources of news for both the networks and the local stations are the news services. The Associated Press provides its regular Teletype news service only. United Press International maintains a special television division in concert with Fox Movietone News; this service delivers words by Teletype and film by air express. Telenews, an offshoot of the now defunct International News Service, also provides news film, and NBC and CBS sell their surplus news film to affiliated stations for use on local broadcasts.

But backing up these basic news sources are the special TV reporters and cameramen who avoid the routine and cover only the big stories. The networks maintain staffs in Washington and in the major foreign capitals. These men do direct reporting. The local stations also employ reporters to chase down the big stories of the day and sometimes feed these to the networks.

CBS for years was considered far superior in coverage of news, but in recent years NBC has caught up. ABC always has been 'way behind. "We've just never caught on," says ABC program director Tom Moore, "and I think it's because we don't have the personalities the others have." Former White House Press Secretary James Hagerty was hired by ABC to make up the deficiency in coverage and to search for the personalities who will sell.

CBS and NBC have news commentators who actually are far more famous than the men they interview. Furthermore, men like Walter Cronkite of CBS and David Brinkley of NBC were skilled and seasoned reporters before they went on TV. However, the fact that TV is a personality medium tends to detract from the primary mission of reporting the news of the day.

When NBC grabbed a great edge in the ratings for its coverage of the 1960 political conventions, the industry analysts made no claim that NBC's actual coverage was superior to that of the other networks. They attributed the edge solely to the personality and whimsy exuded by Brinkley and Chet Huntley.

The local station's commentator likewise is one of the best-known men in the community, although he does not always have the background comparable to that of the network men. Too often the local news is read straight by a former radio announcer who knows no more than the man in the street.

Nevertheless some local stations do fabulous jobs of news coverage. Typical of the better performances is that of KWTV of Oklahoma City. Its news director, Bruce Palmer, travels the world over seeking out stories only for KWTV's viewers. He made a ninety-day tour of military bases in Europe, interviewing 716 Oklahomans. His staff covers the national political conventions with the accent on the Oklahoma delegations. (There were 1,000 TV men, in all, accredited to cover the 1960 conventions.) A KWTV cameraman accompanied an Air Force mercy trip that carried badly needed drugs from Westover Field, Massachusetts, to the flooded areas of eastern Kansas and northwestern Missouri. KWTV cameras were at Little Rock for the integration at Central High, in Europe and the Middle East with President Eisenhower, and at the Orange Bowl in Miami with the University of Oklahoma's football following.

All of this costs KWTV about $125,000 a year, but the station is convinced that the Oklahomans somehow get the feel of the news better when an Oklahoman is doing the reporting. KWTV maintains its own airplane, a fleet of automobiles, and a staff of part-time correspondents throughout the state.

Unfortunately, however, TV is often kept out of areas where it could do some of its best and most valuable reporting. TV generally cannot enter courtrooms, and it is kept off the floor of Congress.

The American Bar Association has its Canon 35, which states: "Proceedings in court should be conducted with fitting dignity and decorum. The taking of photographs in the courtroom, during sessions, and the broadcasting of court proceedings are calculated to detract from the essential dignity of the proceedings, degrade the court and create misconceptions with respect thereto in the mind of the public, and should not be permitted."

That is thirty-five years old. It was enacted after the excesses of the tabloid press during the Hall-Mills and Peaches Browning trials of the not always glorious 1920's. Every attempt in recent years to get Canon 35 repealed has failed.

However, in the final analysis it is the judge who runs the courtroom, and a few have chosen to ignore Canon 35. Judge D. W. Bartlett has permitted the televising of murder trials in Waco, Texas, since 1954. These trials are presented live in their entirety by KWTX-TV. Naturally, they hold great interest for the local population.

After the first experiment the Waco-McLennan County Bar Association endorsed TV coverage as being no more distracting than coverage by newspapers or any other media. The association said it found no effect on the judge's conduct of the trial or on the jury's verdict. "The courts belong to the people," said one attorney. "They deserve to know what's going on in them."

Nevertheless, there are few Wacos in the nation. Most judges will not permit TV cameras in their courts.

Supreme Court Justice William O. Douglas maintains that television would imperil a fair trial. In the first place, he says, it would make the general public the real jury; mass opinion should have no part in rendering verdicts, he maintains. Then, Douglas adds, the presence of TV in the courtroom tempts everyone—witnesses, lawyers, judges—to "exaggerate or clown or make the proceedings a vehicle for getting public attention."

This is a special danger, Douglas maintains, when the judge or prosecutor is a candidate for re-election.

Since the first success of the Kefauver hearings on TV no Senate committee has been the same. Advance men for traveling investigations always inquire delicately if the local station will carry the hearings live, and frequently the decision on the length of the hearing or whether to hold it at all is based on this answer. Senator Joseph McCarthy became an adroit TV performer. It was through television that he retained his power and, again, it was through a televised hearing that he lost it; on the defensive McCarthy was an unreasonable and even irrational figure, and the nation could see this for itself.

On the other hand, the House of Representatives will not permit its hearings to be televised. This is partly a reaction to the McCarthy excesses. Justice Douglas, in addition to opposing the appearance of TV cameras in the courts, objects to their use at legislative hearings. Because the public concentrates on personalities and not issues, these hearings become a trial with the ill-informed mass as jury rather than as information-seeking surveys. A psychologist hired by CBS after the McCarthy hearing said the TV audience made its decision on whether or not it liked McCarthy, not on the issues which were at stake.

Although Congress will permit many of its sideshows to be televised, it won't let the TV camera into the main tent. The truly great opportunity for the citizen to see his government in action is never permitted. State legislatures, on the other hand, frequently allow their proceedings to be telecast. It was partly because of television that Louisiana ousted Governor Earl Long. His antics could never be adequately described by the newspapers, and a reader might distrust the reporter's interpretation anyway, but television made it possible for the voters to see for themselves just what was happening in their legislature.

There is some question as to how much government-in-action TV would present even if there were no restrictions. For some years TV protested bitterly about not being permitted to film the President's press conferences. Finally, in 1955, the doors were opened. ABC televised the completed half-hour Eisenhower conferences for only a year. NBC and CBS never did. As soon as the novelty wore off, the press conferences wound up as two- to five-minute segments of regular news broadcasts. Interest was re-awakened when President Kennedy authorized live telecasts of his press conference, but it was not certain how regular this would turn out to be in practice.

Despite the restrictions on television at the source of the government, television has become somewhat a source of government on its own. It is impossible to run for public office at the city, state, or national level without using TV. This is a touchy matter. A candidate who wants to speak to "all of my friends out there" might make a few enemies by pre-empting the time of a favorite program. He may also be wasting at least part of his breath. People in Indiana tune in regularly to Chicago stations and don't care a mite for the speech of a candidate for mayor of Chicago.

But in elections TV not only covers the news; TV becomes the news. When Richard Nixon wanted to explain the famous "Nixon Fund" in the 1952 campaign, he felt his only hope of vindication was to go before the people personally with an emotional appeal. TV was the medium. When Harry Truman wanted to assault the candidacy of John Kennedy for President, he called a "TV press conference," which meant a TV appearance at which reporters could ask questions. And when time came for Kennedy to reply, he, too, chose TV as his medium.

The Nixon speech in 1952 undoubtedly was the greatest demonstration of TV's impact on politics. As Emmet John Hughes, an Eisenhower confidant, subsequently wrote, "Hours, even minutes, before that telecast Mr. Nixon stood an excellent chance of making history as the first candidate on a national ticket ever to be stricken from the lists in mid-campaign as an insufferable embarrassment to his own party.

"So nearly definite was this stern verdict of the party leaders that it is not enough to note that television remarkably served the man: it saved him. No other kind of apologia—nothing but television, with impact both massive and instantaneous—could have spared Mr. Nixon swift retirement. . . ."

At the advent of television, politicians thought that eventually they would campaign exclusively on the medium. This was especially enticing to national and state candidates who foresaw at last an end to the exhausting whistle-stop trips.

Now the political professionals realize that they cannot depend solely on TV. The personal appearance remains valuable. But they have adopted many TV tricks, with skilled professionals like Robert Montgomery directing presidential TV shows and even with candidates for sheriff buying singing commercials from national concerns. (One of these companies ironically tapes the music for American political jingles in Europe because the musicians cost less there.)

Former Democratic National Chairman Paul Butler cites the percentage of electronic voting since 1948 as evidence that TV does not increase interest in national elections. He also joins many in fearing that TV, that medium of personalities, has shifted the emphasis completely away from the issues of the day. A survey of political-science department heads at twenty-eight universities produced a 50-50 split on the question whether TV increases or decreases respect for the democratic processes. These professors agreed that their students learn the "how" of politics from TV, but not the "why."

Nevertheless, politics will lean heavily on TV hereafter. Local stations even conduct schools for candidates before each campaign, briefing them on how to sit, how to appear friendly, how to appear sincere, how to make the carefully prepared speech seem spontaneous and what color shirt to wear.

The greatest test of television as a medium for political campaigning came in 1960. The debates between John Kennedy and Richard Nixon had significance far beyond this one campaign, for they were an experiment to determine whether all the arduous travel and personal appearances could be eliminated in favor of face-to-face encounters by the candidates on a series of TV programs which could be watched simultaneously by millions of voters in the comfort of their homes.

As conceived originally by the late Senator Blair Moody of Michigan as far back as 1952 and first presented jointly by the three networks in 1960, the "debates," while not strictly that, were the finest opportunity the nation has ever had to see and hear both candidates present their views on the same issues.

The experiment was only a partial success. It showed that in politics, as in anything else, television belongs to the personality who can best project warmth and believability. It showed that on the morning following the debates the voters talked about who "came over best" rather than the issues which were discussed.

There seemed no doubt that these TV debates of 1960 helped greatly to elect Kennedy to the Presidency. Because so many voters are haphazard newspaper readers at best, they are moved by vague impressions and instinct. One of Nixon's great assets at the start of the campaign was a feeling of many that he was mature and experienced while Kennedy was immature and unschooled in government. Kennedy dispelled this in the first debate with his confident tones, his straightforward look, and his instant command of facts. "Do you know what it meant to us to have the issue of immaturity knocked out six weeks before the election?" Bob Kennedy, his brother's campaign manager, asked the morning after election.

Sindlinger & Company sought to find through a poll the full effect of the debates on the electorate. It discovered that before the first debate 37.3 per cent of those questioned thought Nixon would win the election and 23.4 per cent thought Kennedy would win; the day after the fourth and last debate 31.2 per cent thought Kennedy would win and only 29.1 per cent thought Nixon would win. The same survey indicated that about 9 per cent of the electorate switched personal preference from Kennedy to Nixon during the period of the four TV debates.

President Eisenhower thought Nixon was wrong in agreeing to the debates in the first place. He reasoned that Nixon was better known and that he therefore was giving Kennedy an undeserved assist by sharing the TV platform with him. He felt also that a man in a top-level government policy job—certainly the President and probably the Vice President, too—should not put himself in the position of being cross-examined by a political opponent. This, Eisenhower thought, might force indiscreet disclosures or promises that would in the long run be harmful to the nation as a whole.

There is little doubt that the 1960 TV debates will not be repeated in 1964 if President Kennedy is a candidate for re-election. No President will subject himself to such cross-examination. But, at the same time, there is little doubt that these debates did establish something of a political campaign custom for lesser offices throughout the land, and they may well be repeated between two presidential candidates who do not bear the responsibilities and secrets of the White House.

Congress has worried about giving one man the advantage over another on TV. At first it passed the equal-time law—that which required the television stations to give any candidate equal time to answer his opponent. On the surface this was fair as fair can be. But in practice it made the TV stations reluctant to give any candidate time. The law did not distinguish between the candidates of the major parties and the countless splinter candidates perennially seeking office. Furthermore, the equal time reached past the paid political program and into the area of news broadcasts. So in 1960 the law was repealed, and now the stations can use their judgment on granting equal opportunity to the candidates.

The national political conventions are geared to TV. They start, not at an hour that is convenient to the delegates, but rather at an hour that will embrace prime time in the Eastern Zone. (Thus the 1960 Democratic Convention was attended by hungry delegates; sessions started at 5:00 P.M. Los Angeles time, long after lunch but too early for dinner.) The old forty-five-minute nominating speeches have been cut to fifteen minutes and may be cut more, all to fit in with the TV schedule. The campaign platform, once a prodigious written document, now is presented to the public via a slickly edited film.

And because TV is so important to the conventions, TV can draw up the ground rules. The demands of the networks have already streamlined the conventions, and they will streamline them more in the next eight years. The TV men want to halt such time wasters as the demonstrations for favorite-son candidates who have no hope whatever for the nomination. ("I just want my twenty-five minutes on national TV," insisted New Jersey's Governor Meyner when he refused to withdraw his name from the 1960 Democratic Convention.)

Yet too much streamlining could eliminate the one manner in which TV convention coverage actually furthers democracy. Today, with the TV cameras turned on him, no convention chairman would dare gavel down a delegate who insisted upon arguing with the party bosses. The delegate who needs a national voice can usually get one on television.

The networks appreciate this fact and they are proud of it. But they bemoan the waste of time that is the result of their present "gavel to gavel" coverage of tedious procedures. "The political parties must recognize that they are no longer playing to delegates, but addressing themselves to 150,000,000 Americans," says NBC's Robert Sarnoff. To hold audience interest, a TV news presentation must be edited down to essentials. The viewer won't wait for the news to happen.

Because politicians are so impressed by the power of TV, they will save important announcements to make their television appearance more compelling to the viewer. They will submit to tough questioning that they would never permit in the sanctity of their offices.

One of the major make-news programs is NBC's "Meet the Press," one of the oldest continuing shows on TV and yet, ironically, one that employs a small panel of newspaper reporters to question persons prominent in the news. It was originated by Lawrence Spivak. When he and his partner, Martha Roundtree, first attempted to sell it as a radio show they were told "It'll be too dull" or "It'll be too controversial" or "You couldn't get top people to submit to the sharp questioning on the air." But the Mutual Broadcasting System took a chance on it in 1945, and the program has been broadcast continuously ever since, moving into TV in 1947.

It was on "Meet the Press" that Whittaker Chambers dared Alger Hiss to sue him when Chambers called Hiss a Communist, and this touched off the chain of events that sent Hiss to prison. It was on "Meet the Press" that Thomas E. Dewey, then titular head of the Republican Party, revealed that General Dwight Eisenhower was his candidate for the Presidency. It was on "Meet the Press" that Adlai Stevenson gained the national prominence that permitted his first nomination. It was on "Meet the Press" that Senator Walter George called for a summit conference, and this inspired the Geneva meeting of 1955.

There are many imitators of "Meet the Press" on TV now, usually confined to Sunday's Intellectual Ghetto, and the Monday newspapers carry story after story that stem from these make-news interviews on television.

Although one of TV's major problems is the sponsor's insistence that he have his say about the content of a program, there is no interference with coverage of the news. The networks produce their own news broadcasts without help from outside packagers (except the news services to which they subscribe), and no sponsor alters the content.

Nevertheless, TV is a timid industry and does react to pressures. For many years the television network news directors have toyed with the idea of presenting a humorous commentary on the news. They know this would be popular in the old Will Rogers tradition. However, the networks are afraid to present any such show for fear of the reaction that the jibes might produce.

There was serious consideration once that the late Fred

Allen, a true humorist and well informed as well, take such
an assignment, but no sponsor or network dared go into the
project. Mort Sahl came close to appointment as a network's
commentator on the 1960 national conventions, but timidity
conquered art again. Sahl was engaged by an independent
Los Angeles TV station to interview celebrities and generally
comment on the Democratic convention. He was rather funny,
but not as funny as his sponsor, Bart Lytton, who rushed from
the control booth one night in the midst of the broadcast and
shouted, right on camera, "I will not permit this show to become an Adlai Stevenson rally!" This undoubtedly convinced
the networks that they were correct in not risking Sahl's barbs
on their air during the touchy period of selecting candidates.

Sarnoff, in a speech marking the thirtieth anniversary of network broadcasting, told just how much pressure is put upon
the network. He cited a single night in 1956 when the Steven-
son-Eisenhower presidential campaign was at its peak and
the United Nations was embroiled with the Suez crisis. NBC
attempted to cover the news and maintain a reasonable program schedule at the same time. This, taken from the network's
Night Executive Officer's log, was the result:

6:00 P.M.—50 calls protesting that Stevenson was not being
granted equal time to answer Eisenhower's speech of the night
before. "General tenor of the calls: highly irate."

6:15 P.M.—NBC announces Stevenson will get equal time.
"The switchboard lights up, like a Christmas tree. We are accused of giving in to political pressure."

6:30 P.M.—NBC is covering the UN live. "Complaints from
viewers who miss their regular programing."

6:45 P.M.—NBC cuts to its regular program, a world news
roundup. "A barrel of protests for leaving the United Nations,
the callers saying that NBC cares more about making money
than keeping the public informed of impending disaster."

7:00 P.M.—Adlai Stevenson goes on. "The calls continue furi-
ously through his speech, some protesting that we are not at
the UN, some protesting at giving Mr. Stevenson time, others

angry at missing their regular show. Some in fact were so angry they hung up without fully explaining what they were angry about."

"And so on into the night," related Sarnoff. "On the news summaries and bulletins we brought in from the UN, we got telephone protests because our commentators referred to England and France as allied powers.

"The crowning blow came two days later in a letter from a mother berating us because we inserted urgent news bulletins into a children's program. This had upset her young child."

Little wonder that TV stations generally by-pass their right to present editorials of the air. In some instances TV stations have done very well with editorials. WDSU-TV in New Orleans says interest in its editorials mounted considerably when a merger resulted in a newspaper monopoly for the city. But mostly TV news tries to walk the straight and narrow.

This is not necessarily a vice. Marya Mannes of *Reporter* magazine said in an address to the American Society of Newspaper Editors: "Television lives on advertising to a greater extent than newspapers do, and since advertising is big business, advertising is by nature Republican. Yet nowhere in network newscasts or network commentaries on current events have I encountered the intense partisanship—the often rabid bias—that colors the editorial pages of the majority of newspapers in this country."

Television news departments have covered the South's integration battles without concern for the prejudices of the South, and Southern stations, with some exceptions, have carried these programs without audible protest. Television covered Joe McCarthy with less timidity than most newspapers. By its very bigness, TV is forced to be fair in its coverage.

Yet with its time, TV is stingy. With its personnel, it is more concerned with charm than with brilliance. But with its power, it has become a great force in the making as well as the reporting of the news. Truly it is America's fifth estate.

TAKE ME IN TO THE BALL GAME

"Sports is what TV was born to do best," says American Broadcasting Company program director Tom Moore. "There's no drama we can do on the stage that will match the drama on the ball field."

The result has been a revolution in sports. For all the ways that TV has touched upon national life, from entertainment to politics, no field has been so affected as sports. The lad who once begged his dad to take him out to the ball game a few afternoons a year now slumps beside Pop in the living room, following the fortunes of the local stalwarts.

From its earliest days, TV knew it had a vital stake in sports. NBC began experimenting long before it launched its commercial service. It brought both amateur and professional boxers into its Radio City studios for exhibition bouts that permitted the cameramen to study movement and lighting.

Within a month after regular TV service began in 1939, NBC

194

went to Baker Field to telecast a Columbia-Princeton baseball game. It also went to Madison Square Garden for a six-day bicycle race and to Randalls Island for an intercollegiate track meet.

The first big boxing match to be telecast was that between Max Baer and Lou Nova in 1939. It turned out to be a dull fight, but the telecasts received in radio stores caused so much excitement that police ordered the sets turned off so they could get traffic moving again. In the Bronx a riot broke out when the cops tried to force entranced viewers out of a radio store during the fight.

There was immediate talk among promoters of banning the TV cameras from their arenas forever. Obviously no one would pay to see an event that could be viewed at home for free. This was not a surprising attitude. It had been expressed previously in the infant days of radio and, indeed, there was once consideration of barring newspapermen from sports events so that the fans would have to pay admission fees even to learn the final score.

But at the same time that the less-foresighted promoters built their barriers, clairvoyants like Mike Jacobs, then the Number One impresario of boxing, saw TV as the instrument of a great new age for sport. Jacobs predicted the day when there would be no arena at all, when sports events would be staged in a studio exclusively for the television audience.

Jacobs was not quite right, but boxing, his sport, was TV's first big hit. It was boxing that sold the television sets in the first years of mass production. Some decried this, as Gilbert Seldes subsequently wrote in reviewing that period of TV's growth:

"The telecasting of sports was a turning point in the first phase of television history. It shocked the idealists who saw a great instrument of imagination and social significance turn to the mean estate of reporting not only a World Series, but phony wrestling matches and third-rate prize fights as well; and it shook the practical men, because for a moment it seemed that television was moving from the atmosphere of the home (an ideal place for selling clothes, soap, cars and other commodities supporting radio) to the saloon, where, according to persistent rumor, it didn't even increase the sale of beer, the spectators being so attentive to the sport that they forgot to order."

For all these qualms, sports stayed with TV and TV stayed with sports. Television moved out of the saloon and into the living room, carrying the fights and the wrestling and also the roller derby and the World Series and the Kentucky Derby.

The revolution was so great that it reached the halls of the United States Supreme Court. For generations organized sport has been free of federal antitrust laws. This was based on an old Supreme Court decision ruling that a party, such as a theatrical enterprise or a baseball team, that went from New York to Philadelphia for a performance or game was not in interstate commerce. No business was actually conducted across the state line, the court ruled; the business wasn't conducted until the performers arrived in Philadelphia.

Radio actually had changed that, but the stakes weren't high enough to worry about. TV's stakes were high enough, however, and it was an easy matter to prove that this ball game in Philadelphia actually was being played all over the United States if it was being televised. Thus sport was now in interstate commerce.

The International Boxing Club had enforced a monopoly of major professional boxing purely through its TV contracts. The money that television sponsors paid for the rights to exclusive broadcast of the fights was far more important than the money paid through the box office, and the IBC had exclusive contracts with both network boxing-match sponsors. The federal government, acting under the antitrust laws, consequently ordered the IBC to dissolve. It responded first by cutting itself in half, into "competing" organizations, and later by going out of business.

The fees sports promoters charged for TV rights rose fantastically. NBC's first contract for rights to the World Series was signed in 1947 for $65,000. Within two years the price jumped to $200,000. A year later it was $800,000. By 1957, ten years after the first $65,000 contract, the fee was $16,250,000. Today it is $20,000,000.

The Gillette Safety Razor Company, a natural sponsor for sports broadcasts, became synonymous with the nation's big events because it acquired a near monopoly on their sponsorship—the regular weekly fights, the World Series, the Kentucky Derby, the Rose Bowl. With the stars of these events often used in the commercials, Molly of "The Goldbergs" was moved to acknowledge her introduction to Mickey Mantle by saying, "I've never seen you play ball but I have seen you shave."

Sports promoters had to go to the United States Supreme Court to establish legally that they owned the radio and, subsequently, TV accounts of their games. Because newspapers have never paid for permission to report games, there were many radio stations that felt they need not pay either.

The major-league baseball teams and most college football teams succeeded in selling exclusive radio rights to their games, but this was challenged by Gordon McLendon, a radio-station owner of Dallas, Texas. He built an entire radio network on the piracy of major-league baseball broadcasts.

He thus set up the test case which eventually reached the Supreme Court. McLendon, who was the baseball announcer as well as the network president, was barred from the stadiums, but this did not deter him. He would set up his microphones in a hotel room and then subscribe to the Western Union play-by-play service, which is available to anyone. Using this telegraph report of the game, some appropriate sound effects, and a vivid imagination, McLendon broadcast the games to his network without paying a cent of royalty to the team owners.

He lost his case in court. The Supreme Court ruled that the sports promoter does indeed have a property right it could sell exclusively to a radio or TV station. The promoter could halt McLendon's type of piracy by a court injunction.

Television had great effect on the attendance of sports events. At first the matter seemed to boil down to whether the fans had to pay to see the event at the arena or whether they could remain at home and see the same thing for free. Actually, sports promoters learned that this was only one of many factors.

On one hand, they had to consider all the things that always affect sports attendance—the standing of the teams, the weather, the price of admission, the transportation to the stadium, and so on. On top of that they had to consider TV as competition—not simply their own ball game televised on TV, but the programs competing for attention. Would the people leave home to see a ball game on Milton Berle night? The Berle fans stayed home whether the game was televised or not.

Several major-league baseball teams made pointed tests to determine if televising their own games hurt attendance. The New York Yankees decided in 1952 that it did not. In the same pennant drive the Yankees played the Boston Red Sox in a game without television and the Cleveland Indians in a game with television. The no-TV game drew 59,212. The game that could be seen at home on TV drew 75,854. The Yankees thereupon decided upon unlimited television: they felt they could collect huge fees for the TV rights to their games and still not lose at the box office. The Washington Senators found practically the same thing. But some teams still balk at TV.

The National Collegiate Athletic Association, on the other hand, decided that television cut college football attendance by as much as 27 per cent. It adopted a plan whereby one game a week would be televised and the remainder would not.

The boxing promoters, characteristically perhaps, have their cake and eat it too. The routine fights that would scarcely draw a bridge foursome in the old days are presented for free to the TV audience. The big championship bouts certain to attract large paying crowds are staged without benefit of TV cameras.

Television has not only affected the attendance and finances of organized sport. It has affected the players themselves and their performance. In the first days of baseball telecasts the players had to be warned that because of the camera's telescopic lenses they should watch their language (the viewer may be able to lip read) and also be careful where they scratch. Professional football teams call a special time out every period to permit time for the sponsors' commercials.

But the effects of TV on sport went deeper than that. Dan Parker, sports columnist of the *New York Mirror,* wrote bitterly:

"The various branches of sport which have had traffic with television because they couldn't resist the lure of fool's gold have furnished enough tragic examples of what happens once this electronic lamprey eel sinks its fangs into the sports body. Little by little, the sport loses its identity and becomes merely a branch of the Television field. The worst example of all is provided by what happened to boxing. Television now runs the show.

"Its principal object is to build up program material, synthetically, well in advance, so that twice a week a main bout will be available to provide the framework for sales pitches as preposterous as some of the bouts, for the product that is footing the bill. Once, when boxing was its own master, there had to be an excuse for matching two boxers, besides the purely commercial one of making money. There was keen competition between rival promoters who operated in all the key cities where boxing was legal and this made for a healthy condition of the sport.

"There was a steady output of new talent, which had plenty of time to develop, promoters bid for the most attractive matches and thus the most deserving boxers in due time became the champions.

"Now there is no competition, except the synthetic type provided by two divisions of the outlawed IBC which still run the show. Virtually all the top-line boxers (most of whom would have been preliminary boys in the pre-television days) are managed by a criminal underworld syndicate which synthetizes the champions and supplies the 'talent' for promoters to line up for the TV people who have the last word. Boxing commissions accept their subservient role with a docility that is a sorry commentary on what is going on as the once-thriving sport is sold out to the hucksters at every turn. The National Basketball Association is another captive sport, run to suit television's demands.

"Baseball can no longer call its soul its own. The one-eyed lamprey eel has already drained the life blood out of the minor leagues but the TV show must go on and our so-called national pastime has become a mere advertising medium for beer, cigarettes, cigars, etc. Who can remember when baseball magnates wouldn't even permit such advertising to be pasted on their fences? Pro football is thriving on its TV arrangements which calls for time outs at intervals in every game so that TV sponsors can sneak in their commercials."

Sport is so tied in with television that the telecast of a baseball game is not a reporting job at all, but a package deal. The ball club owns the package. It makes the contract with the TV station and then sells its package to a sponsor. The "reporter"— the announcer—works for the ball club.

Insiders chuckle when they hear fans argue whether a Mel Allen broadcasting the Yankees or a Connie Desmond broadcasting the Dodgers games is too prejudiced in favor of the home team. It is not a matter of prejudice. It is a matter of salary. The announcer is on the same payroll as the players and manager. He is not the independent reporter sent to the game by a newspaper.

Yet TV has brought far superior sports announcers than those who held sway in radio's heyday. One of the most famous of radio's sports announcers was known privately as "football's greatest lateral passer." This was because of a little trick he devised to cover up his mistakes in identifying the ball carrier. Jones would streak down the field, but the announcer would mistake him for Smith and yell into his microphone, "Smith is away, going for a touchdown!" Near the goal the announcer would be prodded by a spotter and handed a note saying it's Jones, not Smith, toting the ball. "Smith laterals to Jones and Jones scores the touchdown!" the announcer would screech. Actually, Smith was on the bench at the time, figuring out his withholding tax.

This sort of thing would not work on television, of course, because the fan could see for himself that there was no lateral pass. The TV sports announcer, despite his unfortunate loyalty to the team rather than the fan, is far better versed in the intricacies of the sport than was his radio predecessor.

The major-league baseball teams cannot decide among themselves just what to do with television. The Yankees in New York televise all of their home games and some fifty of their out-of-town games. The Detroit Tigers televise far fewer games, but feed these occasional telecasts to eight other stations in the area as a promotional stunt. The Milwaukee Braves and the San Francisco Giants permit no television at all.

Most of the teams straddle the fence. They permit TV of an average of twenty home games a year, hoping that these will be an enticement that will lead fans into the ball park. Baseball's big hope is that pay television will someday permit huge TV audiences that shell out for what they see on the ball field.

The greatest effect of TV has been on minor-league baseball. Once these minor-league teams served two functions—they provided baseball for the smaller towns as well as a proving ground for young players on their way up to the major leagues. Today the minors are still proving grounds, but they are supported as liabilities by their major-league parent clubs. Television has stolen away the paying customers to such an extent that some minor-league teams play with fewer than one hundred persons in the grandstand.

Minor-league owners have pleaded with the major leagues to prevent telecasts of big-league games from entering minor-league cities. The majors have turned deaf ears to these pleas, or perhaps they did not hear them at all over the jangle of the TV gold.

Boxing has been affected in somewhat the same way. The small neighborhood clubs that profitably provided a place for a youngster to break in have died off, unable to meet the competition of Milton Berle and Desi and Lucy and Jack Paar over the years, not to mention the competition of big-city fights coming over the networks twice a week.

The quality of boxing has also tumbled because of TV. Promoters with TV contracts must provide a show every week. If there aren't two good men to match, then the promoter must match two bad ones. The show must go on.

College football and basketball are based on intense local rivalries and followings, yet they have chosen a different road to TV. The NCAA controls all college football telecasts and generally permits only one game to be telecast live a week. A power such as Notre Dame can sell movies of its games for subsequent telecast the day after the game, but few teams have such box-office appeal to permit so synthetic a performance. College basketball is televised generally. Locally these programs are extremely popular, but ABC found it couldn't find a sponsor when it attempted to put together a national TV basketball schedule for presentation on the coast-to-coast network.

The participant sports have been affected little by TV. There are golf-instruction programs and telecasts of the tennis championships from Forest Hills and local fishing and hunting programs, but these have never been sports that lend themselves to great crowds; hence there is little interest in widespread television of their matches.

Horse racing is a natural for TV, and the big races draw large viewing audiences. However, television, so subject to government scrutiny, is wary of too close an association with a sport that is tied directly to gambling.

Because of its early interest in sports, NBC for years was the dominant network in sports. It had the best of the weekly fight programs and it also held exclusive contracts for the

World Series, the Rose Bowl, the Kentucky Derby, and the NCAA football games. But ABC has now moved up.

ABC likes the idea of sports because it considers itself the network with a special appeal to young America, that part of the nation which is most often buying boats and cars and furniture and cigarettes and beer.

There's another thing about sports: The games are played at a time when the network has difficulty selling any other type of program. Saturday and Sunday afternoons are the key periods. ABC's Moore thinks TV eventually will be almost entirely sports on those days. The ratings aren't so high as those attracted by other shows, but the weekend daytime period goes begging anyway; and besides, sports moves advertisers' products out of proportion to the ratings. The only losers here are the intellectuals, who may soon face eviction from even their ghetto.

For the 1960–1961 season ABC got the boxing matches and NCAA football from NBC. However, these were things NBC was willing to give up. Officially, NBC said it was cutting itself loose from boxing because of the unsavory characters who dominate the sport. The inside story is a bit different. Gillette owned the fight contract, and NBC collected only its time charges for that hour each Friday night. Were NBC to rid itself of the fights and replace them with a network-owned show, it could collect both the time charges and the profit it derived selling the show to the sponsor. As is usual with big decisions in the TV industry, the guiding principal was money, not morality.

NBC retained the big sports extravaganzas—the World Series, the Kentucky Derby, and the Rose Bowl. These are the most valuable television properties in sports.

The charms that music hath are quite limited as far as television is concerned. For all the notes that pour out of the loudspeaker, ranging from the commercials to the NBC Opera, the men who run TV are convinced that music can only be an incidental.

There are, to be sure, music programs on TV. There's the NBC Opera, the Bell Telephone Hour, Dinah Shore, Lawrence Welk, and Dick Clark. But the rule is that the music must always be diluted with something else—a personable singer, comedians, dancers—to hold the viewers' interest.

"You can think up only so many trick shots of the brass section or the bass fiddle and then you're only repeating yourself," says NBC music director Samuel Chotzinoff. "Music is made to be heard, not seen, and television primarily is a visual medium."

Each network maintains a permanent staff of forty-five musi-

cians and actually employs many more during the course of a
week. The Bell Telephone Hour alone will use fifty-nine. Some
singers, such as Perry Como and Dinah Shore, have been continuing successes on TV. The popularity of Lawrence Welk's
orchestra was a phenomenon in itself. But these are the exceptions.

Andre Kostelanetz, who has sold 42,000,000 records in fifteen
years, can find no place on television. Fred Waring, who for
years presented a fresh and imaginative musical program, was
told flatly that he was "washed up" when he attempted to
continue his show on NBC.

Television's interest is largely in personalities, and its inclination is to parade the popular stars of the moment through a
series of safe variety shows, disposing of them the moment
their popularity wanes.

To go on TV today a singer doesn't have to be good—only
personable. The modern microphone is such a talented tool
that it will do the work. The mike of today takes a small voice
and sends it out over the air booming. The echo chamber will
provide resonance.

Furthermore, any musical sound can be changed electronically. It is just a matter of switching frequencies in the control room. Too, magnetic tapes of many performances can be
spliced together into a single song that sounds magnificent.
Once this voice is concocted electronically, the "singer" need
only mouth the words in pantomine while the control room
plays back the tape. Called "lip synchronization" or "lip synch,"
it comes out over your set like a simple singing performance.

Because teenagers are the principal consumers of popular
music, the popular singing stars of the day are apt to be teenage idols and frequently teenagers themselves. This puts TV
in a ticklish position. It minimizes the teenagers' buying power
and hence is loath to lure them to shows where the commercial
will fall on deaf ears. On the other hand, the appearance of a
Fabian on a major variety show will increase the show's rating
and probably reach adults who are in the living room when

the teenager flicks on the dial. Thus the inclination of TV is to have the cake and eat it too: It will spot these teenage idols on show after show, but never give them their own programs where they must be the entire draw. The idea is to give Pop Bob Hope and Daughter Bobby Darin on the same show.

The musical requirements of such a variety show are great. Perhaps the greatest strain is placed on the talents of Ray Bloch, who for years has been musical director of the Ed Sullivan show. Because of the great variety of acts that Sullivan presents, Bloch and his orchestra of nineteen men must be prepared to play everything from rock 'n' roll to the Royal Ballet's music and the accompaniment of Metropolitan Opera stars. And, because of Sullivan's penchant for importing European acts, the orchestra must be prepared to deal with performers in any language.

The orchestra has only a week to get ready, but is so systemized that it requires only one day of rehearsal with the other members of the show's cast.

To provide music for a variety show, one member of the orchestra is assigned as a sort of liaison between the musicians and the other members of the cast. When Les Brown's orchestra plays for a Bob Hope or Steve Allen show, for example, it works this way:

Donn Trenner, who is the orchestra's pianist and also carries the title of "music integrator," sits in on all conferences from the beginning. He is given a list of guest stars and told by the producer which of these will require music. Sometimes it's simply a few bars of introduction for a comedian. At other times it's a full score for a singer.

Trenner then discusses with the writers the music they'll need for comedy skits and for bridges between one act and the next.

He will face his trickiest problem when presented with a "personality," someone brought to the show for name appeal with no special talent for TV but with an important reputation in another medium. Take an appearance of British actress Diana Dors on an Allen show:

She is of the movies. She was brought to the show by booking agent Henry Frankel as a "sex symbol" to bolster the rating of the show. She is not a singer, not a dancer, and not a comedienne in her own right. Yet she can do a little of each. What should her part be on the show?

After a conference with Allen and Miss Dors' manager, the decision was that she would do one song-and-dance number and one comedy sketch. The song-and-dance number fell to Trenner and associate producer Bob Scheerer.

They first looked at movies of her past TV appearances, especially the musical bits. "We made the fast decision to make this a simple production number," Trenner says. "The idea was to use four chorus boys as a sort of distraction. The idea was to keep the boys moving always, to keep her in some motion but assign her no technical dancing. We would have the boys move her about a bit, lifting her, putting her down, crossing in front of her and then behind her. She actually would only walk backward and forward while singing, but on the screen, with the music and the boys' movement, it would appear to be a full song-and-dance staging."

That was the assignment, then, and all that remained was to score the music—"Hooray for Love" was the song selected—and block out the movements. This Allen show was live. Therefore the day before the show Miss Dors' song was recorded as she sat on a stool before the orchestra. On the night of the performance this was played back while she danced and silently mouthed the lyrics. Thus the song continued without puffs for breath while she pranced and was tossed about the stage.

Meanwhile, Trenner penciled onto music sheets the other music required by the show. This consisted largely of incidental bits called for by the writers—"a futuristic-sounding bit for this sketch of the space age," "a prancy sort of march for when Louis Nye walks on," and so on. There was no lengthy discussion. Trenner knew from these phrases what the writers wanted. Once the only requirement was a "boom." Trenner wrote down the "boom" for the drum. By doing so he alleviated a possible union jurisdictional problem; if it wasn't written as music the sound-effects union might claim the "boom."

Two nights before the show went on the air Trenner turned over his work to Frank Comstock, the arranger. Comstock has converted his garage into a sort of musical assembly line. He sat at the piano and orchestrated Trenner's work. As fast as he finished a page, he handed it to a copyist who moved down a long desk on the opposite side of the room, transcribing each musician's part onto a separate sheet.

By morning the job was done. It was time for orchestra rehearsal, then dress rehearsal, and finally the performance itself.

Music for dramatic shows is another matter. This can be played live or it can be taken off tapes. The network music libraries have great files of pretaped music (it's called "cue music") for use by the dramatic shows. These are slotted by subjects and moods, one of the biggest files at NBC being labeled "unrequited love." Some shows have had background music taped especially for them in Europe to cut costs.

There is a trend now, however, to use original music as background for drama shows. The great success of the theme for the now defunct "Dragnet" program helped this cause; there was scarcely a person in the nation who did not recognize those four notes. The jazz written by Henry Mancini for the "Peter Gunn" series created a mood the producers thought furthered the spirit of the show as much as the drama itself. Once "Peter Gunn" presented an entire ten-minute segment without a word of dialogue—only music and visual action.

The shift of TV from a live production in New York to a filmed production in Hollywood also has furthered the use of original music as background. The film composers became available to television, and they brought with them the skills they had acquired in scoring backgrounds for hundreds of theater movies.

The orchestras that are used to score TV-series backgrounds are much smaller than those used to score a motion-picture's background, but the composers consider the smaller group easier to work with. They also are learning to add instrumental combinations to get unusual sounds. In TV they are seeking a double goal: They are providing the background music that supports and furthers the mood of the drama, and at the same time they are providing a sort of musical identification. They want something distinctive for each show, something that will call to the person in the next room and say "Life with Sister" is on now.

But, as always, Hollywood must mix its great talents with great mechanization. The musical directors have devised a system whereby they can provide the background music for several shows in one sitting. This is done through the use of what is called a "click track." The musicians are provided their orchestrations, and the director, equipped with a set of earphones, cues in the music from a series of coded beeps put onto the sound track of the previously filmed program. The musicians never see the drama itself and indeed may not even know the name of the show for which they are recording. What mood they put into the program comes written on that sheet of paper.

There is considerable dancing on TV, but just about all of it is the same. The limitations of the medium are great—the camera can absorb just so many people, just so much action, just so much area.

Choreographer Jerome Robbins, in an interview with columnist John Crosby, said:

"I might say there is too much dance on television. Too much that is mediocre, that is. Like comic strips, a lot of these dances are on a certain level and happy enough to keep in the style of the time. I don't know what the problems are but you'll notice that television choreographers are not really the top ones. As far as the dancers are concerned, second, third, or fourth teams have come in."

TV is just not made for dancing, he said. "If the cameras

get the feet, they lose the face; if you get the face, you lose the body; if you pull back and get the whole dancer, you lose the expression. The screen robs of the dance a lot of personal energy; it takes away much of the effort and daring of the dance. This is removed because the television screen is so flat; you can't tell how high, how far off the ground, what distances the dancer is covering. I saw the Kabuki dancers for the first time on television and I didn't know what was going on."

Robbins said he likes the daytime teenage dancing shows. "I got a few ideas for the dances in 'West Side Story' by watching these shows. I once went to a dance hall in East Harlem and noticed that none of the dancers were anywhere near their partners. I asked someone, 'How do you know who is dancing with who?' and the guy said, 'Try cuttin' in.'"

The hope that television would bring truly great music into the American home has largely disappeared. There are bits of it, but good music simply is not for TV. It is not only a matter of ratings and sponsors. It is a matter of the quality of the loudspeaker and the means of presenting the music on the screen without boring the viewer to distraction.

NBC has done well with its original operas because the opera presents dramatic action to fill the screen. "We've never been successful with concerts," musical director Chotzinoff says. "When Toscanini was alive he did some interesting shows because he was exceptional. For the start of his concerts we did the usual shots of the fiddler, the French horn, and so on. But that got too monotonous. Then we got an idea to put the camera on Toscanini the whole show. It was wonderful. But without him attempts to put concerts on TV were flops. Most conductors are either too dull or else corny showboats. Close-ups of individual musicians are distracting. It's just simply that concert music is not for TV. It's for radio and records."

Conductor Leonard Bernstein would not agree with that assessment. His periodic TV appearances have not only been critical successes but, he said, there is also concrete evidence of great audience appreciation. His tours with the New York Philharmonic-Symphony have attracted record-breaking crowds everywhere.

"It is television," he explained. "There is obviously a special relationship between us and our audiences that obviously know about us from television."

Chotzinoff's great achievement is tailoring the opera for television. He says:

"At the Met you are a block and a half away from the stage. On TV the camera is right up there with close-ups. This presents problems. It makes casting much tougher, for one thing. The voice still must be there, yet when *Salome* opens and the captain of the guard sings, 'How beautiful Salome is today,' you can't have a 200-pound blowzy blonde appear.

"So we have tailored the opera at NBC. We have tailored it into what it really is, a musical drama. We have translated it into English to bring in a wider audience, and our success has been felt. The Met, too, is going more for translations, especially in comedy. We get grateful letters from people saying, 'I didn't know opera was like that.' Well, opera is not like that, but opera should be like that and so we are making it like that."

An NBC opera goes into production a full year before it goes on the air. The big hunt is for a cast—the combination of voice, looks, and acting ability that TV opera requires. Some operas are abandoned only because they cannot be cast properly. The next job is to produce a good translation, especially one that will not lose the humor involved.

Then begin weeks of rehearsals. The NBC Opera does not have the facilities of the Met and consequently does not have three or four standbys available in the event that a major singer suddenly cancels out of a show or becomes ill, but only twice in twelve years has Chotzinoff been forced to dub in a voice for another performer. Once Ethel Barrymore Colt went hoarse during the last five minutes of *Die Fledermaus* and silently mouthed the words the rest of the way while another member of the cast sang offstage. The other time, Chotzinoff simply couldn't cast the baritone who also looked the part of St. John the Baptist in *Salome*. So he hired an unknown young actor named John Cassevetes to play the part while someone else sang it offstage.

Chotzinoff may find more problems in the control booth than on the stage, however. It is in the booth that the music will be sent out properly or out of balance. He said: "Once Stravinsky was conducting a piano concerto with a guest pianist. The show was on the air and I wandered into the control room. I couldn't hear the piano in the piano concerto! I yelled, 'Where's the piano?'

"The engineer said, 'Oh, do you want to hear it? I thought it was too loud so I turned it down.'"

That doesn't happen any more. David Sarser, a violinist with the NBC Symphony, became interested in electronics as a hobby, and now doubles in the control room when the delicate balance of music becomes vital.

WHAT'S THE SCORE?

The rating services, says George Jessel, work like this: "You walk into Lindy's and you see three people eating sour cream. So you say everybody in the United States eats sour cream."

It's not really that bad, but Jessel certainly is on the right track. The ratings, just one outgrowth of the great American game of poll taking, depend upon a few thousand persons to tell them what the nation's millions watch on TV.

Television must have some means of measuring its audience. The advertiser spends millions of dollars to deliver his commercials and obviously he needs to know how big an audience sees them.

When the same advertiser uses a newspaper or magazine, there is an audit to tell him the exact paid circulation of the publication. When he erects a billboard, the highway department can tell him how many cars pass that spot on an average day. When he mails his ad directly to the home, he knows how many postage stamps he bought.

But the nature of TV prevents such accurate measurements. The advertiser can learn how many television sets are in existence, but this is meaningless unless he can also learn whether they are tuned in to his particular program.

The ultimate rating, as far as any sponsor is concerned, is in the sale of the product. But he can't wait for the months to roll by before he can detect a rise or fall in sales after he begins sponsoring a new TV show. By that time he will have spent millions on the show. Besides, a top-rung advertiser like Proctor & Gamble sponsors so many shows that even an increase in sales could not be attributed to any one show without an estimate of its audience.

That's the why of the rating services. They do estimate the audience, and if their methods and figures are questionable they nevertheless thrive on the old principle of operating the only wheel in town.

There are many rating services, and the advertisers are so desperate for an evaluation of their audiences that they will always examine a new system of measurement in hopes that it will be better than what they are now using. The major organizations are these:

A. C. NIELSEN, which uses an electronic device attached to the TV set in 1,050 homes spotted throughout the country. The gadget records on film what hours the set is on and to which channel it is tuned. When the recorder runs out of film it coughs up two quarters, payment to the home owner to put in a new roll. (A TV repairman once called the FBI when he saw this Nielsen gadget attached to a set; he was certain he had discovered a secret homing device for Russian bombers.) Every two weeks the tape is picked up, tabulated, and the results issued to Nielsen clients.

TRENDEX, which polls by telephone calls. Some 3,600 interviewers man the phones in 25 cities, asking if the TV set is on and, if so, which program is being watched. Trendex makes about 1,000 phone calls each half-hour of the evening. There is no attempt to characterize the homes by income group, location, and so on; the numbers are picked blind from the phone book. (One Trendex girl in St. Paul was thrilled to learn that thirty people were all watching KSTP at one number she called; later she learned that the number was that of the KSTP studio.)

AMERICAN RESEARCH BUREAU, which pays a small fee to the heads of 2,200 households to keep a diary of which programs members of the family watch. ARC also has introduced in New York City what it calls the Arbitron, an electronic recording device similar to that of Nielsen but which reports instantly to Arbitron headquarters.

In addition to the big three of the rating world, there's Pulse, which sends about 3,000 women into the homes with questionnaires; Videodex, which uses a diary similar to ARB's in 9,200 homes; and the Sindlinger Service, which uses random telephone calls but seeks more detailed information by attempting to drag these out for as much as a half-hour.

Of the three major rating services, each serves a specific purpose. Nielsen, by telling electronically how many of the test homes tuned into a program, is considered the most reliable of the ratings. Trendex's advantage is speed: it doesn't require the two-week waiting period that is a Nielsen drawback. Trendex produces a rating the morning after the program is aired. The ARB diary provides an important piece of extra information—who was watching. The advertising agencies live in constant terror of discovering that their commercials for a beer will be watched by an audience composed entirely of six-year-olds.

In addition to collecting their information in different ways, the rating services report them differently too. Nielsen is the most pretentious. It automatically assumes that its 1,050 homes are representative of the entire United States. A Nielsen rating of 25 actually means that 25 per cent of the Nielsen homes were tuned into that particular program. But Nielsen then takes this figure and projects it into a total audience. Nielsen figures that 25 per cent of the 44,500,000 TV homes is 11,120,000; not being satisfied with that, he next assumes that 2.7 persons watched each set, and so he announced the audience as 30,000,-000.

Trendex will not go that far. A Trendex of 25 means simply that 25 per cent of the homes checked by the telephone pollsters reported that they were watching the program in question.

The development of the Arbitron instant reporter and the subsequent installation of a Nielsen Instantaneous Audimeter means that the networks now can trace the popularity of their programs every five minutes during the day and every ninety seconds at night. They can see when the audience begins tuning out a show if it doesn't live up to early expectations.

The harassed show-business folk, already badgered by rating pressures and sponsors' taboos, foresee the day when the producer will march up and down a bench of singers and comedians like a football coach. When his glance at the scoreboard shows the act on camera is losing the audience, he can send in a substitute. They might even be able to find Major Bowes' old gong somewhere in the warehouse.

The major complaint against the rating systems is the ludicrously small sampling they take. Nielsen checks only .00002 per cent of the TV homes in the country. Furthermore, because of the expense of installing and removing the electronic device, these are apt to be the same 1,050 persons checked for considerable periods. If by coincidence Nielsen caught 1,050 who hated situation comedy, the television industry would be revolutionized; it would assume all America hates situation comedy.

But at least the Nielsen device reports the truth. Trendex and ARB know that people fib when they are asked either by phone or diary to tell what television they are watching. Some are inclined to say they're watching "Omnibus" when actually they're looking at a Western. The pollsters assume, however, that *most* people tell the truth.

The rating services defend their small sampling by saying they are nevertheless large enough to be indicative. They point to the fact that the Department of Commerce uses only 500 persons to report conditions of 3,000,000 in manufacturing jobs or that the Federal Reserve Board bases its statistics on the reports of only 2,500 families.

The Nielsen sales brochure says, "A scientifically selected sample need not be large in order to provide relatively accurate estimates of population which it represents. For example, samples of 300 representative homes are entirely adequate for measuring radio listening in cities as large as Chicago and with a substantial degree of accuracy.

"Old-fashioned straw polls relied almost entirely for their accuracy on *number*. Modern sampling polls rely for their accuracy on an entirely different principle—the careful selection of a small but representative cross-section of the population being measured."

For all their insistence that their methods are absolutely scientific, the one thing the rating services cannot explain is how they all come up with different figures for the same programs. Furthermore, Nielsen ratings for any program always seem higher than the Trendex rating for the same program. Faced with this question, each rating service defends the accuracy of its own system and shrugs its shoulders at the opposition's discrepancies.

The biggest boosters of the ratings are the networks. They need these figures to show the advertiser what he is getting for his money. The sponsor also grasps at the ratings, especially when they indicate he's not getting his money's worth out of a show. The advertising agencies generally are more skeptical. The performers defend the ratings when they are high and assail them when they are low.

The network men say that the importance of ratings is exaggerated by those outside the industry. The ratings are only one indication of a program's popularity, they say. Furthermore, the ratings are figures to be interpreted by experts, not simply taken at face value.

Hugh M. Belville, who is NBC's vice president in charge of

research, says: "As long as we have our commercial system of
TV we'll have ratings. It's inconceivable that any advertiser
would spend $10,000,000 a year for a TV show without meas-
uring its audience size.

"If properly used the rating service is adequate for us to
decide when to renew or cancel a show. But ratings are often
misused. The only remedy for that is education of broadcasters,
sponsors, and agencies.

"I would also suggest that the press—newspaper critics and
columnists—are not expert enough in ratings to interpret them.
Ratings should have no place in the press."

The fact that television programs live and die by the ratings
makes them too important to be hidden in the executive suite.
Even as entrenched a performer as Ed Sullivan concedes the
terror of the ratings week after week.

"Sunday night you don't sleep too well," he says. "You're up
at nine in the morning to reach for the ratings. Your top rating,
of course, is the sale of your sponsor's product. But meanwhile
you've got to watch the ratings week by week.

"One of them doesn't mean a thing. But if all the ratings
services agree that your audience is falling, you've got to believe something is wrong. And if it happened five weeks in a
row then the joint will be jumping."

Senator Mike Monroney of Oklahoma, who led a congressional investigation into the rating systems, blamed this pressure for the rigged quiz programs. TV insiders back him up.
The quiz shows started out as economical gimmick shows
which presumed that the suspense of an honest contest would
be sufficient attraction for an audience.

But the producers soon began associating high ratings with
some contestants and low ratings with others. The next step
was obvious: to keep the high-rated contestants rolling at any
cost and bounce the low-rated blokes from the show before an
opposition program grabbed off all the audience.

There is even one tale along Madison Avenue about the
sponsor of a quiz show who was told the program had an

especially high rating on the night a bearded contestant won top prize. The sponsors reaction was predictable: "Beards!" he screamed. "Get me more beards!"

That's what the show-business people most deplore about the rating pressure—the need for more beards whenever a bearded contestant draws well at the box office. These people are accustomed to the theatrical roller coaster of hits or flops, but no entertainment enterprise has ever been measured minute by minute until Arbitron erected its big electronic board for TV.

With such pressure, the next charge had to be that the TV ratings, like the quiz shows, were rigged. The stakes are high— an advertising agency may be imperiling millions of dollars in a single account if it urges onto the sponsor a low-rated show— and so the motive for connivance is certainly there.

Robert Hurleigh, the president of radio's Mutual Broadcasting System, did make the charge of rigged ratings, but he was unable to substantiate it and Senator Monroney said his committee's investigation produced no evidence of rigging. The rating services say that attempts to "reach" some of their personnel have been reported from time to time, but these are rare in the first place and not effective in the second place; no one in the rating service has enough authority to tamper with the figures.

TV producers do watch for ways to hypo their ratings, however. They know, for example, that Trendex takes its sample the first week of every month. So naturally they put on their best guest stars during that week. They also buy extra newspaper ads that week.

The sponsors and advertising agencies, however, are showing increasing concern over what the ratings *do not* reveal. The men who finance a TV program want to know *who* is watching, not merely *how many*. Robert Foreman, executive vice president of Batten, Barton, Durstine and Osborne, said: "We have counted noses long enough. Qualitative investigations must be broadened, made more readily available, improved."

The possibilities of more detailed investigation of television audiences actually were demonstrated by an entirely different type of survey. Campbell Foods engaged a research firm to send interviewers into the home to sit at the dinner table with each family in order to see what was served, what was liked, what drew comment. From that idea researcher Miles Wallach progressed to television: if his interviewers could sit with the family at a dinner table, surely they could sit in the living room and watch TV, too.

The first test was in Syracuse, New York, in January of 1957. The researchers selected 10,000 homes, and they divided these into two groups, one to be visited personally by an interviewer and the other to be called upon by telephone. (This convinced Wallach that people fib over the phone; they'll say anything to rid themselves of the nosy caller.)

The first firms to try this TV research were Colgate, Campbell's, Ford, and Revlon. There were major repercussions. For one thing, Ford pulled Mercury off the Ed Sullivan sponsorship because Sullivan's fans weren't Mercury types. On the other hand, Campbell's renewed the "Lassie" show because these were soup eaters.

Part of the interview was to determine whether the people who watched the show used the sponsor's product. Phillip Morris cigarettes had learned that the millions who loved Lucy didn't love Phillip Morris. Anacin, on the other hand, had known that the comparatively few who would watch the low-rated "Original Amateur Hour" were typical Anacin users.

The interviewers found that 21 per cent of those who watched a Kent cigarette show smoked Kents, while only 11 per cent who watched a rival show smoked Kents. They assumed that the show's commercials accounted for the 10 per cent difference.

This sort of thing can't be done every two weeks in the fashion of a Nielsen rating, of course. And it certainly won't produce the instantaneous audience ratings the new Nielsen and Arbitron electronic devices provide. But for long-range program buying, for decisions on whether to renew a show next year, this is the rating of the future.

This qualitative rating system already has told the advertising men some unpleasant truths they could never get from the flat audience-size ratings. They have learned that for as much as 29 per cent of the time the TV set may be on, there may be no one in the room watching. They have learned that in some areas the station with the clearest picture will be watched in preference to other stations no matter what program is on the air. They have learned that Americans now are trained to sit in front of the TV set and do many things besides watch—read, talk, eat, drink, and goodness knows what-all during the Late, Late Show.

But the perfect rating system has yet to come. Perhaps it will be the one just developed by Dr. Charles Allen. He calls it the Dyna-Foto-Chron. It's a small camera that fits into the set and photographs the viewer while he's watching a program. The day is nigh when the network will call in a comedian and say: "Waltham, you're through. Last night 29.3 per cent yawned, 11.7 per cent scratched, and a lady in Hopkinsville, Kentucky, was seen emptying the sponsor's soup into the kitchen sink."

"—— THE TORPEDOES!"

TV is the nation's most censored mass medium. The man in the gray flannel suit wields a blue pencil that makes television performers turn white with anger and red with embarrassment.

Yet according to law TV is as free as any other means of mass communication. The federal criminal code does make the use of "obscene, indecent or profane language" a violation of the law punishable by fine up to $10,000, and it also forbids the broadcast of information about "any lottery, gift enterprise or similar scheme" or fraud.

But beyond that the laws leave television unfettered. The first attempt by a state to censor TV was thrown out by the courts. The Pennsylvania motion-picture censorship board, in 1949, claimed jurisdiction over movies shown by TV stations, but the courts ruled that only the federal government can regulate television.

So in the absence of outside censorship, television has provided its own censorship. It operates generally from a code drawn up by the National Association of Broadcasters, and it adds further restrictions through network regulations, the taboos of the advertising agencies, and the dictate of the sponsors. It is ironic that television finds self-censorship the only means of preventing government censorship. The barn is burned down so it can't catch fire.

The TV code is in the tradition of the movie code adopted in the 1930's and the comic-book publishers' self-censorship installed in the early 1950's. These, too, were voluntary steps taken to avoid compulsive legislation. The broadcasters first adopted their regulations in the 1930's for radio. TV inherited this document, and enlarged upon it to account for the new dimension of sight.

But when television comedians make cracks about "the censor," they speak not of the code's administrator but of the network's own continuity acceptance director who must approve every program and advertisement that goes on the air. Stockton Helffrich, until recently head of this department at NBC (and now chief administrator of the NAB code), recalls that so many borderline cases arose "I had to work out my own code."

"I came to the conclusion," he said, "that he who censors best censors least. But there are great pressures from both the broadcasters and from the audience. You've got to consider them both. Sometimes the problem is to persuade the client away from being too cautious. The public will not support unintelligent censorship."

One of Helffrich's most cherished memories is a little book published by the author, Kendall Banning, in 1926. He called it CENSORED *Mother Goose Rhymes* and dedicated it to "The censors who have taught us how to read naughty meaning into harmless words." One rhyme:

> "Peter, Peter, pumpkin eater,
>   Had a wife and couldn't xxxx her;

> He put her in a pumpkin shell
> And there he xxxx her very well."

The touchy race issue is, of course, one of the network censor's major concerns today. He finds himself in the position of the man who got two neckties from his mother-in-law for Christmas and wore one, only to have her say, "So you didn't like the other one?" Anything conspicuously favorable to the Negro will bring protests from the South. Anything unfavorable will bring protests from Negro and Northern liberal groups.

The general policy of the networks is to strike out any potentially offensive lines or caricatures and at the same time to guard against the total elimination of the Negro or the Jew or the Italian from the TV scene by producers and writers who play it too safe.

Helffrich is especially proud of a positive accomplishment at NBC. He persuaded the producer of the "Big Story" newspaper drama series to place a Negro reporter at a desk in the background of one scene of one episode. This hardly appears earth-shaking, yet for supercautious TV it was as radical a case of integration as the election of a Negro to the Poplarville, Mississippi, school board.

The sponsors are not nearly so liberal as the networks or the performers in racial matters. The sponsors don't like to have mixed Negro and white singing groups, for example. They certainly don't want Negro and white entertainers embracing, even in that perfunctory hello hug which is the standard greeting of show business. On the other hand, some of TV's biggest stars, such as Dinah Shore and Ed Sullivan, refuse to be bound by these rules and can usually circumvent them if they're vehement enough.

The toughest decisions come on jokes. In the mimeographed bulletin Helffrich distributed at NBC he posed this problem: Which of the two following gags is acceptable?

a. A Southerner says that up North these days chiggers are called Chiggroes.
b. There's a farmer who crossed a Guernsey with a Holstein and now has a cow that says "Nu?" instead of "Moo."

Helffrich ruled that the "chigger" joke was out because it "perpetuates a malicious epithet." He ruled that the "Guernstein" joke was in because it does not malign anyone.

The matter of religion is even more frightening than race to the network people. And they are confounded by the fact that religious groups cannot even agree among themselves what they approve. The West Coast Chairman of the National Council of Churches Broadcasting and Film Commission announced one day that he had persuaded NBC to cancel a play concerning a minister who committed adultery. The next day another official of the council denounced the censorship and said the organization had no desire to hold such power on the networks. NBC then further complicated the whole matter by saying it never planned such a play anyway.

It doesn't take a play about a minister's adultery to arouse the ire of thousands of viewers. The most innocent crack can do this. Perry Como remarked on one of his Saturday night programs that "my wife made me a turkey sandwich yesterday." The protests began pouring in. Como is a Catholic, and fellow Catholics were outraged that he ate a turkey sandwich yesterday—which was a fast day. The next week Como had to explain that the "yesterday" he mentioned was not the yesterday of the TV viewer; the program had been taped two days before it was shown on the air. Furthermore, Como added whimsically, all he said was that his wife *made* him a turkey sandwich. He didn't say he *ate* it.

The latest sensitivity in the network censorship departments is mental health. Words like "crazy" and "nuthouse" are out. But "zany" is all right.

Obscenity is, of course, a ticklish matter because in the first place no two people agree on what is obscene and in the second place it is one area which the federal government actually does have strict authority. Thus it took considerable research before television permitted its first "damn."

That came on an NBC presentation of F. Scott Fitzgerald's *The Great Gatsby* in 1955. There is one line, near the end, when the hero is told, "Jay, you're better than the whole damn bunch of them." This is a key line, a very appropriate line, and Helffrich recognized this immediately. He went to the network legal department for approval of the word. The lawyers burrowed themselves in books for days and finally located a ruling: One U.S. Court had decreed that "damn" and "hell" are not profanity "except by divine implication." The script was approved. TV got its first four-letter word.

But that didn't open the dam for damns. NBC and CBS continued to strike them from subsequent scripts. Then a few years later Hume Cronyn and Jessica Tandy were to appear on NBC in their Broadway hit *The Four Poster*. The original play's manuscript was submitted to the network. It was peppered with damns and hells, and these all were duly penciled out.

Then Cronyn telephoned Helffrich. "I agree with you on most of those," he said, "but there's one spot in the play where I'm having an argument with my wife and then I throw her a compliment and she immediately stops arguing and hugs me. I look over her shoulder and say, 'I'll be damned if I understand women.' Now, Mr. Helffrich, can you imagine me saying anything else in a situation like that?"

"No, I can't," agreed Helffrich, and the "damned" was restored. Helffrich anticipated a storm of protests from viewers, so he ordered his department to start a careful check of the "damns" and "hells" permitted on NBC. They totaled twenty the first year, and after that he stopped counting.

The men who turn out the filmed series shows in Hollywood maintain that words and themes forbidden to them are accepted by the networks on the bigger, more expensive shows. This is true. The networks feel that the "Playhouse 90" type of audience is more sophisticated and more serious, that a one-hour or 90-minute play has more time to develop a touchy theme properly, and that these programs frequently use the works of top authors and playwrights who are entitled to more license than a by-prescription scenario writer.

The time the program is shown must also be taken into consideration. A "damn" at 11:00 P.M. is not nearly so damnable as a "damn" at 6:00 P.M. when the tots are at the set.

When TV was young and live it had a physical censorship problem—the bosoms of actresses who had a lot to show and wanted to show it to a lot of people. Burke Miller, the NBC Night Executive Officer, became a "keeper of the tulle" to cover up some of these charms just before the shows went on the air.

He was acting in direct conformity with the TV code, which states, "The costuming of all performers shall be within the bounds of propriety and shall avoid such exposure or such emphasis on anatomical detail as would embarrass or offend home viewers . . . camera angles shall avoid such views of performers as to emphasize anatomical details indecently."

The National Association of Broadcasters has practically no enforcement machinery to back up this code, but it doesn't need any. The broadcasters adhere to the code because they want to, because they are convinced its censorship prevents something more odious. The attempts to circumvent the code are almost always by writers, performers, and producers rather than by station or network officials.

Based generally on the old motion-picture producers' code, the NAB regulations are printed in a fourteen-page booklet that has been amended five times in twelve years.

The code bans obscenity and also warns about perfectly acceptable words which might acquire "undesirable meanings" (as, for example, "had a wife and couldn't *keep* her"). It bans attacks on religion, insists upon reverence in any mention of God, and urges accuracy in any religious ceremony performed on the screen. It insists that divorce not be "treated casually"

and that illicit sex relations not be treated "as commendable."
It calls for a "de-emphasis" of the use of alcoholic beverages
and an absolute ban on the administration of illegal drugs.
Gambling devices can be used as background in a play but not
in a manner that would "excite interest in, or foster, betting nor
be instructional in nature." Criminality should be presented as
"undesirable and unsympathetic," the code says, and furthermore the crime should never be committed in a "frivolous,
cynical or casual manner."

You can show real criminals and real animals on the air, but
the real criminals must be bad and the real animals good. You
can show physically deformed persons on the air but you must
be cautious never to ridicule them; you may show fortune-
tellers on the air, and it's best to ridicule *them*.

The code calls for news broadcasts that are "adequate and
well-balanced, factual, fair and without bias." It forbids drama
shows which might be mistaken for news shows.

The code embraces advertising as well as editorial content
of the TV programs. It specifically bans advertising for hard
liquor, fortunetelling, occultism, astrology, phrenology, numer-
ology, palm reading, mind reading, and so on, and it bans the
use of ersatz doctors or nurses in commercials. It warns against
such words as "safe" and "without risk" and "harmless" in the
advertising of medical products. It calls for fairness in all prize
and premium contests.   The NAB stations seem to adhere to
the code in direct proportion to the outside pressure placed
upon them. In early 1959, when the code office called for a
ban on a questionable drug advertisement being carried by 84
stations, only 49 dropped the commercial. The other 35 either
resigned from code membership or else were dropped by the
NAB.

Subsequently scandal hit the industry, and the station owners became frightened by the threat of government interference. So of the 35 that left code membership over that one
commercial, 33 dropped the ad, and returned. But today there

are still some 75 stations that don't even pretend to adhere to the NAB regulations.

The code also sets up time standards for advertising. In the evening hours it limits total advertising time to 2½ minutes for a 15-minute show, 3 minutes for a 30-minute show, 6 minutes for an hour show, and 9 minutes for a 90-minute show. In the daytime it permits about a minute more per half-hour.

This is the part of the code most often violated because this is the part of the code that could cost the broadcaster money. Besides, the increasing amount of multiple sponsorship on single shows has made it more difficult for all the sponsors to get in their commercials in the maximum time period allotted by the code.

Although officially the code is the censorship bible of TV, any scrawled letter to a network might have the same result as this august document. Television is supersensitive to the complaints of its viewers. It remains so, although the TV executives know these viewers can never agree among themselves.

Robert Sarnoff testified before Congress: "Even within groups presumably bound by the same interests spokesmen have sometimes been at odds. The representative of one farmers' organization with 700,000 members says the networks 'strangle' good programs, and the representative of another farmers' organization with 850,000 members thinks the networks are doing a good job. A professor from Harvard warns that advertising on the air is repelling the audience, and a professor from Columbia testifies that, according to his research, most people 'love' commercials. A distinguished magazine editor urges that the government regulate broadcasting as a monopoly; a distinguished newspaper editor urged that broadcasters be permitted to solve their problems in freedom. And within the ranks of educators we have heard a striking difference of opinion as to whether the depiction of violence may incite passions or release them vicariously."

You would think that the networks, faced with such exasperating differences, would throw up their hands and begin to run their own business with no concern for the outsider. But the opposite is true. The letters from "outraged viewer" are read and studied and often acted upon. TV always runs scared.

There's this one which NBC received:

"Sir:

"We in Wannatosa, Wis, do not particularly care for those overly-personal advertisements such as laxative, muccous membrane, toilet bowl and sanitary napkin type.

"Most of your ads are all right, some in fact pretty good in fact.

"Don't pay any attention to any cards or letters that complain about too much violence or immodesty on the regular programs. I believe that you must face the facts of life and that includes murders, robberies, beatings and divorces, rapes and sexy dolls! Keep these on."

A letter like that is good mostly for laughs around the studio, but there are others, almost as ludicrous, that get serious consideration. Many come from special pressure groups. Dentists complain if a tot is afraid to go to the dentist in a TV play. Toupee manufacturers don't like toupee jokes. Taxi drivers don't like smart-alecky taxi drivers in TV. One manufacturer objected to Dickens' *A Christmas Carol* because Scrooge was an unattractive boss.

Charles Winick, who did a study of TV censorship for the Fund for the Republic, pointed out:

"Labor unions have been one of the very few major groups that have almost never complained about a representation on television. One reason for this may be the comparative infrequency with which workers or work situations are shown in television drama. Even the shirt-sleeves drama of television's early days was built around the kind of hero who was enough of an entrepreneur to want to own his own butcher shop, like 'Marty.' "

Winick pointed up the complete absence of discussion about labor negotiations on TV. One network specifically bans advertisers from commenting on the subject, but no advertiser on any network has ever attempted to bring up the subject; they don't even use their commercial time to present their views when their employees are on strike.

A strange facet of TV's obedience to the letter writers is the networks' knowledge that most people don't write. A program like "Gunsmoke," with an audience estimated at 47,000,000, will get only 25 or so letters per program. The networks say that their mail generally runs three to one in favor of the program concerned.

The censorship on TV extends past the words and into the field of music. The code specifically warns dancers to keep their movements "within the bounds of decency," and the network censorship bureaus are forever tinkering with the lyrics of songs, especially songs brought over from the more liberal Broadway stage.

In *Brigadoon* a song entitled "My Mother's Wedding Day" contained these lines:

> It was a sight beyond compare;
> I ought to know for I was there.

On TV the words were different. On TV the lyrics were:

> Until today the folks declare
> It was a mess beyond compare.

And in Cole Porter's *Anything Goes* the original words were:

> Good authors too who once knew better words
> Now only use four-letter words
> Writing prose.

On TV they didn't use four-letter words. On TV the good authors used "three-letter words," whatever *they* are.

There are other musical taboos. Stephen Foster is to be avoided because of the perennial argument over his mention of "darkies." A man can't sing "My Heart Belongs to Daddy" because this would stamp him as a homosexual, or worse. And, of course, there can be nothing like "Bewitched, Bothered and

Bewildered's" "wouldn't sleep, and couldn't sleep, until I could sleep where I shouldn't sleep."

The networks, in their dread of controversy, also censor what some performers consider their right to speak out on major issues of the day. The *cause célèbre* was that of Jack Paar. He temporarily walked off his NBC show when the network censored a hoary joke about a water closet. However, the joke was not the real basis of the argument. The network had become increasingly concerned about Paar's outspokenness on other subjects, notably his defense of Cuba's Fidel Castro. NBC just picked the moment of the water-closet joke as the time for a show down.

Performers on one hand maintained that Paar's freedom of speech was being violated by NBC's gag.

The network maintained that Paar was hired as a variety-show master of ceremonies and that he had no right to use the network's facilities to espouse his personal views on political matters.

NBC made its ruling stick. Paar returned to the show subject to the same censorship as of yore and, it appeared, a bit chastened by the experience.

It was one more victory for the network censor. He is a man who always wins. He is, after all, that man who made certain that everything didn't go in *Anything Goes*.

MADISON AVENUE—WEST

Hollywood fought off television as though it were an invading horde of barbarians. The movie people first scoffed at it, and then berated it, and next battled it, and finally surrendered to it.

One generation of show business never seems prepared to accept the next. The legitimate stage scorned vaudeville and forfeited control of it. Vaudeville impresarios scoffed at the birth of the movies and eventually found themselves on the outside of their own theaters. The movie people, in turn, could not predict the vast opportunities in radio and, despite that lesson, also looked upon television as an enemy to be despised rather than a companion to be embraced.

The July 14, 1937 issue of *Variety* carried the headline, "Pix Biz Sees Television Only as a Novelty." The February 28, 1944 issue of the *Wall Street Journal* carried this: "Two facts stand out, movie men argue. They are that Television need not constitute a threat to the movie business; instead, if used properly it can be a boon to theatre attendance. The majority of movie houses after the war will install television equipment."

The movie people were begged to go into TV. Rod Erickson, a former executive of the Young & Rubicam advertising agency, recalled: "We went to see people like Darryl Zanuck to urge them to go into TV. We got turned down. I don't know where Zanuck is today. Probably he's still making pictures that don't make money."

Although it was only natural that TV would seek to lure the movie stars onto the smaller screen, the studios resisted strenuously. "I'll never forget the way Paramount President Barney Balaban reacted, and the many wires I got from exhibitors telling me I was crazy to go into TV," Bob Hope said. "I told Balaban that if he would make me the same offer NBC made me I wouldn't sign with NBC. He didn't answer."

Whenever the movie moguls could, they forbade their stars to appear on television. In countless interviews they berated the "cheap" brand of entertainment TV was grinding out hour after hour, day after day. It was strange to see the men who invented the B picture suddenly writhing over a cheapening of our culture, yet they did so, the crocodile tears gushing down their cheeks.

In fairness to the movie-studio operators, it must be said that their resistance to TV was not entirely foolish or even voluntary. It was based to some extent on pressure from their customers, the movie-theater owners. These were the men who would suffer first and most directly from the competition, and these were the men who could never accept compromise with the upstart medium.

Yet television surged forward and took an awful toll of movie patronage. Within two years after TV was big time, motion-picture attendance was down more than a third. It continued to drop, and the studios in Hollywood panicked.

They cut loose all their stars and featured players from long-term contracts. They farmed out their production to independent producers. They sliced exploitation expenses and fired the talent scouts who might bring in new stars. And then they went into competition with themselves in a grab for quick cash. They sold their old backlog to television so that now even a person who wanted to see a movie didn't have to visit the theater; he could sit at home and see a nice vintage picture on his TV screen.

A cost accountant would undoubtedly approve of the studio retrenchment, but cost accountants have always had trouble in show business. It was true that the elimination of the long-term contract saved the studios from paying actors between pictures, but it also was true that these actors demanded double, triple, and sometimes ten times their original salaries when they were approached for a one-picture deal. (Also, free of ties to the studio the actors were able to appear on TV as often as they wished.) It was true that the farming out of pictures to independent producers distributed the risk, but it was also true that these independents were then cut in for portions of the profit and that the studio lost all control of the product it had to sell.

Eventually Hollywood surrendered. Today it is a television town. The old RKO, Universal, and Republic studios have been taken over completely by TV packagers. Columbia Pictures and Warner Brothers depend largely on their TV-packaging subsidiaries for bread and butter. Paramount, M-G-M and 20th Century-Fox moved into TV later than the others, but they are in now and in to stay.

The pretty girls in the skin-tight toreador pants no longer badger the receptionists in the movie studios. They are all after TV commercial assignments now, for this is the new entrance to show business. The writers, the directors, the technicians—they're all in TV.

The big studios still make motion pictures for theaters, but mostly they are idle except for TV production. They have plenty to offer television. 20th Century-Fox's TV series "Hong Kong" uses three sailing schooners—a flat-bottomed full-sized ship built on the studio pond, the same ship built full scale on an indoor sound stage, and a tiny toy-sized model to be tossed about in the bathtub for storm scenes. Only the Hollywood movie studios' storerooms, mammoth lots, and know-how can provide such facilities.

Because a TV show is created on a much smaller budget than a motion picture, the opportunity to work on a big studio lot is sheer heaven for television producers. They will find a $150,000 movie set standing idle and use it for free just because it's there. The set is worth three times the entire show.

The TV people remain second-class citizens in the big studios. The movie men have surrendered, but not gracefully. They look with scorn at these quickie artists. The result is that the TV producer on a big lot becomes a sort of scavenger, snatching use of facilities when the motion-picture elite aren't around. An entire Japanese village was built for a movie on the Fox lot. The movie company went on location for four days, and while it was gone a Fox TV unit moved in and filmed an entire show on the set.

There is a reason for the discrimination. The movies are much bigger money—they make more money and they pay out more money—when they are hits. Warner Brothers, for all its dependence on TV, will make more out of one motion-picture hit than out of the entire TV operation. The trouble is those motion-picture hits don't come often enough; meanwhile, television has to pay the rent and the butcher.

The result is that in Hollywood today the big studios are employing 15 per cent fewer people than they were twenty years ago, but are paying them 129 per cent more.

The actors who switched from movies to TV say they notice a difference in the reception they get from their fans. Movie stars were looked upon with awe by the outside public. TV stars are looked upon more as chums. The taxi driver who picked up a movie star was almost speechless with ecstasy. The taxi driver who picks up a TV star wants to chat. Is it because the TV star is seen in the fans' own living room? The actors think so.

The end of the long-term contract with the big movie studios plus the lush profits to be realized from residual sale of TV films has transformed the Hollywood actor from employee to employer. Not only do Lucille Ball and Desi Arnaz own their own studio, but Red Skelton bought the old Chaplin Studio and Dick Powell is president of the highly successful Four Star Television, Inc., one of the top TV packagers.

The producer who needs a star now deals with the star's corporation. Robert Taylor starred in a TV series for Four Star. But he wasn't a Four Star employee. The Robert Taylor corporation was engaged in a partnership with Four Star, which, incidentally, is owned by David Niven and Charles Boyer in partnership with Powell.

This corporate show business, in direct contrast to the great individual showmen like Ziegfeld and Frohman, in turn produces corporate shows—by formula, using materials drawn from the company storeroom. TV manufactured by the big Hollywood studios means TV shows conceived in the front office and then turned over to an underling to produce. The producer, having no say about the idea, the story, or the cast, is not likely to turn in any brilliant results. He will turn in efficient results. He will stay within his budget.

In New York TV was different. New York got first crack at television for the simple reason that New York is the headquarters of the networks and of the advertising agencies.

When TV was a live medium, the shows were almost all done in New York. Caught without space to stage these productions, the networks bought up legitimate theaters and old movie houses and warehouses all over Manhattan and even in Brooklyn.

TV eventually fled west, however, for several reasons. One was that labor costs are much higher in New York and the union demands were much more stringent. (A TV producer who decided to postpone production of a show from summer

to fall was told that in the interim he'd have to employ a theater maintenance crew at a cost of $750 a week whether he
needed them or not.) The networks could never hope to build
sprawling studios in New York because real estate is too high
and there isn't the space available anyway. And when TV
switched to film from live production, it was only natural that
the home of film would be the new home of TV.

By 1960 many TV artists, writers, and performers, were
forced to move to Hollywood whether they wanted to or not.
There was no work left for them in New York. The few who
refused to move found themselves riding the jets to Los Angeles as though they were trolley cars, sometimes making
round trips twice in a week.

The Beverly Hills Hotel, once the temporary palace of the
visiting movie potentate, now is a headquarters for advertising-
agency men momentarily west on inspection tours. One wag
even tacked a sign, "Madison Avenue—West," on the hotel
entrance. The ad agencies all maintain branch offices in Hollywood to watch the production of their programs and to make
commercials with the town's vast resources.

The networks maintain newly built studios in the Hollywood
area, gigantic brick barns especially constructed for the needs
of TV. This is a far cry from the cramped converted theaters
of New York. There also is a noticeable contrast between the
tradition of the legitimate theater in New York and the tradition of the movies in Hollywood. The difference is that between hand-tooled quality and mass production.

The ad agencies and the networks keep their headquarters
in New York, however. Hollywood is only the factory. It was
like this in the halcyon days of the movies, too. The top brass
of the motion-picture companies has always resided in New
York.

Chicago was also a production center in the very earliest
days of TV, but that didn't last long. Chicago's problem was
that it could offer only talent. It didn't offer the administrative
headquarters of New York nor did it offer the technical reser-

voir of Hollywood. Chicago turned out some brilliant early-vintage TV—the original Dave Garroway Show, Kukla, Fran and Ollie, and the "Ding Dong School"—but it was much easier to ship those people to New York than it was to ship television to Chicago.

There is, in the TV trade, a continual argument over whether Hollywood television is invariably inferior to New York television. A favorite crack is that you can always tell a Hollywood show because the only thing believable in it is the horse.

This seems to be a matter of opinion. The Steve Allen Show, when at its peak, moved from New York to Hollywood and continued live on the West Coast. It was the same show, same people, same format, even the same writers. Did the show suffer from the move? It depended upon whom you talked to.

Allen himself said there was no difference creatively. The physical facilities were better in Hollywood, he said, simply because he worked in an NBC studio built expressly for TV as opposed to the New York studio, which was a converted theater.

But an Allen writer insisted that the difference in atmosphere made the Hollywood show more a formula production even though the same people were doing the work.

Henry Frankel, the Allen booking agent for guest stars, maintained that it was much more difficult to get top names for a Hollywood-based show. "Hollywood actors live in an ivory tower," he said. "You approach them with an offer in Hollywood and they want to argue about the money and the billing and the script. But you transmit the very same offer from New York and they respect it. They think of the free trip and the publicity in the New York papers and the very importance of a message from New York and they are quick to accept. I've noticed that the same people are 80 per cent more apt to take a guest shot if it's in New York."

In the case of dramatic shows, on the other hand, the New York show must be all indoors. Because of the unpredictable weather, it is mighty risky to plan an outdoor scene even on

film. In Hollywood the consistent sunshine means more working days per year for outdoor shooting and also better lighting conditions. Then too, the unique terrain of southern
California is what attracted the movie industry in the first place.
You can shoot desert scenes, mountain scenes, beach scenes,
metropolitan scenes, suburban scenes, and rural scenes all
within the radius of a few miles.

It is the writer who complains most about Hollywood, and
usually he complains about the Hollywood rut. Some have
given serious thought to what makes the difference. They generally agree that the two principal factors are the suburban
living and working conditions of Hollywood (as opposed to
urban New York) and the provinciality of Hollywood.

In New York it's almost impossible to go to work in the
morning without becoming engaged in a conversation with an
outsider—the elevator man in the apartment, the taxi driver,
the elevator starter in the office building, if no one else. In
Hollywood the writer drives from his garage to the office park-
ing lot without speaking to a soul. Writers get fresh ideas from
talking to other people, even doormen and elevator operators.

In New York a man may confine his friendship to those in
his own business, but he lives among other types. In Hollywood, a Los Angeles suburb made up almost exclusively of
film and TV and advertising-agency people, the man next door
is in the same general business as you and everyone else in
the block. Again there is no outsider to spark an original
thought.

The writers feel, in other words, that they are insulated
against the outside world in Hollywood. Elsewhere, they think,
they could not have such insulation even if they wanted it.

On the other hand, Hollywood is good for TV because
Hollywood is oriented to the United States as a whole. New
York is the most provincial city in the nation in a way. Its love
affair with its legitimate theater and Metropolitan Opera and
Carnegie Hall (it loves them even if it doesn't support them)
gives it a sophisticated culture foreign to the bland Holly-

wood diet that has nurtured the nation for three decades. The Hollywood producer is much more apt to know what the people in Oklahoma like in the way of entertainment.

The newest thing Hollywood is giving television is its films made after August 1, 1948.

The pre-1948 pictures brought fabulous sums. Howard Hughes sold his backlog for $25,000,000. Warner Brothers sold its files for $21,000,000. Fox did even better, renting its old pictures for three years for $18,890,000 and still retaining ownership. Other firms, such as Columbia, M-G-M, and Republic, set up their own distributing companies to rent their old films to individual stations.

With this sort of money to be made from out-of-date pictures, it's obvious what the newer films will bring when eventually they are released. And "eventually" is a word Hollywood accepts. Few believe these movies will be kept off television forever.

As in the early days of television, however, the big studios find themselves facing pressure from their customers, the theater owners. The old gripe about providing additional competition that will empty the theaters still stands. But now there is a new complaint. The theaters say that they themselves may need these old films to fill the void created by the curtailment in movie production. Once a major studio turned out sixty pictures a year. Today the average may be less than ten.

The big effect of TV on movies has been fewer pictures. Pictures that cost more money. And by and large better pictures. They are certainly more adult. They make more money when profitable and they lose more money when they flop. This has truly become an industry of feast or famine.

The general trend has been to take Hollywood talent and key technicians to points far from Sunset Boulevard to make the modern movie. This is mostly an economy measure, although it also bears the artistic merit of realism. A Mexican peon will play the role of a Mexicon peon for $3 a day and will be grateful for the opportunity, while a standard Hollywood extra will play the role of a Mexican peon for $30 a day and grumble about the skimpy box lunch the studio provides on location.

As Hollywood has converted from a movie town to a TV town, the theater owners have been left in the lurch. Those remaining in business now find there aren't enough pictures for them to show. Where once Hollywood turned out four hundred features a year, today it is turning out less than half that. Theaters are forced to continue running unprofitable pictures for the simple reason that there are no replacements available.

The first rush from the theaters to the TV sets in America was not matched overseas, and for several years Hollywood maintained a good box-office business in foreign lands. Soon more than half its take came from overseas theaters. By 1960, however, the TV trend was catching on far beyond our shores.

The big studios will continue to make motion pictures for theaters because of the high profit of a hit. They will continue to pay the grocer off the proceeds of television. The independent movie producer, meanwhile, flourishes in the void. Some foresee the time when each movie will be a separate business, organized into an individual corporation as is each Broadway stage production.

This will be a return to the very first days of the flickers when a D. W. Griffith and a Cecile B. De Mille made movies instead of production charts. The organization man has moved to TV.

FEE VEE

The motion-picture business and the television business both could be revolutionized by the advent of pay TV. This has been a topic of discussion and experimentation for many years, but only recently has such a system approached being practical.

Why pay TV? Why shell out money for something that already comes into the home for free? Its advocates answer that pay TV would provide entertainment that *does not* now come into the home for free. It would release for television many things—Broadway plays, recent movies, special sports events, operas—that are not now available. It would also release TV's entertainers from the tyranny of the advertiser.

It is, however, premature to look on pay TV as the panacea for all the ills besetting commercial television today. For one thing, there is no assurance that the pay-TV producer won't be just as apt as an advertiser to bid for the lowest common denominator in entertainment; after all, the more $1 fees he collects, the richer he'll get. For another thing, there may be not enough talent in the world to supply superior entertainment in the quantity that television consumes it.

There are two basic systems of providing pay TV in the home. One is to send a scrambled picture into the air from a standard television station; the signal then is unscrambled in the subscriber's set and visible on his screen. The other system is to pipe the show by wire from the station into the subscriber's set.

The advantages of sending out through the air are obvious. The wires don't have to be laid and maintained. It certainly should be cheaper in the long run. It can reach remote and sparsely populated areas where wire is impractical.

But, on the other hand, the wire system could be developed much more quickly. There already is a shortage of TV channels on the spectrum, and wired TV would not tax these limited facilities. Also, the broadcast system would require approval and supervision of the Federal Communications Commission, while the wired system would not. The FCC is notoriously slow in authorizing new systems and new stations.

Largely for these reasons, four of the five pay-TV organizations are now struggling for a foothold plan to use wire. The five organizations are:

1. International Telemeter Corporation, a partly owned subsidiary of Paramount Pictures, which operates under the trade name of "Telemeter." This company is now considered the leader in the field because of experimental telecasts already well under way in Canada.

2. The Zenith Radio Corporation, which plans a broadcast type of pay TV under the name of "Phonevision." Zenith will conduct a three-year test of its system in Hartford, Connecticut, under the jurisdiction of the FCC.

3. TelePrompTer Corporation, which, as "Key TV," plans to feed pay programs through community antennas.

4. Skiatron Electronics & TV Corporation, which, as "Sub-

scriber-Vision," would feed programs by telephone wires. This company has been in hot water with the Securities and Exchange Commission because of the financial manipulations of its president, Matthew J. Fox. It has attempted to merge with a top Hollywood movie studio.

5. Teleglobe Pay-TV System, Inc., which, as "Teleglobe," would send its picture by normal television means but would send in the sound by wire on the assumption that one is no good without the other.

The duel of the next five to ten years probably will be between Telemeter and Zenith, partly because they seem better able to finance the necessary costly tests and partly because their systems appear most practical to men in the TV industry.

The FCC cannot limit the tests of pay TV by wire. But it has laid down some stringent regulations about such tests through the air. Among other things, it says that tests will be approved only in cities now receiving four or more free TV stations, that there can be only one system tested in each city, that the pay-TV station's signal must not interfere with the signal of any existing station, that the test must be completed within three years, and that the public shall not be forced to buy any new equipment or attachments during the test.

Pay television has been tried in the United States several times previously. The first test came in Chicago in 1951. Zenith operated it, putting special receiving equipment in 300 homes. The subscriber could telephone Zenith and order a movie piped into his set. The charge of $1 was added to his telephone bill. This experiment was a flop. Zenith blames two things: the customer's horror at seeing how much he had spent when the phone bill came in at the end of the month, and the fact that the movies offered were no better than those being shown for free on commercial channels.

The next pay-TV test came in 1953 in Palm Springs, California. This was operated by Paramount's Telemeter in about 250 homes, and the movies initially available were good first-run pictures. The subscribers, who paid their fees through a coinbox on the set, didn't exactly leap at the opportunity. A test family averaged only eight to ten pictures a month. Then a movie-theater operator in Palm Springs began screaming about the competition, and the big studios withdrew their top shows. In 1954, when the experiment ended, the subscribers were more than weary of a dreary run of fourth-rate motion pictures.

In 1957 still another attempt was made, this time in Bartlesville, Oklahoma, by a chain of movie theaters. It charged a flat fee of $9.50 a month for the service at the start, but it failed, and the producers' losses ran as high as $10,000 in a single month. Henry Griffing, head of the theatrical chain that conducted the experiment, blamed the failure on two mistakes —charging a flat fee and offering only one program a night instead of giving the subscribers some choice.

Then in 1960 Telemeter started anew in Etobicoke, a suburb of Toronto, Canada. This was the first test that bordered on success, but everyone involved agreed that it would take several years before they could be certain that they have built a lasting system and not merely a novelty doomed to eventual oblivion.

Telemeter works like this in Canada:

The subscriber (originally there were 1,000 but the present number is some six times that) orders an attachment placed on his regular TV set. He pays $5 for the installation (Telemeter's costs are between $100 and $125 per installation, but it absorbs the difference) and after that he pays only for the attractions he watches.

To see a pay program, he first tunes the regular dial on his set to Channel 5, which is not a commercial channel operating in the area. Then he adjusts the dial of his special pay-TV gadget to Channel C. This channel is the "barker." Through it he will hear an announcer telling him what programs are scheduled, how much they'll cost, and what time they begin.

When he's ready to see a program, the subscriber turns the gadget to Channel A or B, depending on his choice of program, and then drops coins in the meter to pay for the show. The fees run from 25 cents to $1. If he doesn't have the correct change, he puts in a little extra. The meter registers the extra payment and saves it for him. If he wants to apply this extra money to the next program he sees, he simply pushes a black button when the time comes. As soon as the coins are deposited, the scrambled signal of the pay TV transmitter becomes unscrambled and the subscriber can receive the program on his regular screen. Periodically a Telemeter man drops by to empty the coins from the meter.

The Canadian plan is to present first-run movies on Channels A and B each night, and to use Channel C for special programs, such as hockey games, when it is not being utilized as the "barker."

The first reaction of subscribers was good. Few complained about missing commercials, of course (although one man did say the continuous movie allowed him no time to scoot into the kitchen for a beer), and most were satisfied that they'd prefer to see a first-run movie in the home rather than in a theater even if they had to pay an admission fee either way.

The top hits were drawing from 25 to 35 per cent of the possible audience. Telemeter noticed, however, that its business fell off sharply when an especially popular show was being shown for free by the Canadian Broadcasting Corporation.

Is this enough business to make pay TV profitable? It is too early to tell. It cost $2,000,000 to build the station. Each subscriber's coin box cost Telemeter $90 in addition to the installation expense. It must lay special cables at 55 cents a foot, frequently adjust the subscriber's antenna, pay the telephone company for lease of its wires into the home and, of course, it must pay big rentals on the movies it runs. A Toronto newspaper's survey indicated that the average subscriber was putting $2.35 a week into the meter; Telemeter refused to confirm this figure, but says it can show a profit if 10,000 homes contribute $2 a week.

It is Telemeter's plan to lease its system to local operators throughout the United States. The chain that ran the defunct experiment at Bartlesville already has switched to Telemeter and has lined up fifty or so towns in the Southwest as its first areas of operation.

But at the same time Zenith is ready to test through-the-air pay TV in Hartford. In conjunction with RKO General, Zenith is buying WHCT, which is Channel 18 in Hartford, to operate the experiment. This station will function as a commercial station during the day, and then will switch to its pay-TV status for two hours each night.

The Phonevision system will not have a coinbox. The set will be unscrambled by some sort of decoding key, perhaps an IBM card issued to the subscriber. Within the set will be a tape that records the programs watched by the subscriber. At the end of the month he'll remove the tape and this will be his bill. This he will send to the station with a check. There will be a second tape in the set that the subscriber can't reach. The station's people will check this every so often to make certain the subscriber isn't cheating by destroying some of his bill.

If this doesn't prove practical, Zenith will switch to a coinbox.

The FCC's rules forbid selling the decoding units to the public, but they can be rented, and the test-period charge will be between $1 and $2 a month. In addition, the subscriber will be charged about $1 per attraction.

Another system of pay TV is through the use of the community antennas. This setup, known as CATV to the trade, is designed to improve reception and do away with the individual antennas jutting from the roofs of homes and apartment buildings throughout the nation.

The idea is to build one superantenna in the town and then pipe its reception by wire into the subscriber's living-room set. The second Floyd Patterson versus Ingemar Johansson heavyweight championship fight in 1960 was not telecast commercially but was beamed by closed circuit to theaters throughout the nation.

This was used as an incidental test of a CATV pay television. There was no way actually to charge these subscribers extra for the fight because they already were hooked up to the antenna. But in thirteen cities the antenna operators asked subscribers in advance if they would like to see the fight and, if so, would they "contribute" $2 for the privilege. If enough mailed in the money in advance, they said, they would pipe it in. The antenna operators reported overwhelming success. Some said as many as 80 per cent of their subscribers ordered the bout.

The big question for pay TV actually is not how to operate it, but whether to operate it at all. No one can be certain that there are enough worth-while attractions to merit a permanent pay-TV system.

There is no doubt that the top Broadway plays could multiply their earnings many times by performing for millions through a nation-wide pay TV system. There is no doubt that many Hollywood movie makers see national tollivision as the answer to the half-empty theaters. But there are only a dozen Broadway hits a year at best, and there is a limit to the number of top-grade movies that can be made in a year. Sports events appear the most dependable attraction. The Telemeter experiment in Canada was most disappointing when it came to sports, but this was because usually the same games were offered for free on the other channels. However, should sports swing entirely to pay TV the situation would be different.

The Los Angeles Dodgers baseball team purposely refuses to permit its games to be televised on commercial channels now only because it anticipates the arrival of pay television. This prospect induced the team's owner, Walter O'Malley, to transfer his franchise from Brooklyn to Los Angeles.

It is O'Malley's position that he does not want the fans in the Los Angeles area to become accustomed to free TV and then face the revulsion of later having to pay to see the same games. So he prefers to forego television income completely until he can award the fans the right to pay for watching the games in their own homes.

Leonard Goldenson, chairman of the American Broadcasting Company, says, "My own feeling is that they will have a difficult time finding something they can use on pay TV. They have to compete for pay against something that is free. They talk about running top, new movies on pay TV, but as a veteran theater man I don't think the motion picture is designed for the home. They're designed for the theater. You need a disciplined audience, sitting there attentive. At home the phone is ringing, the kids are running in and out, the wife interrupts with a report of what she did today. TV shows are made to take this into consideration. A movie isn't."

Goldenson's corporation operates both a TV network and a chain of movie theaters. Thus he represents the two greatest forces in opposition to pay television.

Whenever an experiment is seriously discussed, the local theater owners are first to rise in arms. They protest to the Justice Department that pay TV would be in restraint of their trade. The networks unleash major propaganda drives, warning the general public that "they're trying to make you pay for something you should get for free."

Actually, of course, no pay-TV advocate has urged the elimination of commercial TV. It is just that the existing TV stations and networks can't abide the thought of losing even a portion of their audience to pay television.

The FCC was first prepared in 1958 to sanction tests of pay TV, but tremendous lobbying in Washington apparently made its mark on the Senate Commerce Committee. It asked the FCC to postpone the experiments, and it did.

Nevertheless, in a report written for the Fund for the Republic, Robert Horton put a plague upon both houses. He said that the proponents of pay TV are always too vague when asked about the charges they will levy against the consumer, and he said, too, that pay-TV entrepreneurs cannot be specific when they're asked about the "different" type of programing they will present.

Too, there is no guarantee that pay TV would not accept advertising just as free TV does. Everyone presumes that pay TV would contain no commercials, yet only the FCC could forbid the ads and even the FCC would be powerless in the case of wired TV. Although it is unlikely that pay TV would accept advertising, it must be remembered that smaller movie houses did carry commercial messages between pictures in their richest days.

One form of pay TV already operating is the one that pipes its programs not into homes but into theaters. It was this type of television that boxing promoter Mike Jacobs envisioned from the very first. He dreamed of the day when millions would see each championship fight—a few thousand at the studio and the remainder in theaters throughout the nation.

Fights have been presented this way frequently, with considerable success. It would appear that theatrical ventures, especially in cases where great operas and plays could be brought to the smaller cities of America, would also flourish. However, up to now theater TV has been almost exclusively the domain of boxing.

TelePrompTer's first attempt to make pay television the actual promoter of a fight was mired in scandal. The New York Boxing Commission subsequently uncovered a sordid tale of under-the-table payoffs by TelePrompTer to land the first Patterson—Johansson fight. But despite this unfortunate tangent, the TelePrompTer promotion was undoubtedly a sign of things to come. The tail had begun to wag the dog.

MEET THE PRESS

The newspaper is in a terrible dilemma when it comes to the consideration of television news. On one hand the paper considers TV a direct competitor, not so much in reporting the news as in scrounging for the advertising dollar and for the public's leisure time. On the other hand the paper knows that TV news and features build circulation.

In the early days of radio some newspapers flatly refused to print the program listings, and others would do so only if the stations bought the space at advertising rates. Most papers soon saw the folly of this. Nevertheless a few blundered into the same head-in-the-sand attitude at the time television was launched. They, too, conceded their mistake.

Today most papers attempt to use TV as a circulation builder. A number of the big papers publish expensive little booklets on Sundays, listing the programs for the week. A syndicate now has launched a national version of this booklet

for inclusion in Sunday papers much like the big Sunday magazines, *This Week Parade* and *The American Weekly*.

One survey (there's a survey to cover everything in TV)
showed that 51 per cent of the families owning TV sets use the
daily newspaper TV listing to select programs for the night's
viewing. Another 22 per cent use special magazines like *TV
Guide* and only 22 per cent actually remember from week to
week what they want to see. Some men in television blame this
devotion to newspaper listings for the fact that TV viewers are
not nearly so loyal to a program or station as radio listeners
were. They think that the additional newspaper coverage has
made the viewer more of a shopper.

Consequently one of the most widely read men in any daily
newspaper is the TV writer. Some call themselves TV editors,
some TV critics, some TV columnists, and some TV reporters.
Actually they all are all of these things. They are, on most
newspapers, one-man departments who inherit the entire world
of TV the moment they are assigned to the job.

These critics face all kinds of pressures. They get beefs from
readers, beefs from advertisers, beefs from disagreeing editors,
beefs from TV stations, beefs from their wives. A vice president
of one network reportedly conceded that he threatens to cancel advertising from the newspaper whose critic becomes too
offensive. But for the most part the critics remain free to
speak their minds. For one thing, TV advertising brings in so
little money that the cancellation threats wouldn't faze even a
newspaper without enough integrity to resist such pressure on
principle.

Much has been written and nothing has been proved about
the influence of TV critics. Some network people maintain that
they pay careful attention to critics. Others scoff that in an
advertising medium such as television it is the audience ratings
and the product sales that matter, not the writings of one man
on one newspaper.

The most listened-to critics are those of the New York newspapers, not so much because of the size of their readership as

because of the fact that the network and advertising-agency brass live in New York and read these papers daily. The Los Angeles critics were, a few years ago, just another batch of provincials, but with the transfer of TV production to Hollywood they automatically attained great importance because the producers and writers and actors were among their readers.

In a report on TV criticism written by Patrick McGrady for the Fund for the Republic (the Fund for some unexplained reason never published it, but *Variety* did), he quoted one unidentified public-relations man as saying the only critics who "are really important" are Jack Gould, George Rosen, and John Crosby. Jack Gould is the top TV critic on the staff of the *New York Times,* the nation's most influential paper in any field. George Rosen is not primarily a critic but the chief TV reporter for the show-business newspaper *Variety.* John Crosby wrote essays, often humorous, on TV for the *New York Herald Tribune* for a dozen years and then switched to a general column.

The critics constantly harp upon the repetitious boredom of the series program, and no one pays them any mind. The same shows continue to roll from Hollywood. On the other hand all the causes have not been lost. When "The Play of the Week" was canceled, the first disclosure by Bob Williams of the *New York Post,* the subsequent campaigning by Gould, and the editorials and cartoons by Long Island's *Newsday* were credited by station WNTA with producing a new sponsor and saving the program from oblivion.

One question raised about TV critics is their very qualification for the task. Commentator Eric Sevareid, for one, pointed out that a newspaper maintains one critic for drama, one for movies, another for music, still another for nightclub acts, and a whole department for sports; yet the one man who is TV critic is supposed to pass judgment in all these fields and many more.

Furthermore, the critics don't have much time for thought before they write their reviews. Most see a show at home, write the review immediately, and send the copy straight to the office. If they have second thoughts, these might appear in a column later in the week.

There has been some discussion of giving the critics a preview of TV shows a week or so before the broadcast. This would permit more thoughtful reviews and it would also make the reviews more valuable to the viewer. A motion-picture critic or a drama critic tells his reader that you should see this or you shouldn't see that. The TV critic, because the show is presented only once, is in the peculiar position of telling his reader "You should have seen 'Playhouse 90' last night." He says this just about twelve hours too late for the reader to do anything about it if he happened not to have been tuned in.

Some syndicated features preview programs by covering rehearsals of live shows and advance screening of filmed shows. Many TV people think the whole industry would benefit if all critics could do this. It is not practical on a large scale, however. The Los Angeles and New York critics could have such an opportunity if they pressed for it, but it's not possible to ship these programs around the nation for advance viewing by writers in Houston and Kansas City and Pittsburgh, not to mention a host of smaller cities.

The critics get awfully bored and awfully disgusted with both TV fare and the TV audience after a few years of watching the 17-inch screen night after night without letup. Jack Mabley of the *Chicago Daily News* unleashed his bitterness in a farewell. He wrote:

"I am going to abuse the first person singular more than usual in this essay because it's my last column as a television critic. It would have been ten solid years if I had held out a few more months, but I won't. I quit.

"After particularly depressed evenings of viewing, I have often felt that television will turn us into a nation of meatheads. From my present perspective I don't worry about that much. The gunks who sit in front of that screen four hours every night watching every bit of garbage that comes in front of them would be reading *True Confessions* or playing pool or would be stretched out on the couch if they weren't watching television. Nothing gained, but nothing lost.

"In the past few years the experimenters have been slapped down or forced into the mold and the industry now is basically an advertising enterprise. This is not intended to connote an evil thing, but certainly it implies that accomplishment is measured by financial rather than by creative achievement.

"As for other professional critics who have been at it for five or eight or ten years, I don't see how they stand it."

Mabley was conceding that although he couldn't stomach standard TV fare, the "gunks who sit in front of the screen" are satisfied. Many critics disagree with him. Many feel that a great segment of the viewing audience shares the critic's boredom with formula programs. TV replies that the critics are full of malarkey. Robert Sarnoff put this in writing in a letter he sent in 1957 to the radio and television editors of the nation. He said:

"I do feel that the time has come to challenge a position taken by some of the 'dud' season critics—a position which is being uncritically accepted by various observers of the TV scene.

"This position is that the critics' dissatisfaction with the level of television fare is simply a reflection of public dissatisfaction. The public's appetite for television, so this argument goes, is being dulled by a glut of Westerns, mysteries and situation comedies and, as a result, the national audience is turning away from television in droves. The claim has no basis in fact that I know of."

And then Sarnoff turned to that Great Answer of TV, the ratings. They show the audience keeps increasing.

One of Sarnoff's stars, Dave Garroway, saw it all as a diabolical plot. The TV critics, he said on the air, "are paid by one advertising medium to destroy another, and, therefore, their motives are quite apparent, I think."

Garroway was answered by Crosby in the *Herald Tribune:*

"The terrible thing about this is that Garroway is probably sincere in saying it. The great weakness of the broadcasting business is that there is no separation of powers as there is in publishing. In radio and television stars like Garroway live under the immediate and intimate control of their advertisers. They are so accustomed to doing what they are told that it's inconceivable to them that we don't run our business that way. It's unimaginable to Garroway that in 13 years as a radio and television critic I have yet to hear a word from an advertiser or from a publisher to lay off or to do anything except to have a decent respect for the laws of libel.

"This is the normal procedure in the newspaper business but it's almost impossible to explain this to anyone in broadcasting. Even Robert W. Sarnoff finds it hard to believe that the publishers are not ganging up to crack a competitor over the skull. I don't mean to say that publishers don't enjoy the discomfiture of the broadcasters. Of course they enjoy it. It's in their blood. On a lower level it's axiomatic that newspaper men and actors loathe each other on general principle.

"But conspiracy to denigrate the medium—the publishers whipping on their hired hacks to flay television—exists only in the broadcasters' own minds. As a matter of fact, the only recorded instance of a publisher messing with his TV critics was the other way around: William Randolph Hearst attempted (not very successfully as far as I can see) to quiet his newspaper's critics and to make them be a little nicer to people and programs in television."

TV has at times considered returning the compliments of the press by reviewing it. Back in the days of radio CBS did put on a fine program of press review and criticism by Don Hollenbeck. Some newspapers flinched and at least one threatened to halt CBS listings if the program continued. It died, not under that threat but under a mantle of disinterest on the part of the general listening public.

CBS, bridling under press criticism when the quiz and payola scandals broke, announced plans to renew the program as a television feature, but the show never got on the air. A few local stations, WBBM in Chicago and WSAI in Cincinnati, to name two, have presented programs criticizing and reviewing the local press. Actually such a program would be commendable if public service rather than recrimination were the aim, but, unfortunately, there appears to be little audience interest in such projects. The ratings would be terrible.

For all the vendettas that TV plots against the press, the fact remains that the networks employ huge departments devoted exclusively to getting free publicity in the newspapers. No newspaper has a full-time employee attempting to get the paper ballyhooed on a TV station.

TV press agentry is almost an industry in itself. In addition to the mammoth network staffs, almost every local station has a public-relations man. The advertising agencies maintain press agents to pay special attention to the agency's programs. The individual TV stars maintain their own press agents. Sometimes there are three teams of publicists all working to promote the same program for different masters.

The network departments do an excellent job. Because TV news is so important to the newspaper, the ABC, CBS, and NBC press departments are set up as news agencies, feeding information and program listings by teletype to the nation's principal newspapers and news services. The networks also set up interviews with stars and generally provide valuable assistance to the papers.

In this era of the organization man, the flashily dressed press agent who once worked alone for an actor or a few actors has given way to big organizations, such as Roger and Cowan, which take on clients by the carload and service them with platoons of men. These press agents in many cases do their clients little or no good. They are as apt to infuriate reporters with their high handed ways as they are to cajole them into good notices for the clients. Many a TV performer literally throws his money away in hiring press agents who accomplish nothing the networks and the reporters' natural curiosity wouldn't accomplish anyway.

But there have been press agents of the old school in TV. Research turned up a yellowed newspaper clipping dating back to the first days of popular TV. It told of the amazing phenomenon of a Long Island housewife who had turned off her set, and five days later the picture still showed clearly. Teams of experts were sent out and they offered all manner of scientific explanation. No one solved the mystery—not until a veteran press agent recently made a slip of the tongue in a Madison Avenue bar: ". . . and then there was that stunt I pulled for Admiral TV sets out on Long Island where I rigged the set up to show a singer's picture for weeks after the damn machine was turned off. We got reams of publicity on that one."

The newspapers don't exactly relish being made dupes, but they are convinced of television's circulation value. Big TV news is played big, not at the top of the television page but rather at the top of Page One. The quiz-show winners were eulogized as heroes when quiz shows were popular, and the same winners were exposed as frauds when scandal hit the industry. It was Page One either way.

Charles Van Doren's appearance before Congress increased circulation as much as 10,000 for some newspapers. Jack Paar's walkout from NBC sold 10,000 to 12,000 extra papers for the New York dailies, and a lively series on a colorful personality like Arthur Godfrey can hike sales by 20,000. On the other hand, it is only the top personalities that will sell these extra papers. The readers show no noticeable interest in special stories on programing or behind-the-scenes production.

The extra sales have led some newspapers to enlarge their television departments almost to the point where they rival sports in manpower. But this is not done without opposition. The local movie-theater owners complain bitterly about the free space the newspaper gives their rival. The theater owners point out that they buy much more advertising than the TV stations and yet the newspaper persists in furthering TV viewing with this extra publicity. The newspapers take the position that there is more reader interest in TV personalities than in movie actors.

Television has affected the newspapers' coverage of all news. It began with sports. The first boxing matches on TV made the fan at home as much of an expert as the writer at the ringside (or so he thought), and so the writers had to take into account the questions or misconceptions arising through TV coverage.

As a natural progression from this point, the Associated Press Managing Editors Association has now recommended that the AP watch TV carefully during such major stories as the political conventions and make certain that news accounts are pegged to what the viewer saw at home.

Sometimes what the viewer "saw" was wrong. Robert Mason, managing editor of the Norfolk *Virginian-Pilot,* who was delegated by the AP to monitor CBS's coverage of the 1960 Democratic Convention, said that the network—apparently in an attempt to build up suspense and make the convention telecasts more "entertaining"—continually held out the possibility that there might be a strong challenge to Senator Kennedy for the presidential nomination. Meanwhile, the AP stories were saying flatly that Kennedy was a shoo-in. The *Virginian-Pilot* subscribers who "saw" the convention on CBS and read the AP stories in the newspapers were either confused or else suspicious that the paper was trying to railroad Kennedy into the nomination. Eventually, of course, the more sober AP was vindicated.

But, on the other hand, newspaper accounts of Soviet Premier Khrushchev's railing at a press conference following the collapse of the 1960 summit conference indicated he was a dictator gone mad. The TV tapes shown later gave a different impression—that this was a cool, calculated performance.

Both cases—one where the newspaper was correct and one where television was correct—point to the same object lesson, the AP managing editors said: The newspaper must realize

that it cannot ignore TV news coverage; it must either substantiate it or repudiate it, for the reader appears to turn to the
printed word for final judgment after having witnessed a news
spectacle on TV.

Newspapers are not always a separate entity from television.
Some 130 newspapers own at least a share of a television station and, in addition, the Hearst and Scripps-Howard chains
and the Henry Luce magazines operate TV stations. Because
of the high margin of profit in television, a newspaper and its
TV station may both show the same net at the end of the year,
although the newspaper's gross income will be five or six times
that of the TV station.

There were accusations, especially at the peak of the quiz-
show scandals, that the newspapers decried the quiz shows on
their front and editorial pages and yet profited from them on
their TV stations. Sarnoff publicly took Time, Inc., to task for
this. "*Time* magazine criticized the networks for failing to do
precisely what the Time, Inc., stations failed to do about quiz
shows," he said.

The Time, Inc., reply was that Time erred. In addition, Time
said, it was prepared to admit that "we have not as yet met the
standards in local programing that our magazines have called
for, but that is our aim." It added, "We must depend upon the
networks for presentations beyond the reach, resources—and
responsibility—of local stations."

Although newspapers frequently use TV for cash profit
through ownership, the papers seldom take advantage of TV
exposure to promote themselves. Many papers do buy straight
advertising time on TV stations, but few push their star writers
before the camera for the publicity value.

Here they miss a great bet. The writers who push themselves
attain a fame beyond that which they would get from their
printed by-lines. A perfect way is provided by Miss May Craig,
Washington correspondent for a string of medium-sized newspapers. She would scarcely be recognized even in the cities
that publish her dispatches were it not for her frequent pep-

pery appearances on TV's "Meet the Press." But because of this TV exposure she is nationally known, and this opens doors to her that would not be otherwise open to a reporter of her limited circulation.

Some newspapers flatly refuse to permit their reporters to go on TV at all. The Associated Press issued an order in 1959 barring any further TV appearances by its men. The *New York Times* won't permit its writers to appear on TV with politicians during election years. Many other papers are happy to let their men grab the publicity, yet don't solicit invitations to appear. They simply sit and wait.

The *Atlanta Journal* and the *Atlanta Constitution*, both owned by the Cox interests, do actively promote their writers and features on the station they operate. Important series are taken from the newspapers and converted into documentaries for TV, and a regular Saturday-night show utilizes the newspapers' staffs to build a show around the most important news story of the week.

For all the reader interest in television, it has not produced the welter of fan magazines which graced (or, if you will, disgraced) the motion-picture and radio industries. *TV Guide* zoomed from nothing to the largest-circulation publication in this country (it issues sixty regional editions) in a few years, but this was as a detailed program listing more than as a fan magazine. Otherwise the surviving movie magazines frequently publish stories about TV stars and there are a few attempts at full-scale TV fan magazines, but nothing to match the output the movie fans gobble up.

One explanation for this is that the fans don't need special magazines. The newspapers and the general-circulation magazines devote so much space to TV that there is little left over for a specialized publication.

TV does have an excellent trade press. In addition to *Broadcasting* and *Television Age* magazines and the solid and well-informed newsletter published as "TV Digest," there is literate and sophisticated coverage by show business' *Variety* and, because advertising is such an integral part of television, the various advertising trade publications are detailed and accurate in their coverage of the medium. *Sponsor* is a magazine devoted entirely to television advertising and advertisers.

There is no doubt that the sufficiently curious person can find all the news that's fit to print about TV, and perhaps a little that isn't so fit.

AROUND THE WORLD

The television boom that was launched in the United States in 1948 became world wide ten years later. In the first six months of 1958, 130 news station were opened, 23 of them behind the Iron Curtain. The number of receiving sets leaped 46 per cent in 1960. In addition to the United States, there were eight nations with more than a million sets by 1960—the United Kingdom with 10,000,000, Canada with 5,500,000, Japan with 4,000,000, Russia with 4,000,000, West Germany with 3,500,000, Italy and France each with 1,500,000, and Brazil with 1,000,000.

It seemed that everyone suddenly wanted to tune in TV. Well, almost everyone. Telegraph Minister Albert Hertzog did announce that he would not license a station in the Union of South Africa because he wanted to prevent "the effect of wrong shows on children, less developed people and other races."

Elsewhere things are better. But only in Japan, where there are six networks (two government channels financed from fees charged the viewer, one an educational channel and three commercial networks), are the broadcasting facilities as extensive as those in the United States. Many nations permit only a single government-owned channel.

There are three systems of TV—government-owned, commercial in the American sense, and a half-and-half formula developed by the British. TV follows the American plan in most of Latin America, Korea, and the Philippines. TV follows the British plan in Japan, Peru, Uruguay, Canada, Australia, and West Germany. TV is government-owned in the Communist nations plus France, Colombia, Italy, the Scandinavian countries, and most of the Middle East nations.

Of the 56 nations with TV, only 39 permit advertising, and even this figure is misleading. In Italy, for example, television is noncommercial except for one advertising period which runs fifteen minutes each evening. The West German and Finish government networks operate on the same plan, but allow only seven minutes a day for ads. The Italian commercials are such a novelty, however, that many viewers tune in to the advertising period with the same eagerness that they tune in their favorite regular programs. Each commercial must consist of two minutes of "entertainment" leading up to a 30-second straight plug.

Britain has tried to attain the ideal in both government and commercial telecasting. The systems reflect the British love for compromise.

The government's network is the British Broadcasting Corporation, which served the nation all through the days of radio and also launched the world's first regular television service with never a taint of political pressure. The BBC is owned by the government and subsidized to some extent by the government, yet its independent directors are never influenced by the government.

The BBC gets its money mostly from subscribers. The set owner pays the BBC a fee of $8.40 a year and the government a tax of $2.80 a year for the right to receive three BBC radio stations and one TV channel. This gives the BBC an income of about $87,000,000 a year, and it hopes eventually to reach $120,000,000.

The government enforces subscriber payments. Special electronic detector units roam the British countryside seeking out sneaks who attempt to eavesdrop on the BBC without having paid the required fee. Those caught are liable to fine and jail.

Free of commercial pressure, the BBC is able to present first-rate cultural programs far more often than the three American networks. It is able, too, to balance its programs in the way the directors feel best serves the nation; they need not succumb to the fads—Western fads, situation-comedy fads—that give networks in the United States such a sameness when all the advertisers leap on the same bandwagon.

On the other hand, the BBC cannot afford the whopping salaries the American networks pay for stars. It was partly because of this that the British, after having survived the radio era without ever being subjected to a singing commercial, demanded commercial TV as well as the BBC.

The British, as usual, compromised. They created eleven regional networks and farmed each out to a commercial operator. This gives Britain the equivalent of one national commercial network. But while these accept paid advertising, the advertiser is allowed to buy only the time for his spot commercial. He cannot sponsor an entire program and, for that matter, he has no say as to where his commercial will be placed on the network schedule. The idea, of course, is to make all programs free of pressure from the advertiser.

There is no doubt that commercial television is a financial success in Britain, and broadcasters predict that by 1964 there will be a second commercial channel and a second BBC channel operating alongside those now on the air. The eleven existing regional commercial networks showed a combined profit of $41,000,000 in 1959, and they continued to grow during each six-month period. They are authorized to broadcast only eight hours a day, however, and they frequently protest this limitation. They claim that homes receiving both commercial and BBC TV are tuned to the commercial channel 70 per cent of the time.

The British certainly do not suffer from the bluenose censorship that besets American television. Not only are they free from advertisers' pressure, but the networks take a much more liberal view of what is too naughty for the public to see and hear. There was, for example, this gag passed along at the prime viewing hour of 8:00 P.M.:

"Do you have a fairy godmother?"

"No, but I do have an uncle we're not sure of."

There is constant disagreement over whether American commercial TV is better than the British. The Americans think it is. The British think it is not. Will Roland, on loan from CBS to British TV, wrote in *Variety:*

"What has happened in England is a frantic growth of commercial TV in a period of four years. Program objectives in both content and quality are influenced by American examples. Perry Como, Phil Silvers, Fred Astaire and other U.S. shows are seen here on film exactly as they were shown at home sans commercials. When they try to copy these productions the 14 years of practical experience on which our production is based is quite obviously lacking. So are the budgets."

In France television is a government monopoly. The network Radiodifussion Française now operates one channel and plans to open a second by 1962. Some advertising men insist that commercial TV is inevitable in France but Pierre Crenesse, North American director for the network, says that a survey showed advertising would bring in only about 4 billion francs a year, while the government-owned network operates on a budget of 32 billion francs a year.

The network is supported by a tax of $12 per set a year, and provides a program that is about half film and half live. The network cannot pay high salaries, and consequently its stars are not apt to be Brigitte Bardots. It can, however, draw from magnificent talents in the French state theater. The result is that French TV is apt to be *avant-garde* frequently and high-brow most of the time. There are about four hours a week devoted to commercial movies and another two hours to quiz shows.

Crenesse says that the American's idea of French entertainment is 'way off anyway. He told of being asked by an American network to help produce an hour-long spectacular in Paris. "We were told to put on an apache dance," he said. "I told them there was no such thing. We do have a musette dance where a woman puts her arms around the man's neck and he puts his hands on her fanny if they wanted that. They didn't."

The French for some years were apathetic to TV, due partly no doubt to its highbrow atmosphere. But by 1961 set ownership reached 2,000,000, movie attendance began falling, and it was presumed that Frenchmen were beginning to watch TV. Actually, there's no way to tell, Crenesse said. The network tried making telephone polls in the manner of the American rating services, but the Frenchman, an independent cuss, would only say: "It's not enough we have to pay to watch the TV but now we have to tell you what we are watching? It's none of your business," and he would hang up.

In Spain TV is only an incidental. The Franco government operates the lone network as a monopoly, naturally, and there are scarcely 200,000 receiving sets in the entire country. The most popular program, of course, is the bullfight, which can draw an audience estimated at 1,000,000.

In Italy, on the other hand, the television audience is large and voluble. (An entire town filed suit in court when it lost out on a $1,500 prize in a quiz show.) The Italian government has licensed a monopoly network under a contract that extends to 1968. This authorizes RAI-TV to operate its existing channel and to open a second, which it plans to do in a year or so.

There are some 2,000,000 receiving sets in Italy, and almost every restaurant and saloon has TV. Unlike the American set poised over the bar, the Italian saloon set usually is in a separate room, with rows of chairs graduated up as in a theater. The waiter fetches a drink when the customer wants it.

Italy is inclined to telecast directly from the spot—a play from a theater, the opera from La Scala. It makes good use of its movie industry and, despite the limited period of advertising, can scrape up the money to attract some of the cinema's top stars for regular series programs.

There is so much pressure from Italy's booming manufacturers to get more commercial time on TV that some industrialists are pressuring the government to cancel RAI-TV's monopoly in order to present straight commercial TV. Others are considering the construction of commercial stations right across the border, the idea being to beam Italian programs for Italians from a location over which the Italian government has no jurisdiction.

Russia's government-owned and -operated television functions as a chain of more than 130 regional stations scattered throughout the vast nation. In addition to local programs, they use kinescopes and films produced by the Moscow Television Center, which also operates two local channels for the capital city.

There is great stress on children's programs, some of them charming story hours featuring puppets, and on government news and propaganda shows. But Russian TV is undergoing something of a revolution. Premier Khrushchev was greatly impressed by American newspapers and television stations on his visits to the United States. Largely through his insistence there has been a general move to imitate the method of presentation, if not the content, of our mass media.

For one thing, Russia is showing an increasing interest in commercials. Because the state manufactures and sells all products, Russian TV is not infected with the "hard sell." However, there is an increasing amount of TV time devoted to "display of new merchandise," which is simply the Communist way of saying advertising. For all their scientific attainments, however, the Russians still haven't invented anything like Gardol's invisible shield.

Russian TV is used a great deal for on-the-spot news coverage, especially of Khrushchev's arrivals and departures from major international junkets and of big sports events. It is official government policy to give major news announcements first to the TV and radio stations and later to the newspapers.

A Russian TV set costs between $200 and $300 in official exchange, but considering the Russian's earning power this comes out closer to $800. There are more than 4,000,000 sets in Russia now, and it is estimated that each is watched by an average of seven persons, by far the highest average of any nation. Russian TV operates only from 7:00 P.M. to 11:00 P.M. each evening but Sunday, when it starts at 2:00 P.M.

Russian programs often are topheavy with uncamouflaged propaganda, but they also present the best films—there are no independent drive-in theater owners to protest when TV gets first crack at a new picture—and some great musical and dance programs. The Russians plan to build the world's highest transmission tower in Moscow, and they are dabbling in color TV, although they are far behind the United States in this field.

The difference between television in West Germany and television in East Germany parallels the difference between political influences. The East Germans operate on the Russian state-propaganda plan and the West Germans operate on the British plan.

There has been some concern in West Germany that one out of four TV homes tunes in occasionally to the East German channel for their excellent movies and for their special cultural broadcasts. Will these West Germans also absorb some of the propaganda dispensed in heavy doses by the East German station?

Some West Germans have put pressure on their TV stations for more quality programing, if only to offset this possibility. Too, the East German station goes on the air at 11:00 A.M.

daily, and the West German stations don't go on until five in the afternoon.

West Germany now has two channels. The government network is cut into regional segments, one operated by each of the nation's ten states. This network permits only seven minutes of commercials each day. The other West German network, opened January 1, 1961, is completely commercial, operated under a franchise awarded Gesellschaft für Freie Fernsehen in Frankfurt. Like the British, it permits the advertiser to buy time for spot announcements but does not allow him to sponsor or control any one program.

The West German pays about $1.15 a year for the right to view the government station. For this he gets programing that is very much on the American order. One of the most popular programs is a situation comedy about the "Family Schöllermann." There is considerable importation of American shows, but the peak hours are usually reserved for German programs.

The Scandinavian countries generally stick together, and the question is which will break through the barrier against commercial TV. Once one does, the others are sure to follow. Presently TV is booming in Scandinavia, but only through government-operated networks.

In the Mideast TV is largely government operated, too. The poverty of the area holds down the sale of sets and the expansion of networks. Israel, the most progressive of the nations in the Middle East, nevertheless is the last to get television. Iran contains one of the few commercial outlets in the Middle East, but its station is somewhat self-sufficient since the owner, Habib Sabet, is the nation's distributor for Pepsi Cola and RCA, and thus automatically became his own sponsor the day he went into broadcasting.

The Middle East nations use their government-operated TV for frank propaganda purposes. When Iraq tried seventy-eight revolutionaries as enemies of the state, TV covered the trial live. The cameras studied the manacled prisoners in the box and the microphones picked up long and shrill speeches by the judge, speeches that made it plain what fate awaited these unfortunates as soon as the court got around to declaring them guilty.

But this was nothing compared to the TV appearances of Cuba's Fidel Castro. Before Castro ousted Dictator Fulgencio Batista, Cuban TV was heavily censored as far as any anti-Batista views were concerned; otherwise it operated in the American image. It carried U.S. movies, a number of U.S. kinescopes, and many American commercials. It even filled in extra time with instructional programs supplied by the U.S. Information Service.

But everything changed when Castro took over. Castro seized direct control not only of all TV stations but also of the bank accounts of the stations' owners. He issued a decree saying that any American commercial must be refilmed in Cuba before it could be played on a Cuban station; this made advertising impossible, for, even discounting the cost of this unnecessary work, Cuba did not have the film supply to remake the ads because another Castro decree forbade importation of fresh film.

Then Castro became Cuba's leading TV star. He wanders unannounced into the key station of CMQ, the principal network, and launches into a tirade before the cameras. He has gone on for as long as six hours without a stop. The engineers at the station never know what time they'll get home at night because Castro keeps late hours. He shows up to begin these speeches at nine or ten at night and keeps going until two and three in the morning.

In Canada TV is a hodgepodge of commercialism, government-ism, and compromise-ism. Canada began by utilizing the system of government monopoly through the Canadian Broadcasting Corporation. Then, to ease the taxpayers' burden in paying the deficit, the government authorized the CBC to take in some commercial sponsors, but "not too many."

Still Canada staggered forward. It authorized independently owned stations in eight major areas, and told them they could show American programs but they could not join an American network. This put these stations in something of a hole because many Canadians can receive American stations from across the border and naturally will do so if they get better shows from the rich U.S. networks than from the financially hamstrung Canadian stations.

On top of all this, the large French-speaking population of Canada often makes it necessary for stations (including the CBC) to operate in two languages.

The Canadian effort to hold down the use of American programs is part of an almost universal tendency. Canada now insists that 55 per cent of its programs be home-produced. Britain will permit a network to devote only 12 per cent of its time to American shows. (Some newspapers complain that this 12 per cent is bunched in the best viewing hours and is converting the populace into Western fans.) Japan puts a financial restriction on imports, permitting a maximum payment of $450 for each half-hour show, although a Japanese sponsor will pay as much as $2,000 for the same type of show if produced in Japan.

Resistance to American programs puts the U.S. syndicators in a predicament. They have been eased out of a good share of their market at home because the American networks claim so much of a station's time there is little left for the syndicate's product. Now, with 10 to 25 per cent of their total revenue coming from foreign sales, they are finding all sorts of barriers erected against them. The prices vary greatly from country to country. A half-hour program that will bring $6,000 in Britain will go for $50 in Uruguay.

The American networks also want to branch out overseas. The American Broadcasting Company owns 51 per cent of the Central American network it helped organize. CBS helped design the West German commercial network and operates a TV production center in Argentina in partnership with Goar Mestre of Havana. NBC also shares an interest in an Argentine network and holds minority interests in a number of Latin

American stations. The three American networks also have overseas sales divisions that peddle films of their old programs in competition with the independent syndicators.

There is frequent talk of a world-wide network that will someday link all nations for a single broadcast or series of broadcasts. Actually, this could come very soon if everyone wanted it, but political and other problems will remain long after the engineering problems are solved.

There exists today a European network of sorts. It is called Eurovision. Actually, it is not a network in the sense that it plans and broadcasts regular programs. But it does maintain a co-ordinating office that makes the arrangements when the networks of the various European nations want to join for a special broadcast. Eurovision eventually will hook up with Asian and Scandinavian networks, and Russia plans to link all its satellites into a single network that in turn could also join Eurovision on occasions.

Eurovision is used mostly for major news events and for sports spectaculars with an international flavor. Wimbledon tennis is a Eurovision regular, for example. Eurovision also has staged a few theatrical programs, but not many.

The factors that would prevent a world-wide TV network as a regular thing are countless. There is the political factor, for example; it's not likely that Russia and the United States will share many TV programs for quite a while. There is the difference in languages. There are the differences in taste (Britain doesn't dig Jack Paar). There is the difference in commercial practices. And there is the time difference. (The prime viewing hour of 8:00 P.M. in New York is 1:00 A.M. in London, 4:00 A.M. in Moscow, and 9:30 A.M. tomorrow in Tokyo.)

News and sports are the most likely fare of even a world-wide network that functions only on special occasions. But here again the demand is slight. For one thing, most news broadcasts are not live but for the most part are composed of tapes or film flown to New York. With the jets becoming even faster, such film can arrive from London or Paris in time for the same news broadcast that offers tapes or film flown from Little Rock or Kansas City.

The idea of a world-wide network is a great dream, but professional TV men wake up when they start considering just how practical it is.

THEN THE ROOF FELL IN

The scandal that jolted the American television industry in 1958 didn't break out into the open. It oozed out. Most people assumed that a disgruntled quiz contestant marched determinedly into the New York district attorney's office and told all, whereupon the forces of law and order swept out of the corral like a posse on the trail of Jesse James. Unfortunately, things didn't happen that way.

In December of 1956 a contestant who thought he had been done wrong complained to the Federal Trade Commission about a show called "The Big Surprise." The FTC asked the show's producer if "The Big Surprise" was fixed. The producer said no. That ended that.

In April of 1957 the *New York World Telegram & Sun* published a series of articles hinting at rigged quiz shows. *Time* and *Look* magazines followed with similar stories. That ended that.

In March of 1958 and again in the fall of the same year George Abrams, then a vice president of the sponsoring Revlon Cosmetics, reported to CBS that contestants were charging "fix" on "The $64,000 Challenge." That ended that.

Then in the summer of 1959 a sometime night-club comic named Eddie Hilgemeier blew the whistle on a show called "Dotto." This time the whole world heard. But Hilgemeier did not march righteously or bitterly to the DA's office. He went to the *New York Post* and offered to sell his story of quiz-show fraud.

Still there was no sudden exposé. The newspapers had sniffed scandal in the big quiz shows before this. But although columnists like Jack O'Brian of the *New York Journal-American* dropped veiled hints of hanky-panky in their writings, no one dared publish a story giving the names of contestants and programs, even though Herbert Stempel admitted his performances on "Twenty-One" were rigged. They feared the law of libel. Making the charges of fixed shows was one thing; proving these charges in court was something else.

The *Post* therefore moved cautiously. It presented Hilgemeier's affidavit to the FCC. It waited only long enough to determine that the commission would handle this complaint like all others—it would pigeonhole it to death. Then the *Post* switched to the DA.

The sponsor, Colgate Palmolive, learned of this and, fearing scandal, frantically canceled the show (which, in that day of quiz crazes, was on *both* networks, CBS at night and NBC in the daytime). The *Post* used the cancellation announcement as the excuse to print the story it had been holding.

Inside TV there was considerable concern, but the industry put up a bold front to the public. The networks took the pose that the one bad apple was out of the barrel and so no one need worry no longer.

The newspapers pushed on, still supercautious but encouraged by the first break. The DA continued his investigation, although there was serious doubt as to what a grand jury might do even in a clear-cut case of a fixed quiz show. There was no law that specifically made rigged shows illegal. The DA worked with vague statutes dealing with business fraud.

Stempel's charges that he was ordered to lose to Charles Van Doren on "Twenty-One" were long known and yet never printed because of that fear of libel. Now suddenly he, too, was talking to the DA—and so the newspapers were emblazoned with headlines about his case. The snowball was rolling. James Snodgrass not only added his story of a fixed "Twenty-One" program to the mounting list, but he could prove it: He had mailed himself letters containing prearranged answers and stage directions for his appearances; the postmarks on the still-sealed letters showed he knew all this the day before he went on the air.

In Washington the FCC remained calm and stoic, but Congress did not. Aware of the great headlines in the offing, the House Subcommittee on Legislative Oversight began an investigation, and soon the entire TV industry was in an uproar.

How long had this quiz fixing been going on? Why had it started? Who had known about it?

Quiz shows dated back to radio, and on radio there were so-called professional contestants, regulars who appeared on show after show under an assortment of phony names from an assortment of phony home towns. But the stakes were not big enough to warrant major scandal. Radio had a $64 question. It took television to produce a $64,000 question.

The television quiz fixes were the result of the following factors:

The fight for ratings. In radio a program was good for thirteen or twenty-six weeks, and the sponsor could cancel only after that time. Because of the tremendously high costs, the TV sponsor felt he could not wait out these long periods. He watched his ratings week by week, canceling if the audience rating dipped dangerously at any time.

The medium's need for personalities. The TV audience did not simply watch a man win or lose on a TV show. It rooted

with him or against him. The quiz-show producers, by studying the up-and-down of the weekly ratings, soon realized that
they had villains and heroes on their hands. They soon ad-
hered to the traditional TV plot in which the villain loses and
the hero wins.

TV's atmosphere. Before the jolt of exposure, it never occurred to quiz-show producers that there was anything wrong
with rigging a program. This was show business, not commerce
or sports. The producers felt the beguiled audience was no
more cheated by the false atmosphere of a contest that was not
a contest than by the false claims of the commercials or by the
fact that a play about Alaska was shot on a Hollywood sound
stage. Furthermore, the producers felt no compassion for the
defeated contestant, for if he wasn't an out-and-out mercenary
he at least was sent home no worse off than when he began,
and often a bit wealthier.

The contestants for the quiz shows often came directly from
show business. With the need for charming personalities who
could project to the audience, it became routine for an actor's
agent to send a struggling young player to a quiz show. This
would not be exactly a rigged hiring. The agent would be
tipped off that "Whoopo" would like a schoolteacher from
Nebraska on its next show. He'd send one of his young clients
up to the producer's office, and she naturally assumed the role
of "schoolteacher from Nebraska" when she filled out the preliminary questionnaire.

From there it was an easy matter of fixing the winners and
losers. Each prospective contestant took an examination in the
category to which he claimed expert knowledge. After that the
quiz master could fix the show without even letting the contestant in on the secret. After all, the examination revealed
what the contestant knew and what he didn't. Want him to
win? Ask him a safe question. Want him to lose? Ask him a
question that goes beyond his knowledge. They called this
"program control," and some sponsors sat in on the selection of
the weekly questions to help out. But the quiz-show riggers

couldn't stop there. Quiz shows needed emotion, and the contestant who won or lost with poker face was not nearly so interesting as the one who writhed under the strain before blurting out his answer. So the producers began coaching their contestants in nail biting, and that's when they opened the door to disaster. Now the contestant was in on the fraud, and it was only a matter of time before one would expose them all.

Once caught, the producers might have stood publicly on their private attitude—that certainly the show was rigged, but only to make it better entertainment. They didn't. Instead they panicked and they lied. Furthermore, they went chasing after bygone contestants to urge them, too, to lie before the grand jury and the DA. But Albert Freedman, the producer of "Twenty-One" broke down and recanted his perjury. He told all—how he rigged the shows, how he coached the contestants, how he solicited a cover-up story from contestants once the DA started an investigation. This was the end. A contestant coached for his appearance before the camera might be pure show business, but a witness coached for perjury before the grand jury wasn't.

These contestants had seldom been casual citizens who wandered into the program off the street. They were the young actors with their foolish hope that a big producer would see them on the quiz show and transplant them to *Kismet*.

They were old actors, too, people who had been acting a role of fantasy all their lives in a struggle to rise above the commonplace. Charles Van Doren fell into this category. Born of a famous family, he was desperate to *be somebody* on his own; to Van Doren the role of quiz-show hero was sudden arrival at a destination he had never before been near.

There was still a third category of contestant—the out-and-out celebrities who were openly hired through normal show-business channels to give the quiz show added box-office draw in that eternal chase of higher ratings. Frequently these people demanded that their quiz appearances be fixed. They had professional reputations to maintain and they dared not risk making fools of themselves before the great TV audience.

The fact that quiz shows were not out-and-out contests of skill and knowledge was well known within the TV industry long before the public found out. But did the industry in general know how much fraud was involved? Some advertising and network people knew everything. Most were a little suspicious and too cynical to inquire beyond that.

Some of the insiders did become worried over the danger of eventual exposure. Once he realized the extent of the show fixing, Revlon's Abrams went to the producers of several major quiz shows to suggest that they band together and appoint a czar to police the field. This would head off trouble, he thought. The producers rejected his idea. This would be admitting the shows might be fixed, they said, and they were not prepared to do that. Why rock the boat? The public had no inkling of what was going on.

This was all done in the interest of the advertiser, and yet it was the advertiser who did the loudest—and, in a way, the most effective—screaming when the scandal became headlines. The protest was not entirely on moral grounds, but was based on the fear that the viewer can hardly be expected to believe the commercials if he is suspicious of the entire program's integrity.

With the very backbone of the TV economy thus threatened, the networks acted. CBS sounded most righteous when it banned all quiz shows and then, going ludicrously past the bounds of necessity, even told its comedians they could no longer use rigged laughter. (The network canceled both orders a few months later.) NBC was more prudent, promising diligent supervision but certainly no expulsion of quiz shows. ABC was not caught in the mess because it had ignored quiz shows to pioneer its policy of formula series programs.

But far more important than any change in network policy was the change in Federal Communications Commission policy. It had long been the FCC's position that it had no right to interfere with TV programing. The inevitable complaints that came into its Washington office were dismissed as the work of cranks, and only the most cursory attention was paid them. Now the FCC, with a prod from the Justice Department (a prod the commissioners privately damned as unfair), suddenly decided it would act on complaints about programing, and Congress went so far as to make rigged quiz shows specifically illegal. This federal action and the threat of even more restrictive legislation, added to the fears of the advertisers, became a second force that prodded the networks into a more cautious examination of what they sent out over the air.

But the scandal could not stop with the quiz shows. There was payola, too. Here again was a situation well known in the trade and ripe for investigation any time any government source was inclined to grab headlines.

It costs only a few hundred dollars to press a phonograph record, and hundreds of companies press new records every day. The only effective way to publicize a record is through the nation's radio and TV disc jockeys. The record company could make the record and hope for the best, or it could offer a gratuity to make certain the disc jockey would play it.

This practice is almost as old as the music business. Even before there were phonograph records, there were song pluggers urging the stars of the stage to hypo sheet-music sales by adding particular songs to their repertoire.

But there is always progress, even in the wrong direction, and the wheedling song plugger of the gay nineties became the bagman of the 1950's. First the disc jockeys were paid in free records, and then in free meals, and then in cash bribes, and then they hit the big money with the right to present singing stars at "record hops." The star collected little or nothing for his appearance, and the disc jockey pocketed all the admission fees he collected for the hop (which he had, of course, liberally advertised in advance on his radio or TV program). The disc jockeys were feted royally by the record manufacturers. Their 1957 national convention in Miami Beach became an orgy of fawning attention. Record companies spent more

than $100,000 in one weekend gorging their guests with food
and drink, and a few of the more important broadcasters found
pretty blondes wrapped in Cellophane (and nothing else) delivered to their hotel rooms.

There were raised eyebrows from the congressmen and there
were raised voices from the supposedly outraged station owners when these practices were exposed. Actually, of course, the
station owners and most congressmen had known of these
shenanigans for years. Some stations' owners, it developed
later, had shielded disc jockeys from excessive payola by collecting the money for themselves.

The record plugging did not only involve *sub rosa* bribery.
Even out in the open there was a conflict of interest between
the broadcaster and what he broadcasts. In the first place, the
radio broadcasters deliberately went into the music business
in the 1930's by setting up their own association of composers,
Broadcast Music, Inc., to compete with the long-established
American Society of Composers, Authors, and Publishers. In the
second place many a star also owns a music-publishing company. Among those who do are Steve Allen, Guy Lombardo,
Dinah Shore, Perry Como, Jackie Gleason, Tennessee Ernie
Ford, Frank Sinatra, Lawrence Welk, Pat Boone, Louis Prima,
Ray Bloch, and Garry Moore. When the time comes for them
to select a song to sing on the air, should they choose a song
published by their own firm? Or should they plug the song of
a competitor?

The House subcommittee's investigators found there was no
end to the moneymaking practices of radio and TV station
employees. Some collected kickbacks from any performer who
wanted to appear on the air. Some demanded not one-shot
bribes but continuing royalties on songs they plugged. Some
simply turned over the mortgage on the house or car to the
record company and let it do the rest. The revelations came
fast and furious, and when reporters saw a newcomer in their
midst busily scribbling notes they found he wasn't from a

newspaper at all. "I'm from the Internal Revenue Service," he said.

The adults who deplored the younger generation's devotion to rock 'n' roll found a new complaint. This music was heard only because of bribery, they said. It was a synthetic fad. Without payola, this never could have been forced upon their young. But Paul Ackerman, the music editor of *Billboard*, wrote in *The Nation*:

"It is axiomatic in the music business that a 'bad' song or record—by which is meant a song lacking in commercial appeal—can never prove a hit no matter how much plugging it gets, legitimately or illegitimately. This was true in the payola-ridden 1920's and 1930's and it is true today. But it is also axiomatic that a 'good song'—i.e., a song with commercial appeal—must receive adequate plugging if it is to achieve its potential.

"Elvis Presley was adequately plugged, but he is also 'good.' All the payola in the world used in behalf of competing discs will never dent the popularity of this singer, whose records have already grossed more than $50,000,000 in the last five years.

"In sum: payola may be ethically deplorable, but it is unlikely that it has ever changed, or ever could change, the course of popular American music."

The broadcast industry found it was much easier to downgrade quiz shows than to halt payola. A number of stations indignantly fired disc jockeys, and the jittery record companies became far more prudent. But the American Broadcasting Company made it plain it would not dismiss the star of its teenage dance hour, Dick Clark, despite revelations that he pushed songs published by companies in which he had a financial interest. ABC's billings for the daily Clark show amount to millions of dollars a year, and this comes at an hour of the day when television time normally is very difficult to sell. TV does have its indispensable men.

From payola the congressional investigators moved to "plugola." They moved sheerly from momentum, for plugola is hardly one of the great sins of our time. It is the practice of a manufacturer paying off a TV writer or performer to mention his product on the air. Sometimes the payoff is in cash, but just as often it is in merchandise.

A writer for the mystery series "Johnny Dollar" got a $30 gift certificate or a case of whisky for the plugs he inserted. Another writer got a new lighting system installed in his home.

Plugola was another of those TV industry secrets that everyone knew about. Writers were supplied weekly lists of plug requests and rewards to be collected. Some specialists went into the plugola business, arranging these mentions for fees up to $350 for each plug planted on a network show. Some air lines put the plug on a business basis, paying cash to the program or the network for mention that the guest stars rode their planes.

Plugola became an open joke in TV. A director who immediately demanded a share of the plugola as soon as he joined a new show was put in his place by the writers: they arranged a plug and delivered to the director's apartment the entire take—eight sacks of fertilizer.

All of this was of little real concern to the viewer, unless perhaps he really cared which air line flew the guests to Hollywood. The only man cheated was the program sponsor who paid for the time to advertise someone else's wares. And an indignant sponsor could have halted plugola on his show any time he chose.

When Earl Kintner took over the Federal Trade Commission and began an exposé of deceptive commercials, he reached the point that the sponsors had feared when they first faced the quiz-show scandals: The public's belief in advertising would be undermined. The advertising industry promised great cleanups and the "hard sell" became something to avoid. But the line between lavish boast and outright deception is so thin and so wavy that the advertiser can only hope for the heat to cool.

What did the public think of all this? Characteristically, TV

rushed to the polls and the rating services for the answer. Elmo
Roper conducted a poll for the Television Information Service
and learned, he said, that only 41 per cent of the people considered TV scandals "a serious moral problem." His poll was
a cutey. Those interviewed were not only asked about TV
scandals. They were also asked about juvenile delinquency,
dishonest labor leaders, government officials accepting bribes,
policemen taking graft, international disarmament, false advertising claims, the testing of atomic bombs, fixed boxing
matches, and congressmen putting their relatives on payrolls.
Obviously, after hearing that sordid list, the man being interviewed had very little outrage left when the questioner finally
reached rigged TV quizzes near the bottom of his list.

At the peak of the quiz scandals Nielsen found a minor drop
in nighttime television viewing—a drop of 3 to 4 per cent. Sindlinger conducted a similar investigation and translated the drop
this way: those over the age of twelve were watching TV forty-
three minutes a day less than they had in the past. This caused
no concern in the industry. The loss was temporary.

Advertising and television men rushed into print arguing
that there was no such thing as a TV scandal per se; it was, if
anything, they said, a national scandal reflected partly in rigged
quiz shows, to be sure, but also in the deep-freeze scandals of
Washington, the labor extortions, the police and welfare and
building-code graft of almost every American city, the rise in
juvenile delinquency. They asked why the special concern
over broadcasting payola when it takes a New York plastics
manufacturer two days to deliver all the Christmas whisky he
dispenses to customers' purchasing agents every year. They
asked why the sudden shock at plugola when most newspapers
have always permitted reporters to take junkets and write
about them.

They were justified in their questions, of course. Some of the
very congressmen who were gasping with horror at the revelations of payola soon were defending padded expense accounts
they had submitted for government junkets. The broadcasting

industry was no more corrupt than any other. It was merely more flamboyant than most. Those disc jockeys who received blondes wrapped in Cellophane were neither the first nor the last businessmen to enjoy the delights of professional love on someone else's expense account.

But the TV scandals did have a good result. They frightened the FCC into discharging its duties on behalf of the people for at least the period of crisis. They frightened the advertising industry into at least re-examining its excesses. They frightened the networks and local stations into injecting at least a minimum of public-service programs into their formula-clogged schedules.

They raised the hope that—if you'll pardon the pun—fright makes right.

...AND WHATEVER BECAME
OF RADIO

Radio didn't die with the advent of television, but it didn't live on unchanged, either. Rather it was reborn in a new image, and today it thrives by embracing many policies it deliberately avoided back before the nation became addicted to TV.

There are now three times as many radio stations as there were in 1946. True, these 3,000 stations combined show only half the profit earned by the 1,000 in 1946, but they do maintain a steady and comfortable income and a permanent niche in the community. The radio station has become the small businessman of American broadcasting.

People still listen. The Alfred Politz Research Institute reports that there are radios in 94.5 per cent of the homes and 70.7 per cent of the automobiles. The transistor radio is carted to the beach, to the ball game, to school, and even on shopping trips.

But life in the radio studio of today is a far cry from the

golden days of the 1930's and early 1940's. The big expensive programs with their world-famous stars are gone and, indeed, the big networks are all but gone: they remain as skeletons dangling in the closet for occasional viewing as a family curiosity. Furthermore, the wisecracking fast-talking disc jockey is becoming a relic of bygone days, his replacement a quiet announcer of songs and commercials. Today's radio is music and news and little else.

The networks were selling $133,723,098 worth of time in 1948 when TV surged across the nation, and from there they began tumbling down. They have since curtailed and curtailed and curtailed. The National Broadcasting Company in 1960 cut its service to a program of only twenty-five news broadcasts a day plus the weekend Monitor news and interview show, and the most significant thing about this shrinkage was the reason behind it: not only did the NBC affiliates want to cut off all other service, but the key stations that NBC itself owns and operates were losing audience because they persisted in carrying outmoded network programs.

Even that old standby, the afternoon soap opera, was a victim of the TV age. At their peak, the sob stories ran six to eight hours a day and brought to the networks more than $25,000,000 a year. Proctor & Gamble alone once had nineteen of these programs going at one time. NBC eliminated the soap operas in the early part of 1960. CBS, always the leader in the soap-opera field, tried to hang on, but later the same year also had to give up.

That left network radio in the position where NBC was reduced to little more than a news service; CBS also stressed news but maintained a few still popular personality programs such as Arthur Godfrey; ABC was playing it by ear, trying out programs but never daring to put them on the air unless they were sold to a sponsor in advance. Mutual, the fourth radio network, also lived off a diet of news and commentary.

Many in broadcasting think that these are merely holding actions and that eventually there will be one radio network at most and perhaps none. This could be a serious situation. Even if there is no economic or advertising use for nation-wide radio hookup, there could be a great need in a time of national emergency. Radio remains the quickest and most practical way of passing along urgent information to the general population.

However, the station owners are firm in their conviction that formula network programing is obsolete. They plan continuous outpouring of news and music, and they can make more money supplying this from their own studios from records (which they don't even pay for, thanks to the largesse of the manufacturers) than piping it in from a network.

Although it was repeated many times across the nation, the tug of war between the networks and the local stations was summed up in a single case, that involving the Westinghouse stations. These had been NBC affiliates for thirty years. But when many of radio's advertising dollars went flying to TV and the listeners and stars followed, Westinghouse refused to sign new network contracts with NBC.

Westinghouse maintained that the old clauses, such as signing away option time to the network, were now outmoded because NBC could not sell the time for the old prices. NBC continued to pipe its programs to the Westinghouse stations anyway, reluctant to give them up because they were such an important part of the network's audience.

In arguments over renewing the contracts, Westinghouse suggested that NBC produce programs and sell them outright to the local stations. These stations could then secure sponsorship and keep the profits. NBC refused. It still had hopes of saving the old system whereby it bought Westinghouse's time for a fraction of the normal price and kept the sponsor's coin for itself.

Westinghouse quit. It pulled its stations out of the network entirely and resorted to local programing exclusively. Robert Sarnoff of NBC wrote Westinghouse President Donald McGannon a bitter letter calling him "shortsighted" and took him to task for abandoning efforts to maintain "a basic national communications system."

But the words were in vain. Westinghouse stayed out, and there were others who likewise gave up network affiliations entirely. The franchise that had been so valuable in the heyday of radio had become a liability in the heyday of television.

The Mutual network introduced what it called a "time barter plan," which has been adopted by others. Under the old system the networks paid their affiliates straight cash for the time used, and the network then resold this time at a profit to the sponsors. Under the "time barter plan" the network gives the station the program but does not pay for the time used; the network sells part of the show to national sponsors and the local station is free to sell the remaining portion of the show to local sponsors.

In the place of the networks radio is growing a new arm. It is the syndicate that provides fragmentary interviews and brief on-the-spot news reports that can be used by the independent station at any convenient time during its programing day. These services eschew the old flamboyance of network radio with its complement of engineers, announcers, producers, and other functionaries. The syndicates send out reporters equipped with only a portable tape recorder and sometimes with not even that—sometimes they go with only a dime to put in the nearest pay telephone for a call to the service's studio. The results turned in by these men frequently are far superior to those produced by the network's regiment of self-conscious celebrities.

The radio industry thinks the ideal in TV-age radio is represented by WPAT. This station was losing $73,000 a year as a typically raucous voice of Paterson, New Jersey, in 1950. Today it is a major voice not simply of Paterson but of the entire New York metropolitan area. Furthermore, WPAT has received inquiries from thirty-eight states and thirteen foreign countries since then. The inquiries are all the same: How do you do it?

WPAT, a 5,000-watt station as opposed to some 50,000-watt giants, built up its mammoth and determinedly loyal audience by planning a program for the listener rather than for the station's convenience or profit. Then, having created a formula that would attract a large audience, it went out to sell advertising on its own terms. It worked.

The WPAT program policy is to play music continuously for fifteen minutes at a stretch; there is no break at all, not even to announce the names of the songs. It plays only standard song favorites, never highbrow and never fads like rock 'n' roll. It has weather reports every half-hour and five minutes of news every hour. It inserts commercials only on the quarter-hour during the day and only at half-hour breaks at night. It will not accept unusually loud and harsh commercials. It will not permit the same commercials to be broadcast so often that they become an irritant. It won't permit shouting or fast-talking announcers. (The limit is 125 words a minute.) It has a flat rate for its time and it makes no special deals for volume sales or favored customers.

The result of the formula is that the listener can turn on WPAT in the morning and keep it going all day without becoming irritated by excessive commercialism or raucous music. The comparative infrequency of the commercials actually gives each ad more impact.

There are many WPAT imitators operating throughout the nation today. Their success is largely measured by their adherence to the formula. Many start with it and then begin chiseling themselves with a few extra commercials or by taking an account that might be just a little offensive. Soon they lose the image that they have been seeking to establish.

The WPAT formula (some stations operate in the same fashion stressing classical and semiclassical music) was given impact by the payola scandal, which provided an excuse for many stations to rid themselves of rock 'n' roll formulas and the ever-chattering disc jockeys. Many were prepared to make the change anyway. As with TV, radio has long suspected the buying power of the teenager and has felt more comfortable luring older groups for the benefit of the advertiser.

Some stations trapped themselves into playing largely rock 'n' roll by following a sort of rating system: They checked the local record stores and on the air they stressed the records that were selling the most copies. The idea, of course, was that these record sales proved this was the music the listener wanted.

However, record sales are largely to teenagers, and radio listening is the domain of the housewife, the barbershop, the automobile. These stations are switching to what they call "recognizable music"—music taken from Broadway shows, from movies, and the old standards that are more to the liking of the audience radio wants.

With the decline of the national network, radio became more local and consequently more interested in local problems. Many stations found themselves doing a lot of good for the community—and for the stations—by suddenly developing a social conscience. This is exactly the opposite of radio's attitude in the old days, when controversy was a word to be whispered in the backroom if, indeed, it was uttered on studio property at all. Today there are Barry Grays in New York and Stan Gysons in Miami all across the country deliberately getting provocative and controversial on the grounds that this is one thing TV can't do.

These are just breaks in the broadcasting day, however. Basically, radio is a continuous program of music, interrupted periodically for five or ten minutes of news. This is such common policy that a vice president of the Storer radio chain, John E. McCoy, told the FCC it is "unrealistic" to expect stations today to present any kind of "balanced" programing. It is the balance of yesteryear that these stations must avoid like the plague, he said. The listener no longer tunes in to a radio program. He now tunes in to a station, and he expects it to be carrying the same thing at any time of the day or night.

Many stations have placed the news over the music. KMOX,

the station CBS operates in St. Louis, carries *nothing but news* in the afternoons. These are not all straight broadcasts of the wire-service dispatches. Some of the programs are discussion, some are tips for housewives, some are book and theater reviews. But they all come under the heading "information," and nary a note of music interrupts them between noon and 7:00 P.M.

This may be an extreme, but the National Association of Broadcasters reports that the average station has increased its news-broadcast time by two hours a week in the last seven years. Furthermore, the NAB reports, these stations are concentrating on their local areas. Some three-fourths of radio's news programs are produced in the local studio in order to stress local and regional news.

Station WNEW in New York spends $250,000 a year on news coverage. It maintains stringer correspondents around the nation who call in special broadcasts by long-distance telephones, and it keeps a 15-man newsroom in operation at home. It subscribes to a special news service in Washington and turns out a total of 330 news broadcasts a week. This is not only a proud service. It is also profitable. It shows a $200,000 net on the sale of these news broadcasts.

Radio stations concentrate so much on news, as a matter of fact, that they killed off one of their own pioneers. It was the Standard Oil Company's "Esso Reporter" which for twenty-four years was the basic news broadcast in seventy cities. Standard dropped sponsorship of the "Esso Reporter" in 1960 because the program no longer had any impact: The listeners didn't wait for it because there were dozens of equally good news broadcasts on every station every day.

During World War II radio had thought that the superior qualities of FM would convert the entire industry from the AM band as soon as peace came. They did not anticipate the speed with which TV would eclipse all radio. But if it did not grow with the rapidity and cannibalism that had been forecast for it, FM radio nevertheless did grow, and today it is a significant arm of the broadcasting industry.

The economy of maintaining an FM station (the Beverly Hills station is run by a staff of six) plus the need to find an uncommitted audience has made FM the nation's quality broadcasting service. It is on FM that one can hear the best music. It is on FM that one will hear experimentation in drama and in discussion programs. It is on FM that radio will buck all the taboos of yore as it searches for a sophisticated audience that is neither glued to "Wagon Train" nor washing diapers to WPAT. FM broadcasting is superior-tone broadcasting (the tone is truer and hence the music more engrossing) and so the music lover will be addicted to it if he can hear good programs. He can, and so now the Madison Avenue advertising men who have been listening to FM for years in their homes are now listening to it a bit in their offices.

FM radio advertising is up. Makers of expensive products are especially interested in it as a medium of selling their wares. And, down but not out, the radio networks are showing an interest in FM. The question here is whether the networks would join FM or kill it. FM flourishes by deliberately ignoring the lowest common denominator of entertainment to seek out a specialty audience. The network philosophy of mass sales runs directly counter to this. Actually, FM has made considerable progress as extremely specialized service. Many stations serve small suburban areas.

NBC had an interesting idea for FM. It proposed to build a network purely as an information service for doctors. The programs would be received in the doctors' offices and in their cars. The station would broadcast medical news and advertising, keeping the doctor abreast of new techniques and discoveries daily. In between these news broadcasts the network would play soothing music that could be piped into the doctor's waiting room. The advertising agencies handling the drug and medicine accounts did not leap to the bait. They had serious doubts that the doctor would listen to the commercial, and if he didn't the whole plan was worthless as far as they were concerned.

There will be other attempts to saddle this mustang called FM. The statistics are so inviting: There are more than 850 stations in operation now, playing to 15,500,000 sets. The National Association of Broadcasters says 51 per cent of these set owners tune in at least once daily. Furthermore, it says, only 3 per cent of the listeners are under eighteen years of age. Those persons asked why they tune in FM almost invariably reply "good music."

FM is due to get even better technically. The FCC has authorized the use of stereophonic programs, and these should be widespread by 1963. Mass production of sets is driving prices down to as low as $19. And FM is finally reaching the automobile with the development of a $75 car set.

The FM listener is so loyal that some stations have collected considerable revenue merely by asking their audience to donate money to finance better programing. Basically, however, FM realizes it must stand on its feet as a commercial medium, and this almost certainly means as an advertising medium.

In a sense radio is getting back to where it first started. David Sarnoff's historic memo proposing broadcasting for the home mentioned concerts and lectures and did not mention "Queen for a Day." The very first performers were concert and operatic stars. (The first known broadcast was by Swedish concert singer Eugenia Farrar, who sang "I Love You Truly" just for kicks when she was inspecting Dr. Lee de Forest's experimental station one night in 1907. She almost caused a young radio operator at the Brooklyn Navy Yard to be thrown into the psycho ward because he promptly reported to his superiors that he heard a woman singing through his headset.)

The formula network radio, as most of us remember it, actually lived a very short life. As late as 1925 the NBC log contained such notes as:

Jan. 25.—Robert Burns Program. Not a good event. Speaker did not show up.

Jan. 26.—Savarin Ensemble. A little dispute between Franko and the director Meyerhoff caused a short interruption.

June 21.—Keith McLeod, pianist, on the air from 8 till 10:35 with 15 minutes' rest. Fay Milbar, who was supposed to play the piano for Milton Cross, didn't show up.

In the 1930's everybody showed up, of course. Radio became big business, and the advertising agencies froze their safe formula programs into the network schedules. These lasted until television silenced them. The flannelmouth disc jockey was next, and his sun was dimmed by the cloud of the payola scandal.

Now radio is back to the original Sarnoff plan of concerts and news and lectures. Sometimes the best form of progress is no progress at all.

The men in television remind anyone who will listen that theirs is an infant industry. It will grow, they say. It will mature. They beg compassion for the mistakes and excesses of youth.

But will TV really mature? The motion-picture industry matured and radio is maturing now, but neither did so until forced. Neither the movies nor radio showed any inclination to break away from their infantile formulas until television began devouring their customers.

Television's greatest handicap is the way it is financed. It is a slave to the advertiser, who, in turn, must be a slave to the bland formulas that guarantee him the greatest possible audience at the least possible cost.

Is there a way out of this trap? Is there another means of financing television? Let's examine the three major possibilities.

The first is government-operated television. The second is pay television. The third is the so-called "magazine concept" of TV.

298

There is something about government-operated television that touches off alarms in the American mind. The dangers are great. It is true that the British have managed for decades to operate first a government radio network and now a government TV network that are completely free of political interference. However, the threat is always present: If the government operates a medium as powerful as TV, the administration in power always will be tempted to use it as an instrument of propaganda and apology.

Furthermore, there is no reason to believe that the government could produce better television programs than the commercial networks. The government might excel in some types of public service or public information shows, but it is not a likely source for superior comedy or drama or music. And, anyway, is entertainment of the people a proper function of government?

Few men who understand television seriously think that government TV is the answer, but many look upon pay TV as the panacea. This would free the producers and artists from the tyranny of the advertiser, they say. This would truly make the viewer king.

But pay TV eliminates the greatest virtue of today's American television. It is free. And with installment buying so easy, there is scarcely a citizen who cannot afford a set. Aerials jut from the roofs of countless Southern shantys and Northern slums, making many a mean life bearable by the laughs and songs and adventure that pour from the box in the living room at the end of a miserable day. The people who benefit most from television would be the first casualties of pay TV.

Yet even then the advocates of fee television can furnish no guarantee that their fare will be so superior to the current network programing after the first flush of originality.

It is in the third possibility that I find most logic and consequently most hope. This is the "magazine concept," another of those Pat Weaver brain children and the system that is used by the British commercial network.

Under this plan the advertiser buys time for his message but he buys no program. Consequently he has no control of the programs. He cannot even choose which shows will carry his commercial.

This is the way magazines work. The manufacturer can buy an ad in the *Saturday Evening Post*, but he does not tell the *Post* which articles to publish that week and he certainly doesn't tell the *Post* writers to eliminate all references to blowouts because he sells automobile tires. The magazine publisher naturally does what he can to protect the advertiser from embarrassment. Ads for competing cigarettes are not placed next to one another. An air line's ad is not placed next to an article about plane crashes. But the advertiser never sponsors the articles in the magazine and consequently he is entitled to no control over them.

The networks are not exactly eager to embrace this concept. They like the old way best. For one thing, under the old system the network collected its profit the moment the advertiser bought sponsorship of the show, and after that it was a case of the public be damned. For another thing, under the old system the sponsor paid for the full half-hour or hour of the program, whereas under the magazine concept he'd pay only for the time of his commercial, while the network would finance the remainder of the show.

Nevertheless the networks are being nudged into at least a modified version of the magazine concept whether they like it or not. One force behind the move is the advertiser himself, who is relinquishing his control over specific programs in order to spread his money and his risk of flop shows. Today the tendency is to share each program with noncompetitive products so that for the same cash outlay the advertiser can place his commercial on several shows a week rather than on just one. Another force behind the switch is the network grasp of control of programs as a means of ensuring higher ratings. The networks no longer dare settle for the profit of a "Firestone

Hour" if that program will imperil its ratings for the remainder of the night.

This brings us almost to the format of the "magazine concept" in that the network will be putting on the shows and the advertiser simply buying commercial time on them. But it's not just the format that interests us. It's the new horizons in entertainment that might result.

Unfortunately the horizon today remains the same old one we've been staring at for the past dozen years. In their chase for ratings, and in their unfamiliar position of risking their own money rather than that of the sponsor on new programs, the networks are more inclined than ever to play it safe. Use the old formulas. Stick to those elements that have lured the largest audiences ever since the heyday of radio. Bright new ideas? Don't take a chance.

This is the heritage of the rating system. R. M. Prentice, vice president of advertising for the Ward Baking Company, said: "The all-consuming race for ratings has killed off many excellent programs and ideas. More importantly, it frightens packagers, agencies, and advertisers from anything untried or unknown."

Don't the magazines operate in the same way? Don't they chase high circulation figures by sticking to the formulas they know are safe?

Here is what I found to be the key to the drabness of television programing. The magazines are specialized. Certainly they stick to the formulas that have made them successful, but *Harper's* is sticking to the *Harper's* formula and *True Confessions* is sticking to the *True Confessions* formula and the *Saturday Evening Post* is sticking to the *Saturday Evening Post* formula. You have a choice of which you buy.

In television you don't have a choice. TV is all the same. The networks are the same. The 530 stations are the same. When NBC was berated for abandoning several adventurous new ideas for the bland Hollywood formula programs, NBC explained that ABC was doing so well with this sort of thing NBC naturally had to follow.

Couldn't ABC have one type of network and NBC another? Couldn't ABC be *True Confessions* and NBC *Harper's* or, at least, the *Saturday Evening Post?*

The networks all want to be the biggest, for the biggest means the biggest audiences and consequently the highest rates. The public is the victim. It has no freedom of choice. Even with seven channels in New York, too often the viewer's only real choice is "off" and "on."

This would be bad enough if those ratings carried the authority of a newspaper or magazine circulation audit. But the manner in which they are compiled leaves them always open to suspicion. Even under the principle of scientific sampling, the ratings poll far too few people to pass judgment on American taste. It may be fair to assume that if 5,000 dentists like "Lassie" then most dentists like "Lassie." But it is awfully presumptuous to say that most professional men like "Lassie" because the one dentist with the Nielsen gadget tuned into the show that week.

Yet samplings such as this exercise a tyranny over all television, and the men in the industry who bewail this ludicrous situation find little inclination toward reform.

The only thing that might conquer this devotion to sameness is too much of it. Three networks can get by this way, but could four? Or five? Or six?

If the FCC ever unravels the knot it made and makes possible a great increase in the number of stations through UHF, then surely there will be an increase in networks, too. This might break the mold. This might produce a fifth network that for the sheer sake of finding a new audience would strike out over uncharted programing ground.

The one sign of this has been in New York and Los Angeles —where there are enough independent stations to force new programing as a simple means of survival. Channel 13 in New York particularly shows a great capacity for innovation. Most of these programs soon become as tiresome as the network formula programs, to be sure. But they are something different while they are fresh and new, and, once exhausted, they are replaced by something else new to excite the viewer's imagination.

Thus there is hope that someday we shall have at least the equivalent of BBC Radio's famous "Third Programme," that network which is devoted to programs of symphony and education and drama above the mass-circulation fare of the other networks.

This might well quell the egghead revolt against today's formula programings, but it would not be all to the good. As it is now, the American system of permitting an occasional intellectual program to intrude upon the domain of situation comedy and Westerns forces many viewers to take an unwitting first look at quality entertainment. A few of them even like it. These converts are perhaps more precious to our future than all the "Third Programme" listeners in Britain.

Printers Ink magazine said: "It will prove far more valuable to expose millions of people to one production of *Hamlet* or the Moiseyev Dancers, for example, than it will be to conduct a six-months seminar on the Elizabethan theater, the history of opera in America or Russian folk dance as a reflection of the Slavic spirit for the limited number of people who are deeply interested in those subjects. A further challenge for the medium to present—eventually—such programing in a popular manner that will make it palatable for many millions of viewers instead of the esoteric few."

There has been considerable demand, of course, that the government force television into improving its programing. And as I complete this investigation into the TV industry, I ponder whether the government really could accomplish anything in this field.

Certainly on the basis of past performance the prospects are not encouraging. But assuming that the FCC has now awakened to its responsibilities and is prepared to act, what can it do?

The first step is obvious. The FCC should force stations to make good on those grand programing promises they inserted in their applications for licenses. True, some of these programs that look good on paper may be awful flops on the 17-inch screen, but the stations have no right to ignore these come-ons that were the basis of their original franchise.

After that, what? License the networks? I doubt if there's anything to be gained here. The FCC, although it technically has no authority over the networks, can exert any real control it desires through pressure on the affiliates and on the licensed local stations the networks themselves own.

Pass regulations about programing? This is dangerous ground. The network president may not be the greatest benefactor in the history of American culture, but he certainly is better qualified than any congressman or federal commissioner to determine programing.

However, it is conceivable to me that a few programing laws might be effective. For example, we would be much more likely to get some public-service programing if a law were passed forcing the TV stations to remain on the air sixteen hours a day, yet devoting only fourteen hours to commercial programs. This would leave a mandatory two hours of public-service programs.

This is not contrary to any American principles. The government now forces railroads to run nonprofitable passenger trains for the convenience of the riders if the railroads want to run profitable freight trains over the same route. TV could become subject to the same type of law—run some nonprofitable public-service shows if you want the franchise for the profitable commercial shows.

The stations actually are enjoined to do this now in general terms. A law might be passed to make the requirements specific. Instructing a TV station to act "in the public interest" is one thing, but telling it to put on a minimum of two hours of public-service programs is something else. There will always be doubt about the definition of the first. There's nothing vague about the second.

Of course, this could continue a battle of semantics if the stations began quarreling with the government over what is a public-service program. The local high-school band? Actually, a re-run of "Dragnet" would probably better serve the people then a dreary concert by a tone-deaf batch of local amateurs.

No, public-service programing is programing that will inform the people about issues of the day, about medicine and health, about educating their children, about automobile safety. These shows could well be staged even by local stations if the owners were willing to channel a portion of their profits in the direction. Almost every TV station employs talented people who yearn for an occasional opportunity to break from the commercial mold to produce a documentary rather than just another furniture-store advertisement.

These arguments about good and bad TV programs always bog down into differences of opinion as to what's good and what's bad and what's in the middle. It is all very well for an egghead to demand that the Moiseyev Dancers replace "Lassie" on Sunday nights. But for how long? "Lassie" runs fifty-two weeks a year for years and years. Wouldn't even the most ardent devotee of the classical dance become a little weary of the Moiseyev Dancers if they appeared on TV this often? All of the shows on Broadway and the Metropolitan Opera Company's entire season scarcely fill a week of television's fourteen-hour days.

There is much that is great on TV now. The networks have created a new journalistic form with their news-in-depth shows, and furthermore they have done so at a great financial loss. Too, the spectaculars that click—"An Evening With Fred Astaire" a few years back, for example—are popular entertainment at the highest level.

Because TV devours so much material in a week, there naturally must be drivel. If the great mass of TV programing seems hackneyed, so the great mass of anything is hackneyed: there are trashy books, trashy magazine articles, and trashy newspaper stories.

The writers—those first-line soldiers in the intellectual war against the advertisers—must share considerable blame. Under their union rules, they will not submit a script on speculation. They must be contracted before they write a line. Although the producer does have rights of revision, he still must buy a pig in a poke, and often is stuck with a script he knows is second-rate. The actors and the singers are to blame, too. They consider TV a fast buck. They often save their pride of craft for the theater appearance, the night-club act, the movie role.

And, of course, the economics of the business are to blame most of all. TV shows are cheap by any theatrical standards. The most routine Broadway show costs as much as the most lavish TV spectacular. The weekly TV-series show costs one-twentieth as much as an average movie. You always get what you pay for.

These TV shows, too, must be turned out with great speed, partly to save money and partly to meet the deadline that is always just around the calendar. The retakes of Hollywood and the tryout performances of Broadway are luxuries TV can seldom afford.

The real solution to the viewer's TV dilemma is the newspaper listing of shows each day. He can tune in what appeals to him and ignore what doesn't. There is considerable room for improvement in TV and a little hope that this improvement will be realized, but these facts should not delude the more discriminating viewer from facing this truth: Television is a mass medium, not a quality medium. The viewer shouldn't expect something TV is not designed to provide. He doesn't shop for antiques at the A&P.

In some circles it has become fashionable to do without TV entirely—not only for the adults but also for the children. This form of intellectual snobbery is as intelligent as forbidding a child to read because he might get hold of some bad comic books. The child of today learns much from TV, and so does any adult who is curious enough to shop around the dial.

There is something to be said for the theory that the public ultimately gets what it deserves. In his *Process and Effects of Mass Communication,* published by the University of Illinois Press, Wilbur Schramm says "a discriminating public" is ultimately responsible for what it gets on TV, and in the newspapers and magazines as well. He concedes that the public is "less than a full partner"—that is, there are other considerations, such as the demands of the advertiser and the prejudices of the publisher or broadcaster. But, he concludes, the public can be the final arbiter if it shows some discrimination: "We only deserve what we get."

This system of being selective cannot conquer TV's negative faults. It cannot provide the good programs that might be, but are not, on the air. The children's news programs, the musical-appreciation programs—those are the areas in which TV has failed the community.

This failure is not without cause. As CBS's Dr. Stanton said, "We can help education but we cannot be education." TV often is the object of criticism that actually should be directed at the nation's educational system. Is it the fault of CBS or is it the fault of the county high school when the graduating class goes out into the world completely oblivious to Bach, Brutus, and even Bemelans?

TV will improve tremendously on the technical level in the next few years. Color TV will enhance the medium for the viewer and the advertiser. Transistor portables will cart television programs to the beach, to the picnic grounds and, we might as well face it, into the automobile.

The question is whether the advertising men and the program directors will keep pace with the engineers. They say they will, that their infant will mature. But the experimental shows of the early 1950's were in many ways better than the Hollywood formula product that represents the "progress" to the

1960's. The difference is between the painter and the mimeograph machine.

The advertising is certain to get better, if not tastier. The advertising agencies are demanding more and better research into why people buy. They are also protesting their commercials more often. They are insisting that the rating services tell them who is watching, not merely how many.

The fear of government regulation is the brake on TV advertising today. Remarkably, the industry does not deny the need for regulation, but pleads only for the opportunity to regulate itself. On this, the American public can judge only by the ultimate results. Self-regulation codes have worked for many industries.

Every phase of TV must mature. It is not only a matter of finding a way to put more sophisticated and thought-provoking programs on the air. It is also a matter of measuring the audience with something more extensive than fifteen hundred electronic gadgets. It is a matter of developing commercials that inform rather than hoodwink the viewer. It is a matter of conceiving a form of government supervision that is neither choking censorship nor callous laissez faire.

The professionals in TV may sneer that these are the unrealistic daunderings of a dreamer, that in a practical world they just cannot be. This might be true. But if it is true, then TV will never mature. TV will fritter away its opportunity for greatness.

And the medium is so powerful that its misuse is a sin against the entire nation.

INDEX